The Complete Guide to Church Play Production

John Lewis

Laura Andrews

Flip Kobler

ISBN 0-7673-3437-X

Dewey Decimal Classification: 792
Subject Heading: RELIGIOUS DRAMA—PRODUCTION AND DIRECTION

Printed in the United States of America.

The Sunday School Board of
the Southern Baptist Convention
127 Ninth Avenue North
Nashville, Tennessee

DEDICATION

This book is dedicated to the many pioneers of church drama who bravely ventured into unknown territory...to those who ignored the repressive words, "But this is the way we've always done it," and continued to invent new ways of communicating the gospel to a progressive world. We know, first hand, the hardships of their journey and applaud their courage and tenacity. This book is written to inspire and assist the new young artists who now stand on the shoulders of those early pioneers and have a clear vision of the future.

DISCLAIMER

Many times discovering new and different techniques generates an enthusiasm that disregards the thought of any potentially dangerous risk. Therefore, before using some of the procedures described in this book, evaluate them in relation to your group for any potential risk, for necessary safety precautions and advance preparation, and for possible results. The Sunday School Board of the Southern Baptist Convention and the authors of this book are not responsible for, nor have they any control over, the use or misuse of any activities published in this book.

CONTENTS

FOREWORD

Bathrobes
Flipflop sandals
Animal droppings
Ear-piercing feedback
Muffed sound effects
Falling flats
Exploding budgets
Lawsuits
Empty seats

These are the stuff play production nightmares are made of. I'm honored to present to you a real vaccine for these catastrophes. *The Complete Guide to Church Play Production* is the most comprehensive guide for anyone wanting to produce effective drama within the church. I thank God for the work that has been put into this volume by three of the finest artists in their fields of expertise: John Lewis, Laura Andrews, and Flip Kobler. This book is groundbreaking.

Don't let this book overwhelm you. There's a wealth of information for churches of all sizes. Whether you are producing a show in a large civic center or simply trying to add drama to your worship experiences, this book will help you realize your dreams of effective presentations.

By purchasing *The Complete Guide to Church Play Production,* you have made an investment in quality. Remember that your audience has been exposed to the very best of what the world has to offer in theater and film. Shouldn't we as Christian artists try to be the very best we can be for our Savior? The story of redemption is indeed the greatest story ever told. Let's tell it in such a way that it will bring honor and glory to God.

Our world hungers for the good news. God challenges us to communicate it. Let's seize this opportunity not only to tell them but to show them who God really is. I am convinced that there is no better way to show them than through drama.

So...on with the show!

—— Matt Tullos

CHAPTER ONE

PRODUCTION VALUES

In the beginning God created...and God created...and God created man in His image. God is the Creator; and we, being made in His likeness, have a natural, instinctive compulsion to create.

God, the Perfect Creator, has charged us with the awesome responsibility that accompanies creativity. And believing that all beauty and creativity come from God, it is our duty, as we create, to do so wholeheartedly, attempting to achieve the same quality and perfection that God originally intended for us.

Since the beginning of time, God's people have placed the creative process in high regard. Through the centuries, the church was in charge of, and in fact, controlled the arts. Writers such as Shakespeare, musicians such as Bach, and artists such as Michelangelo were all supported and promoted by the church.

It wasn't until recent history that the church began to condemn the arts and relinquish its control to the secular world. Since that time, people with strong religious beliefs (especially Christians) have lived with the frustration of suppressing their instinctive, creative urges for fear of condemnation by their own church and other religious leaders.

Theater, television, and film are the arts of today, and they are constantly under attack by many outspoken religious leaders. What little contributions organized church/religion make to the entertainment industry through any of these vehicles is usually of such poor quality, that it is well below the standards of the secular world. When we produce film, television, or theater that lacks integrity and production values, we open ourselves up to condemnation and ridicule from a world that now dominates the arts and has clearly established a precedent for extremely high production values. Low quality productions in the church only create a negative witness. This not only goes against our nature, but it is in direct violation of Scripture.

"In everything set them an example by doing what is good. In your teaching show integrity, seriousness and soundness of speech that cannot be condemned, so that those who oppose you may be ashamed because they have nothing bad to say about us" (Titus 2:7–8, NIV).

We, as Christians, would do better to make a well-produced film like *Raiders of the Lost Ark* than a mediocre film about the apostle Paul. Though Billy Graham has more than earned a reputable name in evangelism, he does not come to mind as someone who would be likely to direct the next blockbuster movie. Imagine a film about the apostle Paul, directed by Steven Spielberg. I think it is safe to say that most of us would choose Spielberg over Graham to direct such a film, since Spielberg has more than proven his ability to direct. This same rationale must be applied to the church that wants to re-enter and reach its community through the art form of theater.

A few years ago, we invited a Hollywood agent to see one of our Christmas productions. She reluctantly consented to come, clearly stating her expectation that it was going to be just another "typical church" play. To the contrary, she was so impressed with the production, she said it was "as good as any show in town." She also came to church services the following Sunday where she heard the gospel preached for the first time.

Unfortunately, though it is what we most want to achieve, not all church productions leave this type of impression on the secular world. We were fortunate to be working with a music director who had the professional knowledge, talent, and experience to produce and mount a major production himself. Yet because of his experience, he had the insight to delegate positions to the most creative staff he could assemble. His writers had all written for film and television; the director had directed both television and professional theater; the production coordinator was an established producer of theater in Hollywood; and all set, lighting, sound, and costume designers were of the same caliber. He called his team together at least one year prior to the production date and solicited their advice. Using the combined talents of this team, he produced musical dramas in his church with the quality of a Broadway show.

Almost every church, of every denomination, does some type of presentation sometime during the year. It might be a simple nativity scene at Christmas, a cantata at Easter, or a youth musical in the summer. Usually, these are the highest attended services of the year. It seems as though church members and members of the community want to see these productions, but most of our churches simply do not know how to "mount a play" with professional quality. In other words, there is demand for something we seldom supply. We, the church, have been attempting to regain lost ground for years, but progress has been slow. One reason for this is the lack of knowledge by those in charge of the productions, and another is the material itself.

In the late sixties, there was a surge of Christian pop music by such composers as Ralph Carmichael and Kurt Keiser. These soon expanded into full musicals with a light rock beat and some minor dramatic action placed between numbers. *Good News, Tell It Like It Is,* and *Natural High* were among those pioneer musicals that were primarily aimed at the youth.

In the early seventies, Ragan Courtney and Buryl Red teamed up to create the Christian rock musical, *Celebrate Life.* Ragan was an actor with a theater background, and therefore *Celebrate Life* was written in theatrical style as opposed to "cantata" style. It became the most popular and enduring of the Christian musicals. Ragan and Buryl collaborated again with the somewhat less successful *Beginnings* and then with Ragan's wife, Cynthia Clawson, for *Bright New Wings.* This unique musical had more production and dramatic values than its predecessors and was a major leap forward in the progress of dramatic expression in the church.

Then, in the mid-seventies, the trend reverted to the standard cantata-style musicals or musicals with narration and/or dramatic readings between songs. Music directors and pastors continued to "play it safe" with these types of choir productions. Nothing as unique or as memorable as the first Christian rock musicals was then published. Several churches put on productions of the "Living Christmas Tree," but again these were (and still are) mostly cantatas. Hundreds of other clone musicals were cranked out, telling the same story in the eighties by unwittingly rearranging the script, music, and lyrics from the sixties and seventies.

We are not saying that there is anything wrong with doing a cantata, but we are saying that it must be done well, both in its writing and its presentation. If we are to reach people, we must meet them where they are, both in our choices of material and in the quality with which we present it. Presently the community does not have a positive attitude or high expectations from the church in general and may have preconceived notions of "typical church productions." Therefore, high production values are essential when producing a church play or musical.

One of the biggest obstacles to overcome is the concept of the traditional stuffy *bathrobe drama.* This term comes from the use of department store bathrobes as biblical costumes. This mentality enabled the church to rationalize their substitution of high production values for lower standards, believing that the audience, mostly composed of church family, would accept and appreciate the effort. The term has now expanded to become a catch-all phrase that describes that sense of mediocrity which then carried over into all areas of production, from lighting to sets to performing, and so forth.

The church deserves—and in fact, demands—the same attention to detail as patrons of professional theater. Don't try to get away with less. Your audience is no longer just your church family. It is just as critical and artistically unforgiving as any other audience; therefore your best effort is expected.

Production Values

Since the beginning of theater, there has been a natural tendency to gravitate towards spectacle, or bigger and better production values. Secular theater understands that if people are aware of the quality of a show's production, they will pay more to see it. Therefore a production company can increase its revenue at the box office by improving the look and sound of what it puts on stage. More importantly, in church theater, people will see it. To quote from the film, *Field of Dreams*, "If you build it, they will come."

If you build a reputation as a church that adheres to high production standards and values (not necessarily the same as expensive), then "they" will be more accepting and supportive in their attendance. When it comes to the production values of a show, most well-known playwrights, directors, actors, and designers seem to agree that more does not always equal better. Yet musicals, with their larger-than-life sets, lighting, costumes, and special effects, continue to be the most popular form of theatrical entertainment among general audiences. It isn't the bigger that attracts them, but the better. And we can do better. When we do quality work, regardless of our profession, we earn respect and credibility. Christians are commanded to stand out among the crowd "...so that you may become blameless and pure, children of God without fault in a crooked and depraved generation, in which you shine like stars in the universe" (Phil. 2:15, NIV).

Audiences recognize great production values subconsciously; a lack of production values they recognize consciously. When an audience enters a theater and sees a well-crafted set under exquisite pre-set lighting, they anticipate an enjoyable evening of art. They will then "buy" into the purpose. If they walk into a performance space and see a set that has been obviously thrown together from scraps left over from previous shows, they start the evening being very skeptical of what they are to see and less inclined to care about the purpose.

A scenic design and setting are supposed to communicate something about the play to the audience. They are supposed to set the mood or impart basic information about the content of the show. If a total lack of basic construction standards has been met, an

12

audience is likely to receive a message about the play they are about to watch that is in direct contrast to the message intended.

Good production values can sometimes be evident in a set that is built with great care to *look like* a badly built set which will create a tension in the audience. In too many instances this is the result we get without intending to. Even though the individual audience member who is viewing the set may not notice the small details, he is influenced by the overall statement the set is makes.

In the church, you must think of your target audience and the purpose for your production. Theater is an art form. But in the church it must be much more than spectacle and more than art. We did not say "instead of"; we said "more than." Church theater is art with purpose. When we fail to connect with an audience, the art is worthless. In church theater, purpose without art also will fail to connect with the audience.

There have been many books written on the subject of theater. Libraries are full of reference materials on just about every aspect of the theatrical experience. But if you are considering the mounting of a theatrical production in a church, we have found very little material that addresses the unique problems inherent in church drama. Hence, we hope that this manual will fill that void for you. All the information presented is based on many years of combined experience. However, there is much more that can be learned. Every production presents new obstacles which challenge creative energies.

Although we have attempted to cover every conceivable area of production, don't let this manual scare you with its detail. We realize that you may not wish to use all the information presented. However, we suggest that you read it in its entirety, as it was written as a whole. One chapter is not complete without the others. In this manual, we share our knowledge and experience to equip you with step-by-step guidelines to produce productions of the highest quality.

CHAPTER TWO

CHOOSING THE PLAY

Choosing the play or musical is probably the most important single factor in the quality of any production. Choosing the right play is as important as doing the play right. Generally it is the youth or music department that initiates the concept of doing a play, and so it follows that often the burden of choosing the appropriate play falls upon the youth or choir director. Quite often the people in these positions have little or no theatrical experience. This should not be a problem if appropriate attention is given to certain factors: knowing your audience, theme, and available resources. However, if a director has been selected, he should have major input into the selection of the material.

Let's suppose that the choir director decides he wants to do an Easter musical. Already, the choice has been made to do a musical rather than a straight drama; a seasonal rather than a non-seasonal. He is now faced with the decision of which play to do. If he does not already have a play in mind, there are many sources to which he can turn. Many of the Christian music publishers have theatrical divisions with a variety of dramatic materials.

If the play is being initiated and produced by the choir director, he should utilize the insight and input of his creative staff, especially the director. As a team, they will meet to present and discuss various musicals. These may be obtained from listed publications and/or referrals by colleagues, which would include productions seen elsewhere by one or more members of your creative staff. Another possibility would be that of original submissions.

After all the plays are considered, the team then begins to explore the feasibility of producing one of them. Problems will arise while mounting any production, be it amateur or professional, but many of them can be avoided if enough research is done before the final decision is made.

Target Audience

A very important yet often overlooked question is, "What is the purpose of this production?" In other words, for whom are you doing it? If it is primarily for the members of your church, it's purpose would be to create for the believers a worship experience with entertainment values. If it's purpose is to be an outreach to the unchurched/unsaved community, the emphasis would be on entertainment with an inspirational message mixed in. Now, before you completely disagree, let us explain.

Most churches will want to believe that the purpose for their productions is always for outreach. However, the material they select is usually so full of "Christianese" and Christian buzz words that the unchurched person hasn't got a clue what's going on. Someone who has never read the Bible or has never been to church has no point of reference to relate to the scenes we Christians are presenting. Unchurched viewers don't usually attend a church production to be preached to, nor with intentions of becoming saved. Usually they attend because a church member has convinced them that this production has entertainment value. More often they attend to participate in a celebration of a particular season, such as Christmas or Easter.

Most of the dramatic and musical material that is presented by our Christian publishers is done so without such consideration of the unchurched or unsaved audience. You can argue that people do get saved during your productions. True, and that is by the power of the Holy Spirit, despite the program. If you were to integrate proper play structure with well-developed characters who speak real dialogue and tell the truth of the Scripture, you would be amazed at the jump in the number of decisions.

Know Your Audience

A "good" play in itself is not enough. It must also be right for the audience to which it will be presented. When choosing the play, you must keep in mind the types of persons that will be attending. Although we don't mean to categorize or stereotype, there are certain factors to consider regarding your audience.

Material that would appeal to a West Coast audience may not necessarily appeal to an audience in the South. As theatergoers vary from state to state, differences will also occur from large metropolitan towns to smaller, rural communities. Attitudes towards religion, race, sex, and so forth may be more limiting in a rural community than those of a broader-based audience accustomed to a more culturally diverse lifestyle. But regardless of your location, avoid underestimating your audience's knowledge and appreciation of quality theater.

We once produced an original dramatic musical depicting a very realistic view of the crucifixion. Combined makeup and special effects created an "illusion of reality" that gave the audience a greater understanding of Christ's suffering. The months of hard work given to this realistic approach paid off when the opening night audience responded more than enthusiastically at this very genuine portrayal, despite its realism. The pastor, however, was afraid his people would be offended by the "excessive use of blood" and asked us not to use it during the rest of the performances. Even though he himself was positively affected by the performance, he was being protective of his congregation, thereby underestimating their artistic integrity. Members of the cast and also members of his congregation urged him to reconsider. After speaking with several audience members, he realized his fears might have been unfounded and consented to let the play run in its original form. By closing night he was overwhelmingly convinced of the audience's approval, and many lives were affected.

In another instance and in another church, we were asked by the pastor to produce a series of secular plays in their theater. He believed his people would only support and attend "upbeat musicals," and play selections were made accordingly. Though the plays were well attended, his membership also planned several group outings to attend the local community theater, preferring a more diversified artistic menu. The pastor soon realized that his people were not merely looking for simplistic entertainment, but emotionally and intellectually stimulating works as well.

Another factor to consider is the age of your audience. Avoid choosing material for your church production that will target a specific age group, since the age range of attendance is from baby to great-grandparent; unless, of course, you are intentionally trying to target a specific age group, such as a youth department, for a special function, or such. Decide if the material will appeal to a limited age group or a general age group. When choosing your theme, do not cater to a "church audience" but rather to a general audience who expect to see a good show, complete with moral and spiritual values.

Theme
The theme includes the subject matter, idea, and story of the play. Most churches do their productions either at Christmas or Easter. In this case the choice of theme is no problem. There is a countless supply of seasonal musicals and dramas available. The majority of these are "period" pieces involving large casts, thereby recruiting the involvement of the entire church family. Churches unaccustomed to theater are generally more eager participants of a Christmas or Easter play. Likewise, the community is more apt to attend.

Very few churches do productions on the off-season. It seems it is easier to justify doing theater in the church if it is done as a Christmas or Easter pageant. But, consider the advantages of a non-seasonal production. There is little or no competition from other churches, so their members could freely attend your performances. A great number of church members who leave town during the holidays would have the opportunity to share in a non-seasonal production. It is also a novelty that would draw the interest of audiences at large.

Choosing the right material for an off-season production is critical. A great deal of care and research must go into the proper selection. While still remaining true to your chosen theme, there are many types of plays to be considered. These would include contemporary versus period, traditional versus experimental, and realistic or historic versus fictional. Even these may be presented in a combined form, such as a play concerning a fictional character in biblical times. Let's go back to our example of the choir director choosing to do an Easter musical. If *Celebrate Life,* a musical written by Ragan Courtney and Buryl Red, is chosen, the creative staff has elected to do an experimental/period piece: that is, placing biblical characters into the twentieth century. On the other hand, choosing to do the dramatic presentation of *The Seven Last Words of Christ* by Theodore DuBois would be presenting a realistic/traditional/period musical: that is, the presentation of biblical characters in the traditional costumes and settings of their era.

Resources

Time, talent, facilities, and finances are all factors that should be clearly defined before the final decision of material can be made. Once you have analyzed all that is necessary to get this play running, combine the experience of your staff and the resources you have available to determine if you have enough time to make your opening night date. Remember, you must allow for ample pre-production and rehearsal time. This will all be covered later, so don't panic.

Unfortunately, not every play that is right for an audience is right for the group that desires to produce it. There just may not be enough talent available within your group to competently fill all roles of both cast and crew.

Since some plays require larger performance areas than others, your facility may or may not accommodate your choice of play. The space you have must be adaptable to the required sets and number of performers both on and off stage.

Costs will vary from play to play. Securing the rights, scores, sets, costumes, props, lights, publicity, and so forth will incur varied expenses. Weigh these against your available monies, potential donation of equipment and services, and your group's own storehouse. This will give you a reasonable estimate of your ability to meet the financial demands of this play. Consider also the potential for offsetting these expenses with incoming money, either from direct ticket sales, sale of program advertisements, or general "love" or "free-will" offerings.

Writing Your Own Scripts

You may also consider doing an "original," something that has been written by someone you know or someone you hire. There are a great many advantages to this. A "world premiere" always generates greater publicity and is usually free of royalty rights.

Do not make the mistake of assuming that a published Christian piece is a proven piece by a professional. We have found numerous scripts published by various Christian organizations which are not written by professional script writers and are missing even the basic elements of script and story structure. The Christian community tends to embrace those artists who have church-related credits more than fellow Christians who have experience in the professional entertainment industry. Even professional script writers study for years to learn the craft of storytelling and script structure. They write, re-write, submit, get rejected, and start over again. It is a craft that takes talent, hard work and years of experience. It is estimated that 10,000 screenplays land on desks of Hollywood executives each day and don't even get read. Even the professionals with credits get rejected. So you must realize that it is not an easy task.

Consequently, it would be unrealistic for us to give a script-writing course in this small chapter. There are many great books, seminars, and college courses on the art and craft of script writing. It is worth pursuing (or promoting someone within your church to pursue) the education of script writing. We need good scripts from professional Christian writers.

In summary, analyzing the written material is extremely important. Selecting the material after giving consideration to all the criteria mentioned here is not impossible, but you can see how important it is. Though the final selection may rest with one person, the input of team members may very well prove to be invaluable to him or her when making the final choice.

CHAPTER THREE

PRODUCTION STAFF

During the performance of any production, the audience is only aware of the actions that take place on stage. The audience will not and should not see all of the work that goes on before, during, and after the performance. This supporting work is done by a great number of staff and crew members, most often greater than the number in the cast. The people working backstage and those who work prior to actual performance are all members of the production staff and production crews.

The individual jobs of the staff and crew vary from theater to theater due to the availability of talent and the demands of each situation. In the professional theater an individual is hired for personal talent or capability. In most amateur and church productions people are chosen to fill certain positions only because they are willing to try, with or without any background of experience or training. That is a great place to start. Local colleges, seminars, trade magazines, conventions, and such could provide training materials; all are relatively inexpensive and would be well worth the investment.

A successful production is run like a piece of machinery. A proper order and chain of command are necessary for the machine to run smoothly. Every department head has a responsibility to see that his or her department works in harmony with all others. The entire production will only be as professional as the professionalism of its weakest department. Each must know the duties, responsibilities and boundaries of his and all other departments. Following are brief job-descriptions of all the positions needed to mount a professional production. While the job descriptions may differ from church to church due to politics, necessity, and personal abilities of others on staff, we will attempt to outline broadly the tasks and draw some conclusions about the staff and crew responsibilities.

Executive Producer
The executive producer is usually the person or organization who gives the financial

backing to the production. Usually this entity has very little creative control as far as how the play is mounted. In a church production, the executive producer is usually the church itself. Sometimes groups within the church like to be credited as executive producer. In this case both may be credited. For instance:

The First Christian Church
and
The Praise Singers
present
THE PASSION PLAY
by
John Lewis & Flip Kobler

Even though the sponsor may be the drama, the music, or the Sunday School department, it is still a production of the church and should be credited that way. The church is ultimately responsible for what takes place on its grounds.

Producer

Though the executive producer has the ultimate responsibility, the person actually in charge is the producer. In the chain of command, the producer is second to the executive producer, but the producer is the one in charge. In other words, the executive producer has hired the producer to be the boss. The producer is the one who actually runs the production. Everyone else answers to him. The producer hires and fires, forms the crews, schedules all meetings and rehearsals, and coordinates the entire production. This is an enormous job requiring full attention for months before, during, and after the run of the show. Only an experienced and/or knowledgeable person will do this job justice. Since most church productions are initiated by the music department, the church music director is often by default the producer.

Although a good producer knows how to delegate authority, he must have some basic knowledge and ability to understand each department function. He must be able to speak the language of every department so that they are all striving for the same goal. This is why it is extremely important for the producer to have an excellent production coordinator to carry out most of the production work.

The producer is often heard more than seen. The initial work of selecting a script, choosing a director, and hiring a designer is more than meets the eye. If the producer has chosen well, then his job is only to be a guiding hand and make executive decisions.

Director

The producer handles any business issues and the director handles creative issues. The producer is the one in charge, but his goal is to see that the production stays true to the director's vision. This is the director's show. In other words, the producer has relinquished the authority to choose and implement all creative elements to the director. The director is responsible for everything the audience sees, hears, tastes, feels, and smells from the moment it arrives until the moment it exits. The director is the interpreter of the play as a whole—the one who is concerned with the total picture and decides just how to arrive at that total. The director determines the concept of the production: is it to be realistic, stylized, a fantasy, or expressionistic? The director instructs the actor as to the type of character to be portrayed and defines the creative boundaries for the designers—the boundaries in which their crafts are to create. The director is the one who takes all the individual pieces and carefully shapes, cuts and then fits them together into a finished product.

Production Coordinator

Although the director has the overall responsibility of mounting the entire show, he cannot monitor the progress of the other positions and their responsibilities single-handedly. There are so many details to coordinate, so many people to keep track of, so many cues to remember, there must be one person charged with the overall responsibility of keeping the production together and making sure that it runs without a hitch. That one person is the production coordinator. The position requires strong organizational skills; the ability to relate well to people; and the ability to delegate, monitor, and communicate from a place of authority without insensitivity. Responsibilities for creating calendar schedules, coordinating all rehearsals (music, choreography, blocking, and scene breakdowns), the physical plant (auditorium, stage, shop, rehearsal halls) as well as the crews dealing with these areas will be assumed, to relieve the director of concern for these details. Related issues which involve support staff within the church, music, drama, and worship divisions as well as the kitchen, childcare, and maintenance staff all will be handled by the production coordinator.

Stage Manager

The stage manager's job is similar to that of production coordinator, but it is mostly limited to the stage. This would include responsibilities for all staff, stage crews, and performers during rehearsals and performances, and while they are in the theater or church for a scheduled assembly.

Like the production coordinator, the position of stage manager requires strong organizational skills, the ability to relate well to people, and the daring to dispatch authority. The difficulties inherent in both positions are multiplied when placed in a church or amateur setting. It is difficult to give orders and make strict demands on volunteers who have worked their regular jobs all day and now face a long night of rehearsal. Tension, friction, animosity, anger, and fatigue are just a few of the elements a stage manager must learn to recognize and handle appropriately.

These positions are often misunderstood in church productions and are given to whomever happens to be available. To really do the job the production coordinator and stage manager must have a working knowledge of all of the elements of the production.

These jobs begin during the pre-production period and continue until the show closes. Much of the actual day-to-day work, however, varies depending upon what phase of production the show is in.

The stage manager must be able to: coach actors should the director be absent; intelligently discuss any technical problem with any staff member; and take many of the relatively minor decisions and problems from the director's busy schedule. A stage manager must know when to make a decision and when it must be referred to the director and or production coordinator.

In addition to keeping attendance and contacting those not present during rehearsals, the stage manager creates the prompt book. This is a copy of the script which includes the marking of all of the blocking, business, and cues in order to communicate issues that will directly impact other departments (props, special effects, costumes, etc.).

The major responsibilities during the performances of the show will be to check attendance and work through a refined, even elaborate check list with the production coordinator, verifying calls for pre-show activities for such tasks as prop checks on stage, house open, general assembly, and places for musicians, crew, and actors. Once the performance is under way, the normal communication between the production coordinator and stage manager will be the pivotal factor that enables each show to progress as planned and rehearsed with as little variance as possible. Post-performance duties will be much the same as during rehearsal: monitoring the clean-up and storage of stage, back-stage, and dressing room areas by all members of the cast and crew.

Music Director

There is a difference between the positions of church staff music director and music director of the production team. Although these two positions may be occupied by the same person, they have different responsibilities. Here we will deal exclusively with the responsibilities of the play/production music director.

A theatrical production can be in the form of a musical, comedy, satire, farce, and so forth. In a musical, the music serves to enhance and support the drama. So it follows, the music director will serve to enhance and support the drama as the director outlines. It is his job to see that his musical interpretation coincides with the director's concept. Like all other members of the production team, he is responsible to the director.

One of the problems we have frequently encountered is the protection of imaginary boundaries between groups. Commonly the choir members resent outsiders "taking over" their musical production. This attitude is intensified when the director of the production is someone other than their own choir or church music director. Before the production begins, the music director should alleviate the fears of his choir and encourage them to accept and support the entire production team. There is no room in a church production for territorial friction. The old theater saying "The play is the thing" might be reworded "The message is the thing." Everyone must work together for the good of the play, which is, after all, for the good of the church and its mission.

Choreographer

The choreographer is responsible for creating and staging all musical numbers. But like all other positions, this must done within the framework of the director's vision. The choreographer will need to work closely with the director and musical director. They are more like partners than any other members of the staff. Staging a musical number is much the same as the director blocking the non-musical scenes. The difference is that the director has input and veto power over the choreography, where the choreographer has none over the scenes.

However, the choreographer does help create and rework music with the music director, as it pertains to the choreography. The music director would mostly concede to the choreographer's requests. Again, all of this is subject to the director's approval.

Production Designer

This person is responsible for designing the "look" of the production. The production designer will influence all areas of the look, such as lighting and costumes, but his primary design will be the set. The audience's attitude toward the play is conditioned, at least to some extent, by what it first sees. That is the set. Right away the audience forms opinions, both good and bad, toward the quality of the production. The set establishes, in the audience's mind, the tone, style, and theme of the forthcoming play. So it is important that the set and scenery be an accurate representation of the director's concept. The set designer must give full attention to the smallest details. Even the tiniest inconsistency can weaken the illusion of reality before the play even begins. When this happens, it puts enormous pressure upon the performers and technical crews to recapture the audience and bring them back to the right frame of mind.

Construction Coordinator

This person takes the designer's concept, drawings, or models and makes them a reality. He develops construction plans that his work crew will work from. He should have a knowledge of set construction as opposed to commercial construction. The construction coordinator should be aware of the director's vision, the script, and the actors' needs and should not deviate from the design without consultation with the designer and director.

Scenic Artists

The scenic artist works directly for the production designer and construction coordinator. He simply brings to life the designs created by the designer. Although this requires talent and creativity, the designer is mostly responsible for choices like mediums and colors, leaving the application to the scenic artist.

Prop-Master

The prop-master works directly with the set and/or production designer. He is primarily responsible for all handheld props. The prop-master and his crew must determine what is needed, and determine with the production coordinator how it is to be acquired. Once it is obtained, the prop-master will maintain it, store it, and finally deal with its return or storage.

The prop-master's job begins as soon as he has a script. By the time he has his first meeting with the director, he should have done a complete script and scene breakdown and have a completed list of props. He should meet with the director to assure proper color, style, size, shape, type, and period of the individual items.

By attending the first read-through and selected rehearsals, he will learn what character props are needed and how they fit into the show.

Technical Director

The technical director (TD) is the overall director of the major technical departments: lights, sound, effects, rigging, etcetera. The TD is not the designer nor the head for each of these departments, but the head of the combined departments as a whole. He coordinates the technical divisions together and solves any problems that might arise.

Therefore the TD should have an overall knowledge of each department. He should understand weights, measurements, limits, codes, laws, and so forth. The TD should make himself aware of new innovations in each field. He should be aware of seminars, conventions, courses, and such that might help him in his position. He should read books, subscribe to trade magazines, get on mailing lists, and access the Internet. Whenever there is a problem that he doesn't have the answer to, he needs to know where to go to find it.

Lighting Designer

Visibility is not the one and only consideration for the lighting designer (LD). The lighting should do more for the play than allow the actors to be seen. It also enhances the mood, conveys information, and underscores dramatic moments. If the LD has done his job well, the lighting will not draw attention to itself, but will serve to heighten the audiences's theatrical experience according to the director's concept. Though the main function of lighting in theater is to make the actors visible and is the primary consideration when designing lighting for the production, the LD must make sure that his design allows for coverage of all areas of the set and that all actors can be clearly seen as appropriate.

Sound Designer

The primary concern of the sound designer is to ensure that the audience clearly hears everything that is intended for them. He must do this within the confines of the play, the set design and the director's concept. He and his crew must define, secure, record, and/or produce all sound effects, mood, overture, and intermission music, and/or amplify the production as required by the script and/or the director.

This process should begin with reading and breaking down the script and meeting with the director.

Costume Designer

After the set, the design of costumes is probably the second most critical area of design within the framework of what is on stage. Both must support the concept established by the director and be historically accurate to the period with regards to texture, color, and accessories that will denote rank, position or class, wealth, career, and so forth. Research and attention to such details will be more important than how much time this person has to sew, though knowledge of fabrics and sewing cannot be underestimated. Coordinating the costume crews and dealing with thrift shops, rental stores, costume departments of local schools and colleges and/or community theaters requires a friendly and knowledgeable person in this position.

Makeup Artist

Makeup design can be as critical to the production as any other part of the production design. It requires skill, creativity, knowledge, and experience. It can be learned; but practice, prior to the dress rehearsal, is essential even for the experienced makeup artist. The design for the principle characters will need to be determined by a collective meeting of the key makeup artist with the director and costume designer if not also the production designer and LD.

Publicity

Though this person does not have to be artistically gifted, he will be coordinating efforts regarding advertisements on radio and television and in newspapers, and the design of tickets, programs or playbills, flyers, posters, and such. Their design, appearance, size, information, and function should support the director's concept, and release dates should meet all established deadlines. The person in charge of publicity should be aggressive and energetic. He should explore every available means of promoting the show and attempt to create new ones. His job should begin as early as the first pre-production meeting and should remain constant throughout the production. The timing of certain events is critical to proper publicity and should be planned and executed appropriately. This position requires excellent organizational skills and an out-going, friendly personality.

Safety and Security

Safety should also begin at the first production meeting and continue through the strike (the end of run). Almost everyone involved in the production will be concerned with accomplishing their particular goals; their mind-set will probably not be on safety and security. A separate department with a responsible leader should be formed. Since safety and security are each of such importance, you may want to have a leader for each, depending upon the size of your facility both in numbers and in square footage.

The position or positions should require knowledge of fire laws, insurance, first aid, and so forth. These areas can easily be studied and learned. However, the position requires certain skills and characteristics that are best described as natural talent. The position demands strong leadership qualities. Both the ability to enforce rules without overreaction and to follow-through without distraction are imperative. Investigative skills, being able to "read people," and the ability to smell trouble before it starts are clear advantages that the person in this role might also possess. Physical strength and characteristics are important factors, though not ones that override the others.

Hospitality Coordinator

Usually provision for refreshments such as coffee, tea, fruit, donuts, and such for work crews is planned by the production coordinator. This is usually in the budget and handled by the hospitality coordinator (HC). It can be as simple as beverages for rehearsals or the full-scale meal between matinee and subsequent performances that will be requested of the HC. Whether the meal is provided by the production budget or set up as a pot-luck where all participants are contributing, the hospitality coordinator will take full charge for its preparation, coordination, serving, and the clean-up to follow. This would include the set-up of the room or even outdoor area where the food will be served with tables, chairs, trash receptacles, and all necessary utensils and condiments. It may even include separate facilities for those providing childcare and their respective "charges".

While we are on the subject of charges, let us point out that for practicality, we have designated the child-care division as a part of the hospitality department. It seems that these two functions are already well-established departments within the church and augmenting them with a liaison or additional volunteer personnel may be all that is required by the production team, aside from a printed schedule of requests that you will be asking them to fill. Let it be clear that even if this is true, they may be doubling the normal hours of service they are asked to provide under other circumstances and are in fact serving as members of the production crew while in this capacity and so should be approached as such.

Should there be plans to provide any refreshments to the members of your audience during intermission (or at any time during your run of performances) then everything from the coordination of the menu, the facilities where this will take place, the decorations that may be needed, those who will be serving, and so forth all fall within the perimeters of this department. A tireless spirit and a ready smile are to be sought in those who serve on this team.

House Manager

The house manager will be actively in charge of your team of ushers, ticket sales, and box office personnel and will be integrating with the safety and security leaders as well as the hospitality crews. Though this position is not called upon before dress week, it is important for this person to have a good understanding of his duties prior to that time, so he can coordinate with those he will be responsible for. General leadership skills such as you would find in all your key positions are required for this role. Perhaps your head usher may be asked to assume these duties, but if he is already performing on-stage or in another back-stage crew (or is just over-burdened already), you can ask for recommendations from him which may provide you insight into someone else who is equally qualified.

CHAPTER FOUR

THE DIRECTOR

The director will spend countless hours working and planning, long before casting and rehearsals begin. As captain of the team, the director has a threefold function. *First,* he must determine exactly what effect the playwright was trying to achieve. The playwright is the original creative artist, and it is his concept, his characters, and his ideas that will be presented to the audience. *Second,* the director must devise a plan to ensure that the desired effect reaches the audience. *Third,* he must employ all the arts of the theater to put his plan into action in order to create and sustain the illusion of reality necessary for the audience to appreciate the play fully.

Once he discovers the playwright's intention, the director must mold it with his own creative vision. Then he must pass that vision on to the entire production staff. To do this effectively he must be worthy of their complete confidence and trust. They must believe that he knows what he's talking about, and in fact, he must.

Many directors make the mistake of not learning about each of the departments involved in production. For instance, how can the director convey his vision of lighting to the LD, unless he understands something about lighting? The same holds true for the set, sound, prop, makeup, and all other departments within the production.

To gain their confidence, he must speak their language. When the production team understands and shares the common vision, its input will be invaluable to the director when forming the plan of action. A good director has the ability to maintain creative leadership, while drawing upon the experience, expertise, and ideas of his staff.

Although it is better to have an experienced director, this is not always possible in small churches. You might consider finding someone from a community theater or college in your area to guest-direct your first production. This way you can have someone in your church train as his assistant in preparation for directing future productions. If there is no outside help available, or if your church policy restricts the participation of someone other than a church member, it is still possible for someone in your church to learn to direct—if this someone possesses a lot of talent, energy, and enthusiasm. In this chapter we will give some basic guidelines that would be beneficial to a first-time director, especially as related to a church environment.

When considering a play for production, the director should first ask himself:

Am I capable of staging this play the way it should be staged?

Do I really understand the play?

Do I agree with its basic theme?

Do I have the technique required to stage the most difficult scenes?

Do I understand the character relationships and the motivations well enough to make the action clear to an audience?

Am I really excited by the prospect of doing the play?

Unless a director can answer yes to these questions, he would do better to investigate another play, or yield his position to a director more qualified for that particular production.

Do Your Homework

After you have read the script, there are several tasks you must complete as a director to be adequately prepared for the meetings with your staff and actors.

Of primary importance is the breakdown of the script: that is, the dissection and analysis of its content. Having a clear concept of the playwright's intent, you must now choose the style of its presentation. For instance, we once mounted a production of *You're*

YOU'RE A GOOD MAN, CHARLIE BROWN by Clark Gesner. Produced by Morning Star Entertainment, at the Jess Moody Theater, Van Nuys, CA

a Good Man, Charlie Brown by Clark Gesner. Rather than following the tradition of presenting the characters as the children the cartoons represent, the director chose to have the actors portray the actual cartoon characters themselves. This style was supported with the use of sets, props, and costumes based on the drawings of Charles Schultz. The set pieces and props were bigger-than-life, and the costumes were oversized and hand painted to heighten the effect. So, the chosen style gave the play the appearance of a living, three-dimensional cartoon.

Once the style has been selected, you must now decide how it can best be supported by your sets, costumes, props, and lighting designs. To accomplish this, you should break the script down scene by scene and chart what is required for scenery changes, costume changes, etcetera, and where your sound and lighting cues will be most effective. By having these basic ideas in mind, you will be better able to inspire your technical designers to capture your chosen style in their designs.

The Director and Staff

Once the director has satisfied himself with his own abilities to handle the play, he must evaluate the talents of his staff, crew, and performers.

First he must evaluate the ability of his designers and technicians to construct the physical elements of the play. For instance, if he plans to use complicated lighting in the play, does the LD have the knowledge and resources to pull it off? If not, the director must think of ways to rework the scenes, consider a different LD, or if necessary choose another play. This idea holds true for all positions.

When he feels he has the proper talent and physical properties available, he will meet with the producer. Once they have agreed on the director's vision and his plan to implement it, they can start the ball rolling. With the producer backing the director, a meeting with all department heads will be arranged to discuss this concept. Everyone must fully understand what the director is trying to accomplish before anything starts. Each department head will work on his or her individual designs and plans and submit them to the director for approval. Several different versions may have to be submitted before the director approves them and any action takes place.

The Director and Actors

While the designers are busy working on their various duties, the director must now concentrate on preparation for work with the actors, which is his primary duty. The director will begin with the actors the same way he began with his technical staff—on paper. He will break down the script, scene by scene, line by line, and word by word. Then, a general "blocking" will be sketched into the script. Blocking is the direction of movement and action your actors will be taking on stage. This would include entrances, turns, crosses, stationary positions, and such. Blocking is the physicalization of stage life. This general or "rough" blocking will probably change many times before and after rehearsal begins, but it is important for the director to have a starting point from which to work. As the characters develop, the motivations for movement and action may also change.

It is the director's responsibility to begin the development of a character before giving it to the actor. The actor will need the director's input as a starting point for his own growth in the role. He will start by answering the following questions as they relate to each and every role:

    1. What are the external or physical characteristics, i.e., age, race, build, defects, and speech pattern?

    2. What are the internal or emotional characteristics, i.e., morals, attitudes, and weak and strong traits?

    3. How does this character relate to all other characters in the play?

The director should know, in detail, the basics of acting found in a later chapter of this book.

Once the director has answered these questions and has completed all charts and breakdowns, he is ready to begin rehearsals with his actors. This is a most critical time for the director, because this is where he begins developing his relationship with the actors.

The First Reading.—After proper introductions of actors and appropriate staff, the actors will sit in a circle or around a table and read the play from start to finish. The director will lead in a discussion of the play, allowing the actors to express their personal feelings and concepts. He will ask each actor to give an analysis of his own character, ask the other actors to give their views, and then he will give his own. He will continue this same process until all actors and characters have been discussed.

Rehearsals.—As the sculptor uses clay, as the artist uses color, so the director uses actors. But, they should not be directed simply as marionettes to be moved about the stage against a background of scenery, nor should they be regarded simply as voices speaking the lines the playwright has given them. They should be encouraged to function as artists. At the same time, they need direction to stay within the boundaries of the overall concept and truth of the play.

It is up to the director to set the tone to establish an environment in which creative work can take place. In order to work successfully with actors, he must have their complete confidence. Actors, especially inexperienced ones, feel terribly exposed when they are thrust onto a stage in front of an audience. They are afraid of appearing ridiculous. Consequently, they look to the director to give them confidence and reassurance, to boost their egos, to build them up rather than tear them down. They cannot bear sharp or personal criticism; their ego structure may be too fragile. And once their confidence has been broken, it is very difficult to restore. Actors must be made to feel at all times that if they do what the director asks them to do, they will look good rather than bad, interesting rather than stupid. Without this feeling of confidence, most actors with limited experience will find it very difficult to give the director anything but a very flat reading of a role.

This gentle but firm treatment of the actors is a fine line to walk, even for the professional director, but it is especially difficult to accomplish in the church theater. The director will probably be working with amateurs or people with very little experience in theater. They may not realize how much is required to produce a quality production. Usually in a church production, emotions ride on the surface and feelings are easily hurt. It would be helpful if the director knew a little about the psychology of human relationships and was sensitive to the physical and emotional needs of those with whom he is working.

A common mistake of first-time directors is to allow the authority of the position to go to their heads. By misusing the position of power or simply misunderstanding it, a director can create the opposite effect of what he is trying to achieve. To get the best results, a director should strive to achieve and maintain a correct attitude toward his actors and staff. If a director fails to regard his actors as artists and pay them the respect due them as artists, if he refuses to let them bring their artistic imaginations to bear on the characters they are assigned to play, if he demands that their performances conform exactly to his preconceived ideas of how those characters should be played, then he is cutting himself off from one of the richest sources of creative inspiration he has available. This will likely cause their performances to appear dull and lifeless. They will lack the fire and excitement that the audience deserves to see. Because these are qualities that an amateur actor probably is not aware of in himself, he must be inspired by the director. The director must not stifle creative imagination, but encourage it. His objective should be to help each actor make his greatest possible contribution to the production.

The theatrical process, especially in the church, is a collaboration. You are all working together to reach the end result. The director's job is only a part of that collaboration. Too many directors feel that it must be their idea in order to maintain their importance. The director should be open to all ideas and use them if they do indeed improve the production.

The director still has the vision of the total concept and must make sure that all performances are working together to meet that vision. The actor is working with a partial concept and must depend on the director to guide the development of his role. The actor may have a tendency to overact or overdevelop and thus cause distortion to the character and its relationship to the rest of the play. The director must recognize this and correct it without sounding as if he is personally attacking the actor and/or his ability. The actor, like the scene designer, the costume designer, or the lighting designer, should be encouraged to make his full contribution to the production; but he must not be allowed to tip the balance in his—or any other—direction.

Instead of statements such as, "No, no, you're not saying the line right!" you might try something like, "That was good. What would you think if we tried it this way?" This requirement for both encouragement and restraint is what makes the director's task so very complicated. Yet it is this necessity for keeping an open mind, while making the most careful calculations, that makes this position so fascinating. It is even more challenging when the director is working with amateurs in a church environment.

Blocking.—The stage is divided into specific areas to make it easier to block the scenes. The director must learn these areas and teach them to the actors, so that he can easily communicate where they are to move and position themselves on stage.

The director should have at least a basic idea of how each scene should be played before the first rehearsal. Using the floor plans provided by the set designer, the director will sketch actors' positions and draw arrows for their movements and crosses, making notes at which point during the script each takes place. He is creating the stage picture.

A stage picture should not remain static for long; that is, the actors should be moving. But the director must never move the actors simply for the sake of preventing static; the script or action should have a proper motivation for the move.

There are two kinds of movement which are included in the script and are essential to the progress of the play. Usually movement is included in the stage directions, or if not, it is implied in the lines. The first kind includes such things as the entrances and exits of the various characters. With this kind of movement, the director has little choice. He may alter its direction or location, or he may change its execution to a certain extent; but he must include it.

The second is that movement which, although often suggested by the lines, is not absolutely essential to the progress of the story. It is movement added by the director (or actor) to enrich or clarify the story, to shift attention to a particular character or area, or for purely technical reasons to improve or correct the composition.

Composition is the design or pattern of the stage picture. It includes the actors, their costumes, the scenery, and the lighting effects. The director, of course, must be aware of all these elements as he blocks the actors. Aesthetically, the audience has an unconscious requirement for balance on the stage. The positions and movements must express a mood that is in harmony with the basic spirit of the play; and it must have variety, both within itself and from one picture to the next.

When blocking the actors, it is important to remember that unless the proper characters are emphasized, the audience is given no clue as to the person who is speaking or who may be expected to speak. This will especially be a problem with large casts or when using wireless microphones. When creating the stage picture, there should be a point of emphasis to which the eye of the audience is drawn. Remember that the eye, in looking at any composition, automatically searches for order.

To achieve emphasis in his stage picture, the director can use body position, level, area, space, repetition or reinforcement, contrast, and focus. In conjunction with the scene designer, costume designer, and lighting designer, he also has color and light.

There are certain commands that a director will give to position his actors in the correct body positions. The director and the actors should understand and memorize these commands in order to speed up the rehearsal process.

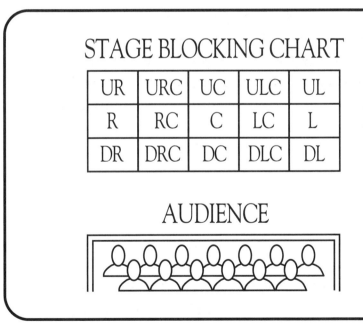

UR–up right, URC–up right center, UC–up center, ULC–up left center, UL–up left, R–right, RC–right center, C–center, LC–left center, L–left, DR–down right, DRC–down right center, DC–down center, DLC–down left center, DL–down left.

Stage right/left is from the character's viewpoint while on the stage looking at the audience. When the director, sitting in the audience, gives a command to move "stage left," it is to his right.

Downstage is down toward the audience.

Upstage is up, away from the audience.

Cross is to move from one place to another.

Project is to project the voice to the back of the auditorium to be heard; using greater volume without distorting the quality of the voice.

Articulate is to speak clearly and understandably.

Never place your actors in a position in which they feel unnatural, uncomfortable, or stiff. Watch for those actors who are frozen, waiting for their cue to move or speak. If they are involved in the plot, listening to or watching the other actors, their posture and movements should be natural. Unnatural blocking is one of the most common reasons for breaks in the established illusion of reality.

The body positions an actor may assume on stage must be considered from two points of view: the actor in relation to the audience and the actor in relation to the other actors in the scene. In relation to the audience, an actor can assume five basic positions. In the order of their relative strength (i.e., their attention-getting ability), these positions are:

- full front (the strongest),
- one quarter front,
- profile,
- three-quarters back, and
- full back (the weakest).

However, these values are not absolute and should only be used as a guideline.

The following illustrations show some of the most common commands for stage positions.

POSITIONS

These are only guidelines from traditional theater. Don't feel restricted by rules. Sometimes it is more dramatic to have an actor's back to the audience or to speak while walking upstage. Sometimes it is more realistic and interesting when you direct against the norm. Too many directors try to create symmetry or even-up on stage. Often unbalance is what is necessary to create the desired mood of the scene.

Unless the proper tempo/rhythm pattern is achieved and sustained, the actors

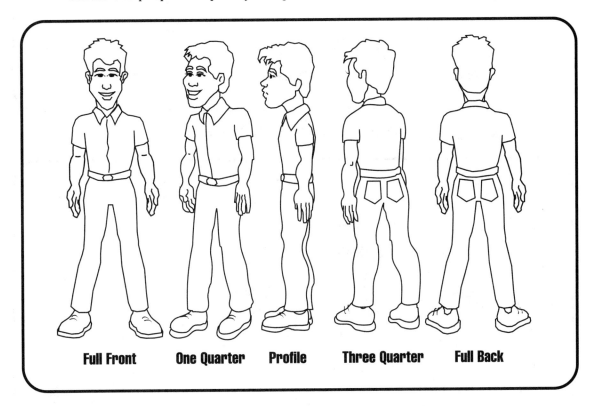

Full Front   One Quarter   Profile   Three Quarter   Full Back

will find it difficult, if not impossible, to feel their parts and give an emotionally convincing performance; and the audience will be unlikely to respond emotionally to the intention of the script, since it will probably be misled in respect to the mood, the atmosphere, and the nature of the characters involved. Keep the scene flowing.

When a director begins blocking a scene, it is suggested that the actors have their lines memorized for that scene. Traditionally, the blocking is done first and the actor carries his script, making blocking notes. We have found that this is not only tedious and time-consuming, but it helps create unnatural blocking.

When the actors know the lines, the director can watch the scene "play," then paint the picture (block the scene) as it develops from natural motivation. The way an

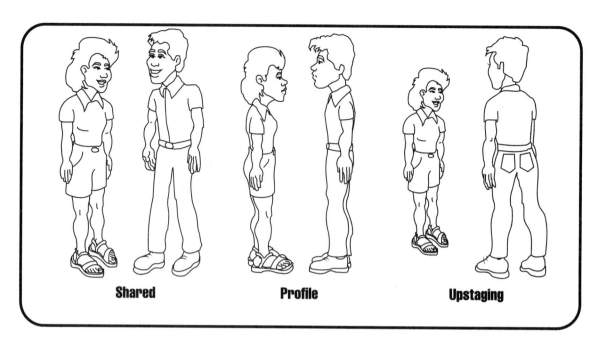

POSITIONS OF TWO ACTORS

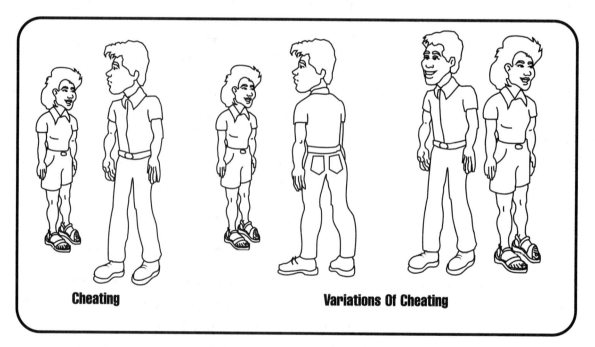

POSITIONS OF TWO ACTORS

actor speaks a line might create different motivations for movement. The director will know when the line delivery and movements work in harmony.

The director is also responsible for bad delivery of dialogue. Bad acting should never have gotten as far as the performance without the director correcting it. He

40

should pay attention to every word spoken by every actor. If the actor understands his character and is listening to the other actors, the words should come realistically from the "internal character".

The director should read "A Study in Acting" (a later chapter), as it goes into great lengths on how to "act" naturally. The director must understand this chapter in order for him to be the actor's guide.

Tech Rehearsal.—Before dress rehearsal, it is very important to have a rehearsal for all of the technical areas of the performance in order to set levels and create cues. This is a grueling and time-consuming process which would be a waste of the actors' time. In most productions, expect the tech rehearsal to take several hours. It is a good idea to have volunteer stand-ins to move around the stage in place of the actors.

The director would sit in a neutral place in the auditorium, while all tech running crews are in their places. If communication is not available through headsets, the director should have a microphone.

Go through the entire script, cue by cue, stopping to set microphone levels, lighting levels, timing of effects, and so forth. This is where the running crews finalize the cues in their tech scripts.

Dress Rehearsal.—Every production should have a minimum of two dress rehearsals. A dress rehearsal should be considered the same as a performance. All costumes, makeup, effects, and such should be used in full. Do not stop to fix problems. Allow the performance to continue. The cast must be allowed to understand the transitions and become part of the whole process. If you as a director can resist the temptation to stop, you will find that most of the problems will fix themselves by the next dress rehearsal.

Take notes. After the rehearsal, bring the cast and crew back out in the audience and give the notes. If necessary, have the cast go back on stage to rework the major problem scenes. Ask actors to write down comments that are given to them.

The Director and the Audience

When a patron enters the theater, he enters into an implied agreement with director, author, and actors to suspend his disbelief and accept whatever premise is set on stage. The audience wants to be caught up in the play, to forget their own preoccupations, and to become involved in the action on stage. The audience will keep their part of the deal and will ask only that the cast and crew not abuse their confidence.

An audience, if it is to participate fully in the theatrical experience, must be made to feel that everything it sees or hears on stage is happening to real people in a real place at a particular time. The director can create this illusion of reality so that the audience will become completely absorbed. This is where the "script breakdown" and "charts" will be invaluable. With thorough research and attention to detail, the director can diminish the possibility of losing his audience through inaccuracy. Maintaining the illusion of reality means consistently maintaining the premise you have already established with your audience.

Regardless of the type of production, you must never deviate from the guidelines you've given your audience. We attended a church production of a play portraying the life of Christ. The format chosen was one of realism and accuracy to that period. Every aspect of the production supported this style, including the performances, costumes, and sets. Unfortunately, the illusion of reality was shattered when one of the disciples entered wearing eye glasses, and another a gold watch. As a result, the credibility of the play was never regained. Even though all other areas of the production were completely accurate, the focus remained on the errors. You may not get your message across if the audience stops to "criticize" the play because the illusion of reality is broken.

One of the first things to break the illusion of reality for the audience is a long scene change or blackout. During this down time, the audience will drift back into their own world and break their relationship to the characters. As a director, you are responsible for creating these transitions from scene to scene as quickly and smoothly as possible. We believe that a scene change longer than ten seconds is too long. It would be better for the actors to make the scene change as part of the story, in full view of the audience, than to have a long blackout. The sets and props should be designed with scene changes in mind. If a blackout is necessary, fill it with something like narration or music. As director, always keep the pacing and rhythm moving.

If it sounds as though we are making the director's position a difficult one to fill, that is precisely our intention. But it is not impossible. It is necessary to understand the enormous amount of problems inherent in the job. These will vary from church to church, person to person, and sometimes gender to gender. (A woman may have a more difficult time directing in some churches because of very old and antiquated attitudes.)

Whatever problems arise, the director has the responsibility of solving them. In his capacity of guide and mentor to the audience, he must determine everything that is needed to give them the illusion of the stage reality from curtain to curtain.

That is the bottom line.

Notes.— At the end of each rehearsal, it is important to assemble the cast and crew together to give your notes. Be wise in the way these notes are presented. They should never be made to embarrass anyone. If you think that a particular note might be of a sensitive nature, save it for a private moment.

"Notes" is also a good time for questions from your cast and crew. Many of the problems that you may not even be aware of can be solved here.

Once the opening scene of opening night begins, most of your job is done as a director. However, a great director stays with the show, taking notes each night from the audience. In a general assembly before each performance, give the notes from the previous performance. Many of these individual notes can be given in private.

What is being presented to the audience is the vision of the director. It's his baby. And yet, the audience will most likely never even know who he is. The reward for the director is the final result. When he sits in the audience and watches lives being changed, he is satisfied that he has done his job well.

DIRECTOR'S CONCEPT

Here the director's concept was to design the set to appear as if the audience was lying at the foot of the cross, looking up toward the sky. The frame was constructed of 2 x 4's, then covered with 3/4" plexiglass painted to resemble stained glass. Note how far the stage extends into the audience.

44

CHAPTER FIVE

MUSIC & CHOREOGRAPHY

The production is shared by an ensemble and its success depends on the "teamwork" of the production staff. "Territorial" divisions will almost always ensure its failure. Most often, in church productions, the Music Director is the one in charge and initiates the entire production. He enlists a Drama Director to handle only the dramatic parts. The Music Director then usually handles all music including the choir and casting of soloists. This divide and conquer approach goes against that which has been proven in professional theater.

It is of utmost importance to the production that a clear distinction is made between the responsibilities of the church music director and the production music director. Although these positions may be occupied by the same person, they must be performed separately, according to their respective job descriptions.

The church music director, while responsible to the church and choir, may initiate the production and may even be the producer. The production music director is responsible to the director and is concerned only with the music of the show. The most successful church productions have been accomplished when the church music director, who also acts as the production music director, yields to this chain of command.

The director should be creatively in charge of the entire production, and the production music director is another one of his team members heading a particular department: music. There should not be a conflict of concept since one person, the director, has that exclusive responsibility.

A great music director will be thinking of the entire production and what it is expressing to the audience, and not just showcasing his music or his choir. That is the way it is done successfully in professional theater, and so it can be successfully accomplished in the church.

Pre-production

In the initial production meeting, the production music director will use the predetermined budget, space, and talent available to determine whether he will use live or taped music, or any combination thereof. For instance, if a taped score is not available from the publisher, and you do not have room for a full orchestra, you can assemble the musicians to record your own soundtrack. This recorded music could even be accompanied by a few live musical instruments, such as the organ and piano. Each church will use combinations best suited to its unique situation and budget.

Once the final decisions have been made concerning musicians, instruments, vocalists, and so on, the music director can begin ordering the appropriate material. Musical scores and scripts can be purchased outright or leased, depending on the publishing company. Deposits, royalties, and/or other fees may be attached. When ordering, be sure to allow ample time for delivery since processing and shipping procedures vary from company to company.

Before the casting of soloists can begin, the music director will need to make specific selections from the score to be used as audition material. These selections should represent the vocal range for each character.

If that the material is not be available at the onset of auditions, the music director will need to select appropriate audition music for soloists, comparable in range and style to that of the musical score.

The director may rely upon the input of the musical director when casting a singing role. Appearance, age, stage presence, acting ability, and projection are some of the many factors to be considered in addition to the vocal quality of a performer. Soloists should be chosen for their performing ability and compatibility with the role, rather than church politics and choir membership. "Paying dues" to the choir should not be a prerequisite for auditions and only tends to reinforce those territorial boundaries.

We once worked with a music director who insisted on final say in casting all leading roles that required solos. The music director was thinking only "music," where the director was thinking of the whole production. Unfortunately, the music director had the unusual authority in this particular production and went against the pleadings of the director. The music director cast a man who had a very beautiful and powerful singing voice to play the part of Jesus. He was also a middle-aged, overweight, balding man with a heavy foreign accent. He looked ridiculous in a loin cloth, and every time he spoke, there were giggles from the audience. There isn't a singing voice in existence that justifies this type of casting. In good theater, it is always better to have an actor who sings than a singer who acts.

Rehearsal

When working with a church choir, it is advisable to begin on familiar ground, with music rehearsals on their established choir night. The music director will begin working with the chorus and soloists prior to and separate from regular cast rehearsals. This will allow them ample time to memorize both music and lyrics before joining the cast rehearsals.

Once the chorus has begun rehearsing with the principal cast, the music director will be there to see that the quality of the musical performances is not deteriorating. He will assist the director in making whatever changes are necessary. He will also give notes pertaining to music at the close or beginning of each rehearsal.

The music director will usually be required to train and rehearse the principals and the chorus, unless an assistant music director has been appointed for these chores. To be most useful, this assistant should be experienced in choral work. Even with an assistant, the music director has a large and demanding job. The average musical has anywhere from sixteen to twenty musical numbers, not to mention the musical transitions, the overture, special effects, segue music, underscore, and exit music. This, of course, adds up to an enormous number of music cues, all or most of which must be executed at precisely the right moment. Even a one-second delay could destroy the pace of the show.

If an orchestra is used, it is the music director's responsibility to make sure that they are fully rehearsed by "dress week." This means that rehearsals must begin far enough ahead to ensure that the musicians will be thoroughly familiar with the score before they are asked to work with the performers. In most cases either taped music or piano accompaniment will be used for rehearsals until the orchestra is fully prepared.

The music director will meet with the director to decide the most suitable area to place the instrumentalists. Then, he will meet with the sound designer to discuss placement, balance, and type of microphones to be used for the orchestra, soloists, and chorus. If you are performing in a large auditorium, it may be necessary to use special amplification, such as a wireless microphone on a soloist. Again, the final decision is reserved for the director. All this must be determined before the first dress rehearsal.

Performances

Before the show each night, the music director will lead the cast through vocal warm-up exercises. If he is also the conductor, he may decide to meet early with the orchestra for warm-up. If an orchestra is not used, it is advisable not to have a music director visibly conducting the choir during the performance, as this breaks the illusion of reality. We attended a production where the music director sat on the front row and directed the choir with white gloves, thinking he was inconspicuous, when in fact he completely distracted the audience and broke the illusion of reality. A chorus is part of the cast and should not break the "fourth wall" to look at a music director. If he is not conducting, it is advisable for the music director to sit in the audience and take notes to improve future performances.

The last responsibility of the music director is the selection and execution of house music. That is the music that the audience will hear pre-show, during intermission, and as they leave. This music should compliment the director's concept of the show. Once, we produced a realistic re-enactment of the crucifixion, with full costume, realistic sets and special effects. To set the mood, five minutes before the opening of the show we had a man, dressed in a modern suit and tie, walk around the set singing, "I Walked Today Where Jesus Walked." This was complimentary in its contrast.

Chorus

Some choir members may not be accustomed to performing without the aid of a book or a choir director out front leading them. Most productions will require the chorus to become characters and therefore part of the cast. In this case the chorus must at all times maintain the illusion of reality since they are the supporting players. If the chorus is playing the mob at the crucifixion and they hold music books, the audience's belief in the scene will be instantly shattered. Compromising any one scene means compromising the entire play.

Since the chorus members are portraying characters, they should be treated as any other part of the cast. They should conduct themselves with the same enthusiasm that the principal actors have. A chorus member should never break the character that he or the director has established. The chorus member should never break the fourth wall by looking out into the audience. He should never assume that he is inconspicuous and that the audience is not looking at him. Even the slightest slip of characterization can be picked up by an audience member, destroying his illusion of reality.

This is why it is so important for the chorus to have all music memorized. There should never be cue cards or cheat sheets to look at. Many church choir members underestimate themselves and their ability to memorize. The books are usually more for personal security than for necessity. We have seen many choirs develop the self-confidence to perform as actors, once they got used to the idea of being on their own, without a music director or music book to follow.

Musical Numbers

This is where the church makes one of its biggest mistakes in presenting quality productions. Music directors usually select some of their favorite songs, assemble them in an order, and ask someone to write "drama" to fit in between them. This is backwards from anything done in professional theater. A musical number in a show, whether a solo or full cast, must be born out of the show. To sum up what a musical number should be: The lyric is an extension of the dialogue and the music underscores the mood of the scene. A "canned" song cannot speak what the character needs to say. Unfortunately, a vast number of the Christian musicals published are written with music first and dialogue sandwiched between.

Choreography

Although the choreographer is responsible to the director, since he is involved in staged movement, he will be working directly with the music director. As such, we have included choreography in this chapter.

For the average church group, the most troublesome problem in doing a musical drama will be the choreography. Not only is it difficult to find the right choreographer, it is difficult to find willing and suitable dancers. Most people can sing, at least adequately; they have been encouraged to sing all their lives. Singing is a natural expression of joy. But, most Americans are not accustomed to expressing their emotions in dance. They are not raised to folk dance like the Irish, the Mexicans, the Israelis, and the Greeks. The problem, then, is to help them overcome their inhibitions and show them how they can derive as much pleasure through choreographed movement as they can through choral singing.

The well-known dancer Ray Bolger once said, "I've never been that great a dancer. It's what's inside me that comes across to an audience that has made me what I am. Dancing, according to the dictionary, is the poetry of motion. If you make this poetry come alive, you can make the audience become a part of you and dance right with you."

This, of course, should be the object of any choreographer—to help the chorus "make this poetry come alive." Unfortunately, that will not be easy. For those churches who have a religious conviction that dancing is wrong, let us emphasize that there is a major difference between "social" dancing and theatrical choreography. Choreography is staged movement. The term applies to the way in which actors and choruses move about the stage during a musical number.

This movement may be simple or complicated, but it is not haphazard. It is well-planned and rehearsed, that is, choreographed. As an example, let us look at a scene where Barabbas is being presented to the mob. Music builds and the crowd begins to chant "Give us Barabbas" in song. The choreographer stages their positions and their movements to start slowly and build in their anger. By the end of the song the crowd will be moving about the stage in deliberate and graceful movements that have been designed to convey the mood of the angry crowd.

We have seen choir members quit the choir and/or the church over this. We have also seen hundreds of people join the church and the choir because of the quality and professionalism performed by the church.

The choreographer will probably be working with largely untrained and inexperienced people. Most of them will have had no experience whatever in the specialized movements required for the production. Many will be older, heavy, out-of-shape; some may even be crippled.

The choreographer's job, then, becomes essentially one of teaching, patience, and use of strategy. He should develop movements and routines that will place those less capable performers in the background or possibly as observers, sitting on rocks, carrying lamps or bread, or just standing and swaying. The more able would be placed in the foreground and given the more complicated routines.

To begin with, the choreographer will meet with the director to discuss the play's concept and style. They will use the floor plan and/or set model to develop a basic design of movement for all musical numbers.

One very critical area of choreography that is often overlooked is the transition into and out of musical numbers and between dramatic scenes. The illusion of reality will be shattered if the actors stand awkwardly on the stage waiting for their music cue to begin dance movement. There should always be transitional movement that is motivated by the trueness of the scene and its characters.

The choreographer must work directly with the music director. However, most rehearsals will be with taped music and an assistant to control the tape player. Sometimes the rehearsal process may go as slow as one musical phrase at a time, played over and over. When an entire number is somewhat mastered, the choreographer will probably want to call in the rehearsal pianist. This person, although too often underrated, is a very important member of the choreographic team. If possible, the pianist should be the same one who will play in the orchestra and the same one who played for the auditions. He should be flexible enough so that he or she can vary the tempo to fit the increasing proficiency of the dancers. Because of this flexibility, a rehearsal pianist is much more valuable than a tape. The goal, of course, is to bring the dancers up to the tempo indicated in the score, so that when they are brought together with the orchestra there will be only minor problems of adjustment.

Scene from "Living Christmas Tree," First Baptist, Van Nuys, California; 1987. The theme that year was "Country Christmas." The choreography was fashioned after a country hoedown. The movement fit the story of a small country town having a Christmas celebration. Much of the choreography was physically demanding and so was performed by the younger groups. However, everyone on stage was given some movement which complemented the livelier action.

Notice the unfinished set and the orchestra wearing street clothes. This is a rehearsal in which the performers are getting comfortable with the restrictions of movement a costume might cause. There are those who mignt object to the use of "dance" within the church. One should be sensitive to those people when designing any choreographed movement.

Rehearsals

Choreography rehearsal will be held separately, well in advance of full cast rehearsals. By the time the director is ready to go through the show in sequence, the choreography should be completed. The movements are the equivalent of dialogue lines: they should be learned first, then polished during rehearsals.

Every rehearsal should begin with at least 15 minutes of warmup and stretching exercises. This would include all those participating, regardless of age or restrictions. This is a good time for the choreographer to "size up" his talent and begin making decisions for placement.

Staging vs. Dance

Most church choreographers make the same basic mistake which gives the production an amateur quality. They create "dance" steps and teach everyone the same steps which they all do in unison across the stage. Most choreography in a musical is not done by dance steps. It is the way actors and chorus are moved about the stage.

Rent and watch some of the great musicals of the past. In the library scene from *The Music Man* every person has a different movement. Some are walking up stairs, sliding down poles, or sitting on a bench tapping their feet. In the chimney sweep scene from *Mary Poppins* they do tumbles, back flips, and slides, and swing brooms. They make use of props and sets and stage levels.

In addition to those mentioned above, rent and study old musicals such as *Brigadoon, My Fair Lady, The Sound of Music, Camelot,* and *Fiddler on the Roof.*

Choreography is creativity at its best.

CHAPTER SIX

PRODUCTION COORDINATOR & STAGE MANAGER

The production coordinator (PC) carries a tremendous responsibility throughout the mounting of any production, regardless of its type or complexity. The PC is the central figure to whom all cast and crew will report progress, concerns, questions, and so forth. This person's job is that of referee, psychologist, den-mother, nurse, child-care provider, secretary, fact-finder. . . in short, the one holding all the answers to your questions (i.e., the Alex Trebec of the production team).

Pre-production
The PC is the director's right hand and will learn everything the director wants to happen in the production, since he will be responsible for "making it so." The PC will coordinate and attend all production meetings (taking and keeping notes) as he will be required to track the progress of decisions made and actions to be taken. He should always be aware of the "big picture" and how the smallest details that the director may overlook at a given moment could impact the course of events during all phases of production. Tact and intervention will be daily honed and refined throughout this production.

Auditions
During pre-production the PC will be the person scheduling and coordinating the auditions to coincide with the format the director has indicated. He will keep notes throughout the auditions as to strengths and weaknesses and general, over-all ability of those trying out, as perceived by the casting team and director.

It is during the auditioning process that the stage manager (SM) will first appear to those auditioning. He will have been involved in the necessary pre-production meetings held to determine how the auditions will be conducted. Usually the stage manager will:
- greet people as they arrive,

- make sure they are on the sign-in sheet,
- give them the parts they may be asked to read or forms they may be asked to fill out,
- collect the forms and scripts when finished,
- direct them to available rest rooms when appropriate,
- keep refreshments fresh (if provided), and
- inform those auditioning as to what can be expected during the audition to make it as comfortable a situation as it can be.

The PC will keep the SM informed as to how it is going inside the audition room(s) so that the SM can answer any questions that may arise from those auditioning.

Upon conclusion of the casting session(s) the PC will notify those who are to be "called back" (seen again for final selection). This notification may be done through an announcement, a posted list, or a phone call. The roles of the PC and SM during the call-back process are much the same as they were for the audition portion. They are conducted much the same way as were the audition(s), but with fewer people; and more attention is paid to all aspects of a person's ability to fill the open role(s). Most times actors will be seen with others who are considered for (or may have already been cast as) characters who will interact with one another to see how they play off each other, how they look together, and so forth. Often an actor may be right for another role that was not considered when he or she was seen at the initial audition.

If there are no call-backs scheduled, parts may be awarded soon after the close of the audition process. The director may choose (for various reasons) to pass this task on to the PC, which is not uncommon and sometimes benefits those involved. It allows the director some distance from the actor who may require some time to get over his personal disappointment before any kind of confrontation is made. When posted or announced by the PC, it is recognized that the PC does not carry the weight of having made the decisions and has some capacity to be a neutral party in the notification process. He may also be able to provide some insight to those people who were not awarded the parts they hoped for while still maintaining necessary confidentiality. It also allows the director time to follow up with those people who, with just a little one-to-one explanation and/or encouragement from him, may be less likely to carry the loss over into other areas.

Note: It is imperative that those auditioning understand the notification process prior to their leaving the audition. It requires a great deal of courage and strength of character for most people to audition for a part, especially before people they work with on a regular basis within the church, knowing they may not get it! Letting them down easy and encouraging them to participate in other areas is vital to the success of the play and its impact on the church and the community as a whole.

Production

Once the show is cast, you are in "production," rehearsing and getting the entire cast and crew show-ready! During this period, it becomes apparent to all that record-keeping is the most valuable part of the production coordinator's job. It would be wise for him to keep a comprehensive and current file containing copies of the following:

- *Designs*—all designs (from initial concepts through final approval) of sets, lighting, sound plots, costumes, props, playbills, tickets, etc.
- *Schedules*—meetings, rehearsals, cast and crew availability lists, construction, publicity deadlines, etc.
- *Phone lists*—cast, crew, production staff, church staff, resources, etc.
- *Forms*—cast/crew availability, medical release, parent consent forms, photo release, sign-in sheets, ticket requests, personal history/biography information, etc.
- *Resources*—potential or available materials, workers, monies, publicity, etc.
- *Notes*—meetings, rehearsals, suggestions/comments/requests, director's comments, producer's comments, casting, etc.
- *Finances*—receipts, budget breakdown, donations of money/materials/services, crew and cast complimentary ticket requests, etc.

The file will begin during pre-production, and will continue through the run of the show and the strike. Many of the items listed will actually be generated or monitored by the PC and responsibility for same will lie with the PC. The idea here is that the PC will be doing just what his title indicates: he will be coordinating the production! Therefore, he will be interacting heavily with the production staff at various pre-production meetings to establish the schedules for auditions and rehearsals pertaining to music and choreography and the dramatic portions—breaking down the given and helping the directors to plot a strategy to allow ample time for:

- learning lyrics and music: keeping in mind the number of songs to be memorized;
- establishing the sequence in which they will be learned in conjunction with the choreography schedule; and answering questions such as:
- Which titles pertain to the entire group verses smaller groups within the whole

or just soloists or featured dancers?

- Will rehearsals require a rehearsal pianist, organist, or other instrumentalist?
- At what point can choreography rehearsals be conducted with taped music only, and when is the rehearsal pianist or other instrumentalist required?
- When will specific scenes be rehearsed? When are the actors to be blocked into those scenes? When will the work-throughs and run-throughs be scheduled? When are the actors to be "off-book" for these rehearsals?
- Which music, choreography and scene rehearsals can be conducted simultaneously? How can you integrate "work days" for various crews with rehearsals already scheduled?
- For which rehearsals and work days will you need to provide childcare? ...refreshments? ...to secure rehearsal and/or work spaces and arrange setup and teardown for same?
- At which rehearsals will various forms be made available for emergency information and to obtain information to construct the resource lists and/or contact sheets of all cast and crew members? Who will monitor and input all the data to determine its accuracy for content and so forth with respect to all forms to be utilized?
- What will be your method of signing-in those attending rehearsals? Will you establish several contact persons or stations, or a general station where even a board can be placed to indicate the building or room where each person can be found at any given time?
- For all children involved in the rehearsal process: How long can they be expected to stay? Will their parents' attendance be required? Who will have full responsibility for those children when parents are not on site? How will children be released into an adult-supervised childcare program once their rehearsal portion is over? To whom can each child be released upon the closure of any meeting, rehearsal, and such, and under what manner shall that release be recognized?

As you can see, this file should be present and accessible at all meetings and rehearsals and should hold the answer to every question concerning any aspect of the production. It will also prove to be a valuable resource when preparing the playbill, as will be discussed in a later chapter.

It is also in this production phase that some key issues must be addressed. In outline form, these include:

I. *Keys* should be issued to the production coordinator that would allow him access to all areas that may be important to any one person on the production team.
   A. These include:
      1. Rehearsal areas
      2. Church storage areas
      3. Bathrooms
      4. Childcare rooms
      5. The kitchen
      6. Access to phones for both incoming and outgoing purposes
      7. Set construction areas: props, costumes, makeup, and wardrobe assembling/storage areas
      8. General production office desk or work space
      9. First aid supplies, etc.
   B. The stage manager may also need to have keys for the more immediate needs (rehearsal, childcare, and rest-room facilities). That way, he can open up those areas as outlined in his job description, mentioned later in this chapter.
II. Another aspect for consideration: *Who approves* the calendar for the work schedule the production team desires to establish? Which church staff members, departments, and/or classes must be notified of the new schedule?
III. In conjunction with this topic, *security* measures and general maintenance issues must not be neglected.
   A. How will the rehearsal and workdays affect the existing work load and schedule of the maintenance and grounds-keeping staff?
   B. Will those duties be altered, or concessions be made, so as best to accommodate the full church and production calendars?
   C. Special preparations for worship services must be acknowledged by the production team. (This is especially critical during the time for which they assume general clean-up duties.)
   D. Will the security of the buildings lie with the maintenance staff or the production team? It is also a good idea to have a contact number for one or more persons on the maintenance staff. Policies which should be reviewed with the maintenance staff regarding the utilities are:
      1. The location of heat and air controls.
      2. Who is responsible for having them set at a reasonable temperature?

3. The location of circuit breakers as well as the main shut-off valves for the water, the gas, the baptistry.

4. The location of the light switches for all areas, and which are to be left on round-the-clock and which are to be left on at the time the production team is scheduled to vacate the property.

5. Is there an alarm system that requires a code or a key to activate and deactivate? If it is accidentally triggered or engaged, who should be notified? How shall its non-urgency be communicated to the alarm company?

6. Areas/offices which are off-limits to certain persons, and those which are off-limits to all persons.

7. The locations of fire extinguishers on the property.

8. Accessibility of the sound system.

9. Activation of lights for the outside grounds and parking areas: activated manually or by a timer? will the timer need to be reset to include days and/or nights now on the calendar?

IV. In the event that there is an emergency wherein a church leader or pastor must be called, a list of those to handle such situations along with contact numbers for them (both day and night) should be on file with the PC, SM and director.

V. Also on file with the PC will be emergency release forms filled out by all members of the production team, including the producer, director, all actors, singers, dancers, stage crew, designers, assistants, child-care providers, ushers, security personnel, etc.

A. These forms will initially be passed out once auditions begin and be given to whomever joins the production team in any capacity. It is a safety measure for the most part, nothing more than providing for the most responsible and efficient means of dealing with the unexpected.

B. Often we assume that because we see various people on a weekly or even daily basis, we would know how best to respond to their needs. Stop and think, right now, of the person other than an immediate family member, whom you "know best." If something were to happen—if he or she were to become unconscious—would you be able to supply the following basic information?

1. First, middle, last name

2. Address and phone number

3. Allergies, medications, or previous surgeries

4. Insurance carrier or family doctor

5. Employer's address

6. Date of birth/place of birth

7. Social security number

8. Mother's and/or father's name, address, and phone numbers both day and night

9. Name and phone number of "significant other" (spouse, parent, friend) who should be contacted in a more serious matter (or one not so serious, depending on the relationship and circumstances of the individual).

VI. Not to be overlooked is the method or policy with which the church responds to the needs of people seeking assistance who will show up after the pastor or pastoral care department has gone home for the day. Is there someone "on-call" to counsel, advise, and/or assist in general to the physical, emotional, and spiritual needs of such persons? Let's not forget that though our immediate response is to reach out to those in need, the situation may be much more than is immediately realized at first observation, and in some cases should be referred to those who specialize in this area of service.

VII. Another aspect is that of the church's insurance policy.

A. Does it indicate the number and age-range of persons required to function as chaperons or child-care providers?

B. Will the church provide transportation of any kind to any persons involved in the production, and what are the insurance restrictions regarding this arrangement?

VIII. Who controls the finances?

A. Does the church have any open purchase orders or accounts with any local vendors to which name(s) may need to be added?

B. How is the production budget separate from the church budget?

C. What is the policy regarding:

1. Purchase orders?

2. Check requests?

3. Cash requests/petty cash, receipts, reimbursement of out-of-pocket expenses?

Most of these points will be answered in the pre-production and early production phases of mounting the show. Each church will have certain idiosyncrasies that we could not begin to foresee. However, these points will set you on course to deal with events in an organized and effective manner that will maximize the talent, energy, and time of all concerned. You don't want to spin your wheels while you wait for the "one person" who is authorized, knows the phone number, has the key, remembers the plan, brings the refreshments, and so forth!

The PC will have a comprehensive file, making sure that all department or staff members have what they need to do the jobs they are expected to perform. Though some items will need to remain confidential, it is not meant that the PC or the SM will have exclusivity with respect to its general contents. This is meant to be a production resource file and the PC/SM will have to monitor its contents and whereabouts at all times.

Rehearsal

The stage manager and/or production coordinator should arrive at the rehearsal location at least twenty minutes prior to call time. They will work together to make sure that the space is suitably arranged to meet the needs of that particular rehearsal. This would include the removal of existing furniture and the setting up of working set pieces and set props. It is the SM's responsibility to set out or assist with any refreshments that are provided. Whether the rest room facilities are in the rehearsal building or in a separate location, the stage manager will see that they are unlocked and adequately supplied. Proper air/heating adjustments may need to be made, the lights and sound systems need to be turned on, the 'sign-in' sheet and 'rehearsal-in-progress' sheet will be posted in their pre-arranged locations—all before the first actor arrives or at least before the first cast member(s) call-time.

The SM needs to be aware of any other meetings or functions taking place on the property or grounds to avoid unintentional interruptions of any function. It also is helpful to know how much traffic to expect in the adjoining rooms, buildings, hallways, and such. If your facility is used by other organizations on a regular basis (i.e., Boy/Girl Scout Troops, A.A. Meetings, etc.) then you may encounter strangers who have permission to be there. It is important to check out the calendar and perhaps introduce yourself to the other group leaders or members so they will also recognize you and approach you with questions or problems.

All these tasks to be done prior to each rehearsal can be easily shared or alternately handled to best accommodate the needs of the PC and SM. As long as the director is aware of which one will be fulfilling these tasks prior to each meeting, there is usually no problem with whatever arrangement(s) they make between them or those who may be working with them. The SM, however, will need to be present, from beginning to end, at every scene rehearsal. Being available at the beginning or end of the initial music and choreography rehearsals is important for dispensing and receiving information from each group and keeping everyone well informed and united in their common goals. Reminding them of pending deadlines and so forth is also important for the SM and/or PC.

As liaison to the production staff, the SM will field questions from cast members as they arrive and get settled for rehearsal. Fielding questions, rather than sending the person to another staff member, ensures that the PC/SM has the most current information at all times and that consistency in policy and presentation of information for the group remains at its maximum. Answers to specific questions that may apply to the general cast can be included when notes are given. These notes would include any information from the church staff, producers, director, production coordinator or the stage manager himself. It is clear that the communication among the production coordinator, stage manager, director, and producer is critical to the continuity and success of the production.

Some production teams find it easier to limit the direct input of the SM to items pertaining to the actual rehearsal. Notes then generated by the SM would apply to such points as:

- encouraging the cast to show up on time
- proper disposal of trash and personal properties
- direction regarding storage of props at the rehearsal's close
- call-time/schedule for the next meeting
- fielding questions to relay to appropriate production staff person(s)
- relaying notes as requested by the Director prior to dismissal
- keeping them aware of safety factors which may change from meeting to meeting

Usually notes given at the beginning of rehearsal are answers to pertinent questions: the purpose and goals of this rehearsal, temporary changes in blocking due to safety conditions, and so forth. During rehearsal the SM will stay near the director to take notes, give cues, and handle minor problems as they arise. At the close of rehearsal, he will again give notes, answer questions, and post the call board. Then he will see that the rehearsal spaces (and all other spaces occupied by any persons involved with the production team) are cleaned and secured.

Notes addressed by the PC would encompass such items as information from other production staff members regarding wardrobe fittings and requests or referrals for props, lights, and other equipment not yet obtained by the production team; and information regarding publicity, ticket sales, playbill information, work days, refreshments, child care, and parking restrictions and so forth. Most of these should be presented at the close, saving encouragement and praise for last. Inquiries for information or items to be collected can be done in the beginning to maximize their use during the rehearsal period.

During the rehearsal period, the PC will coordinate the completion of all departments' responsibilities. He already will have acquired answers to the key issues outlined at the beginning of this chapter. He will now work closely with each department, providing them with the resources they will need to perform their respective tasks within the budget and on time. Resources in this sense would include:

- *purchases* (money, p.o.'s, and/or check requests for the purchases that will be made);
- *inventory* (access to materials in storage to be utilized in your production and the names of persons to contact with respect to your present needs); and
- *acquisition* (contacting outside agencies and organizations from whom items may be borrowed, leased, or exchanged in trade; trade may include services rendered, equipment loaned, space leased at a discount, or free advertisement in the program/playbill of the production).

The PC, director, and sometimes producer or even pastor may be the only persons authorized to arrange such plans. No doubt members of the cast and crew will have association with other companies, agencies, or groups that might want to assist in one of various ways. The PC will need to be made aware of these potential resources by those members and will work to coordinate each with respect to its benefits and limitations. These offers could include:

- the donation of materials used to make costumes, props, sets, lights, etc.;
- the donation of money towards the rental, purchase or construction of same;
- the man-hours required for the making of those items;
- transportation for bringing those items to the church facility; and
- child care workers or refreshments on work-days for all persons working.

The PC will enlist people from all areas of the church to assist the various crews with their assigned tasks. It is important that this effort be coordinated by the PC and not individual department heads, to avoid approaching the same small group of members who may be willing to help, but are unsure as to what to do and how to volunteer in an area (or areas) of their choice. In order to make it easier to obtain such commitments, childcare, refreshments, and meals at reduced costs (if not donated) should be provided for the long workdays scheduled. That way, families can be there together without much hardship on anyone. Other church groups or classes may choose to donate refreshments, provide meals, and/or sign up for child-care sessions.

The PC will need to record the names of all persons who assist in any capacity, even if just for one day, noting the area of service or type of work done by all volunteers or contributors to the production. Recognition will not only need to be acknowledged at the time rendered, but also in the program or production playbill. This applies to all persons, groups, and organizations who make donations of any kind. Appropriate, comprehensive recognition is critical when you consider the benefit to be gained by the production, and more importantly, by the church. One of the benefits is allowing others to see what your church is really like. These people may include those who are searching for a "church home" or a "place to fit in," those who are curious about "the church" their friends are always talking about, or those who have memories of "a church in their past."

Your response to their contribution, regardless of how minor it may be, is important. Their attitude towards "the church" may very well depend upon their observation of your attitude towards them. Is your church one that takes pride in doing things well and has cooperation among members of all age levels and abilities?

In addition to this, the PC will be working with the publicity staff to coordinate all efforts in the areas of publicity. Involved in making the community aware of the upcoming production, he may choose to utilize local newspapers, church or class newsletters, church bulletins, flyers, posters, distribution of tickets, sale of advertisements in the program/playbill, and local radio stations (both secular and religious), as well as local television broadcasting networks. While the PC may not be the person who writes all the necessary submissions for any one or all of those suggested above, he will certainly need to see that appropriate statements are prepared and approved prior to their submission. In conjunction with this, he will see that photos are taken or provided to make the most appealing presentation whenever possible. He will also be responsible for keeping track of all receipts and monies spent by each department and for monitoring the budget on a daily basis. He will need to know the restrictions on the usage of all items "on-loan" to and purchased for the production team. Storage space for all items, regardless of their origin, will need to be arranged.

In general, the PC is the one who keeps the checks and balances, both literally and figuratively, throughout the entire production process. He keeps track of the actual rehearsal process itself. He keeps everyone focused on the original goal. He keeps egos in check and feelings from being hurt, making sure everyone stays on schedule and aware of the benefits to be gained in the end.

As you may well have concluded: the roles of the production coordinator and stage manager are very challenging, requiring an enormous commitment of time and energy. At times these jobs may seem very isolated, yet they are extremely rewarding and fulfilling to the personality that enjoys such a challenge.

The SM's and PC's duties continue through the dress week, the performance run, and the strike. Those responsibilities, along with the duties of all other production Team persons, will be contained in the chapter titled "Opening, Closing, and Strike."

AT LEFT: Tree constructed of wood and chicken-wire, covered with papier-maché, then painted. The leaves were a camouflaged netting obtained at a local Army/Navy Surplus store. The netting was draped from the ceiling. This particular tree was hollow, allowing the actors an exit off stage. Full construction details on page 90.

BELOW: Papier-maché is being applied to a solid base. Once painted, this "rock" will dress the set and support an actor's weight. An interesting note: One of these two workers is the pastor of the church. Full construction details in chapter 7.

CHAPTER SEVEN

THE SET

The Design

The first thing the set designer will do after reading the script is meet with the director. At that time they will discuss the requirements and limitations of the stage, the budget, and the schedule. The director will convey to the designer his concept of the play as it pertains to style. As in the example of *You're a Good Man, Charlie Brown,* the director's concept was to capture the feeling of the original cartoon. In turn, the designer came up with the idea of using oversized set pieces of bright, vivid colors outlined in black, with a high-gloss finish. Once the initial idea was accepted, the designer was then ready for the next step.

When developing a design, the designer will need to know the dimensions of the performing area. This would include the exact measurements of the stage in width, depth and height, and the wing space and backstage area. Keep in mind that your set is not limited to the stage platform and can, in fact, extend into the audience area. This would give the actors a larger performing space as well as more options for entrances and exits.

The problem with designing a set in a church sanctuary is working around existing furniture, musical instruments, and other equipment. Pulpits, communion tables, choir seats, rails, and such will probably need to be moved off stage to make room for the incoming sets. It is not always possible to move objects such as the organ or piano. In this case, it is necessary to incorporate those pieces into your design. In one instance, we enclosed the organ in a wooden structure and painted it to look like the dock of a fishing village. Another time we surrounded the organ with a huge **papier-maché** dome and painted it to become the tomb where they buried Christ. With a little creativity, immovable objects will not be a problem in designing the set you want.

The first phase of the design process will be to draw a top-view "ground plan" of the sanctuary/stage, using the previously obtained measurements. (The church office may already have these plans or blueprints on file.)

Next, the designer will create a top-view blueprint of the proposed set to scale, using a copy of the ground plan as his guide. This set "floor plan" will be taken to the director to discuss possible alterations and to obtain final approval.

Now the designer will complete a detailed drawing or painting of what the set will look like to an audience. Additional drawings should be made if the play requires more than one set. These can be done in watercolors, oils, colored pencils, crayons, chalk, or any medium that will accurately represent the colors, textures, and nuances of the proposed set. Ideally, build a miniature scale model—it is the best way to represent your set. The advantages of using a model are many. The director, choreographer, and actors will have a common base from which to begin blocking. The lighting, sound, special effects, and costume designers will have a more comprehensive understanding of what is required of them. In one production, we even used photographs of the scale model for publicity purposes. When published in the local newspaper, the model appeared to be the actual set and generated greater public interest. Foam core is the standard material used in making scale models. It is relatively inexpensive and is easily cut with a razor knife and glued with a hot-glue gun.

Following, in a detailed order, are examples of the design process.

The *ground plan* is the blue print of the existing stage, steps, and doors, including musical instruments, railings, pews, and so forth. Over this you will draw the set "plan view" of the set.

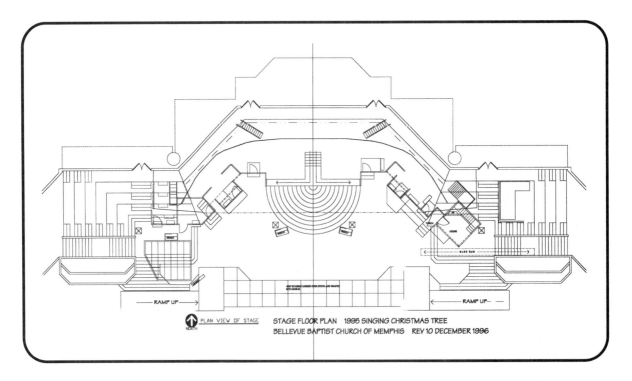

PLAN VIEW OF STAGE   STAGE FLOOR PLAN   1995 SINGING CHRISTMAS TREE
NORTH   BELLEVUE BAPTIST CHURCH OF MEMPHIS   REV 10 DECEMBER 1996

SAMPLE FLOOR PLAN: A top view of the set design drawn to scale by the set designer, taken from measurements in the sanctuary. When compiling the ground plan, special note must be taken of what furniture can be removed or rearranged and what must be incorporated into the set design. The first three rows of pews have been removed to form an orchestra "pit." At this stage of the design it is important to note all legal exits and fire codes.

The *floor plan* (top view), as we have seen, is intended to show exactly how the set is to be placed on the stage, how it is to be oriented, where the openings will be, where the stairs and platforms will be located, where the furniture will be placed, and how the off-stage areas will be masked from the view of the audience. A ground plan is essential even if no other descriptive material is given the builders.

The *designer's sketch* will show what the completed set is intended to look like from the audience's perspective. It will show the audience's view of the set openings, stairs and platforms; architectural treatment of doors, windows, and arches; necessary masking; and furniture arrangement. It will also show, of course, the dressing of the set, the draping of windows, and the use of pictures or ornaments. It will include the colors to be used on the walls, the drapes, and the furniture.

The *designer's model*, if he makes one, will combine the ground plan and the sketch to show the complete set in three dimensions, but on a greatly reduced scale. The purpose of the model is to make it possible for the builders and the director to see at a glance exactly what the finished set will look like from any angle. It will show the relationships between the various architectural features, the spaces between platforms or groups of furniture, and the shape and color of every item to be included in the

Mark Alexander is the production designer at Bellevue Baptist Church, Memphis, Tennessee. Here Mark is constructing the model of the "Singing Tree 1996."

Sometimes a model may be detailed enough to be used for publicity shots as if it were the actual set.

set. In a standard realistic "box set," it is hardly necessary to go to the trouble of constructing a model. However, when a set has complex architectural details, with a variety of stairs and levels, it is almost essential to have a model in order to visualize the construction and the potential use of the set.

Since most churches won't allow the set to be built in the sanctuary until one to two weeks before the show, the set model is necessary for the performers to understand their blocking during rehearsals in relationship to the performance.

Working drawings are the means by which the designer conveys precise instructions to the construction coordinator and set builders. Where standard flats are being employed (either new ones or old ones repainted), it is hardly necessary to prepare a working drawing for the construction of the flats themselves. It is advisable to provide working drawings, however, to show where and how the flats are joined and braced. Where set pieces, cutouts, trees, columns, rocks, circular stairs, or platforms are requested, the designer will be well advised to provide the builders with drawings that are as specific as possible. The construction of many of the most common of these specialized pieces of scenery is described and illustrated later in this chapter.

The completed set during a performance—"Singing Tree 1996," Bellevue Baptist Church, Memphis, Tennessee.

By this time, it should be clear that the set designer is both an artist and a craftsman. He must know much more than merely how to design a pleasing background before which the action of the play will take place. He must be able to create a working environment in which the play can grow and flourish.

Flats sorted out on pews before assembling on the stage.

He is working with real materials such as wood, canvas, metal, velvet, scrim, glue, paint that have highly individualized properties of appearance, strength, durability, drape, ability to reflect light, and ability to take paint or dye. He must know these properties in order to be able to use the proper materials to gain the effects he desires within the budget. He must also know how his set can best be put together and strengthened so that it will not shake every time an actor slams a door. He must know how it can best be shifted, if shifting is a requirement. Should the set be flown? Or run on? Or put on a wagon or turntable? And finally, he should know how it can be (or should be) lit in order to achieve the effect he envisions.

The designer, like the director, the actors, and everyone else who is engaged in the project, is a problem-solver. His problems are different from the other artists' problems, but his efforts are directed toward the same common goal: to give the best and most effective production possible.

Set Construction

By now the set has been approved and the sound and lighting designers are working on their designs. It's time for the designer to meet with his construction team. The set designer will work directly with the construction coordinator. This should be someone with carpentry skills who is capable of working from the blueprints, drawings, and models submitted by the set designer. The construction coordinator will head the actual construction team which will consist of as many volunteers as possible, hopefully with artistic and/or carpentry skills. But, their skill is secondary to their attitude and willingness to work. There will be work for everyone who volunteers, since there are many things to be done.

At the first crew meeting the set designer and construction coordinator will present all the different construction crews, such as carpenters, scenery artists, painters, prop makers, and gophers. The volunteers will be placed in one or more of the above crews, according to their respective skills and availability. At that time the designer will give them the projected work schedule.

The construction coordinator and his crew heads will begin acquisition of all materials. Though your church may be limited in funds, it is still possible to mount a play of high production values with minimal cost. Churches, due to the diversity of their membership, have a greater network of potential resources than most theatrical companies. By tapping into this network, you can greatly reduce your production costs through the donation of supplies, props, manpower, and skills. For instance, one church member may own a lumber company, another an art store, and another a fabric store. These church members may be willing to donate materials or give discounts, both of which are tax deductible. You may want to offer advertising space in the playbill in exchange for materials or services.

Once the supplies are in and the schedule is made, the crews are ready to go to work. To maximize time, the crews should work separately and simultaneously. For instance, the prop crew can be making rocks, while the scenic artists are painting the flats already assembled by the construction team.

Construction time may not coincide with availability of space. For example, church policy may not allow you to build in the sanctuary until two weeks prior to opening night, but your set requires four weeks to construct. In this case, you will want to begin construction at another location and then assemble the set as soon as the sanctuary becomes available. The set designer would need to know this in advance in order to design a somewhat portable set. Whatever it takes, the construction coordinator, in conjunction with the stage manager, must make sure that the entire set is completed by the first technical rehearsal.

If you use professional carpenters and they have never built a theatrical set before, they will probably have a difficult time adjusting. Sets are "make believe" and are not built to last. Strength and durability of a set are primarily for the safety of the cast and crew. Facade walls are usually built with 1 x 3's or furring strips and not 2 x 4 studs.

Stage floors can be built with 2 x 4's and not 2 x 6 beams. Temporary screws should be used whenever necessary, instead of nails where set pieces are braced or joined together. We know of a church that hired a carpenter to build a stage for a TV show they were producing. He used the most expensive and durable lumber available and built it to "construction code." The final cost of the set was $6,000. When it was torn down six months later, we built a much larger set for approximately $500. It was just as durable and safe.

The audience will not know how you built the set when it is completed. The designer will have created an illusion that the audience accepts, not because of the foundation of the set, but because of its "dressing." The fine details and trim that artistically create the realism are what the audience sees. Most people who visit the studio of their favorite television shows are disappointed to see how crude the sets actually look in reality.

As you build the set, it may not look like much until the final days of trim and dressing. This is where the creativity begins to flow as one idea sparks another. Like an artist, you will stand back and look at the set and notice new details to add. The carpenters and painters will probably all have creative input as they work, and a wise designer will listen and evaluate their input for possible use.

When the set is completed, the construction team will be concerned with "masking off" all "sightlines." A sightline is the direct line of vision from any audience member, sitting anywhere in the auditorium, to anywhere on the set. If there is an exit into the wings that is visible from any point in the audience, it must be masked off.

Masking can be done with black cloth (duvateen), a flat, a set piece, or anything that is consistent and true to the set. Masking should also be applied to any visible equipment such as microphones, cables, lighting instruments, or anything that is not true to the set.

Though the audience may never see it, the wing space and backstage areas must be completed also. They should be clear of all debris and equipment that could cause injury to a cast member or create noise during a performance. The floors in the wing areas should be sound-

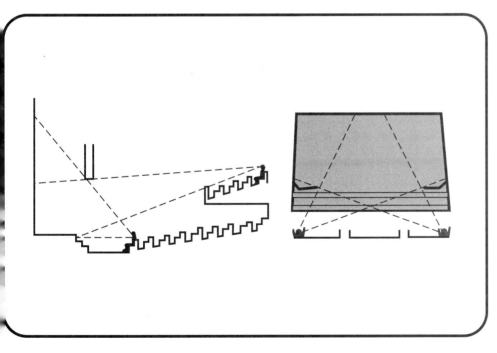

SIGHTLINES (VERTICAL and HORIZONTAL): Mask all areas not intended for the audience's viewing. When designing the set it is important to keep all key areas in full view of every audience member.

proofed to cover the noise of footsteps as cast members prepare to enter the stage. Small lights such as nightlights, christmas tree lights, and such should be at floor level to cover all wing and backstage areas. If lights would create any spill onto the set, glow tape can be used. This can be purchased at theatrical supply houses. Glow tape is a good safety tool that helps mark low hanging beams, bracing, corners, and such because it glows in the dark.

The construction coordinator is responsible for the fireproofing of the entire set; most of it will have been done during construction. When the set is completed, a final inspection should be made of all materials such as drapes, cloths, paper, cardboard, and any other highly flammable substances.

A "running crew" will be selected for set operations and scene changes during performances. Ideally, this crew would consist of members of the construction team because they are more familiar with the set. They will be directed by the director and rehearsed with the cast and other crews as if they were performers. Timing of scene changes and the grace with which they are carried out are critical to maintaining the illusion of reality. They must be well coordinated with exits and entrances of cast members who may be assigned to remove or carry on certain sets or props. The less attention drawn to the change, the better. Unless the change takes place in a "blackout," any crew member who might be seen by the audience should appear to be a member of the cast (in costume) and remain in character during the action.

Making Sets and Props

Aside from donations, making your own sets and props is by far the most cost-efficient method of obtaining them. By storing them between productions, you begin to build an inventory that saves time and money on each future production. Making props and sets can be a challenging and rewarding experience, and it is not as difficult as one might think.

It is an unspoken rule in the theater that those refinements of detail that will not be noticed from the audience area are unnecessary. However, we feel that whenever possible, the extra time should be spent on the detail to create as much realism as possible. As stated earlier, if the audience notices one flaw, however minor, the illusion of reality is broken for the entire play.

Following is a comprehensive and detailed inventory of the most commonly used set pieces for church productions. The instructions can be followed exactly, adapted to your particular needs, and/or enhanced with your own creative talents. They have been designed to be relatively inexpensive and can be stored for reuse for years. Like most of the other sets you will be creating, the one-time cost can drastically reduce the budgets of future productions.

We thought it best to start with papier-maché, since many of the props and sets can be made effectively and inexpensively with this simple formula. Virtually anything that you would spend money on in a professional scene shop can be created with paper-maché. The prop and set crews should know how to make and use this material and should always consider this method. Following is a complete explanation as to paper maché construction:

Basic Papier-Maché

First, construct the basic shape of the set piece, prop, or mold with wood, wire, cardboard, and such. Tear (do not cut) strips of newspaper. Dip these strips of paper into a bucket of 50% water to 50% white glue. Always add in an appropriate amount of fireproofing powder that can be purchased at theatrical supply houses. Apply the strips to the shape, and mold it around all edges. Overlap the pieces, creating several layers on the entire piece. You can build up certain areas, creating contours and ridges and so forth. The more layers, the more durability of the piece.

Tips.—Apply as many layers as you want, but allow every three layers to dry before applying the next. You can wear rubber gloves to protect your hands from the glue, or keep a bucket of warm water near to rinse your hands constantly. If you are doing this indoors, make sure that you are doing the papier-maché project on a large sheet of plastic to protect the floor.

When it is dry you can smooth out any rough lines with a base-coat of paint before applying the artwork. If the edges of paper are too thick to smooth with paint, you may want to apply the following top coat.

Papier-Maché Pulp Paste

1. Tear (do not cut) newspaper, or some other soft paper, into shreds and soak it in water overnight.

2. Drain off the water, then add fresh water and a small amount of caustic potash to assist the breaking down of paper fibers, and boil for several hours in a large metal bucket. During boiling an occasional aggressive stirring and pounding will aid in forming a wet pulp with no lumps.

A plaster mold for a breastplate. Papier-maché will be applied inside this reverse mold. Plaster can be used to create a reverse mold for almost any object. Be sure to use vaseline on the object to make removal easier.

3. Drain off excess water. Cleanse the pulp thoroughly in cold water by straining through a large piece of muslin.

4. In a separate container add two parts of thin, hot flour paste and one part of hot liquid glue to form a mixture with the consistency of thick plaster. Add in an appropriate amount of fireproofing powder.

5. Now mix equal parts of paper and glue paste. Many small objects, decorations, special textures for rocks, and the bark of trees can be molded directly from this substance. Larger objects such as small statuettes may require an inner framework of wood and wire.

6. Smooth with hands or trowel for a finish. Flour on the hands will prevent the pulp from sticking during the modeling.

7. Let the object dry slowly, although placing smaller objects in an oven at a low temperature will quicken the process.

8. The finished piece can be sanded and is very lightweight. Objects that might tip over should be weighted at the bottom.

9. Coat with shellac, then paint.

The completed, painted, paper mache breastplate. The back was also molded and made of paper mache but it could be made of leather or naughahyde with velcro straps or leather ties.

Molds

More complex forms, and those requiring more accurate detail, may require a mold. If you do not have an object to copy, you can create the desired shape with clay. Coat the clay with Vaseline™, then pour a quick-drying plaster over the entire surface. When the plaster is dry, remove the clay shape, leaving the plaster reverse mold. Use a stiff brush to thoroughly clean out all traces of clay. Coat the interior of the plaster mold with Vaseline or a soap solution, and then cover its surface with four or more layers of torn, paste-soaked paper strips (papier-maché) or fill with the paper pulp. Reinforce with a final layer of dipped coarse muslin. Forming the papier-maché in a plaster mold also allows several identical objects to be made from the same mold.

Remove the object from the mold after drying, then paint and shellac. Applying the shellac last gives the object a shiny surface.

Muslin/Plaster

To make a carved-stone look as in Roman architecture, you might consider the use of muslin and plaster. It can be used on statues to drape and create the "costume." It can be used to cover columns or walls or carved thrones. Dip lightweight muslin into a slow-drying plaster. The plaster will dry in the fabric, leaving a rigid, "carved" look in about 45 minutes or less; but let it dry about 24 hours. You can paint it or leave the natural plaster look.

Basic Sets

The basics and "absolute musts" of any theater, including church theater, are platforms and flats. You can never have too many of these, and over the years you will build a large inventory.

Basic Platforms

Platforms can be built to any size and shape you want. We suggest that you build a number of 4 x 8 platforms. With this standard size, they can be joined together to create much larger sets and stages.

The material list for one such platform is:

- Five 8-foot 2 by 4's
- One 4 by 8 half-inch plywood sheet (For best results use the more expensive three-quarter-inch plywood. For safety reasons, never use one-quarter inch.)
- Abundance of sixteen penny "sinker" nails

- One box of 1¼-inch or 1½-inch drywall screws (Drywall screws in various sizes will be your most commonly used item.)

Platform Construction Details

Cut five 2 x 4's at 45 inches. Nail two of these 45-inch pieces between the ends of two eight-foot 2 x 4's. Then nail the remaining three 45-inch pieces at the two-foot, four-foot, and six-foot marks. Be sure to split the board at the marks.

Stand on the boards when nailing to push them flush with the floor. When finished nailing, turn the frame over so the flush side is now up and run a line of wood glue around the upper surface of the frame. Lay the 4 x 8 plywood on the glued frame and flush and square one edge and secure it with drywall screws. Then flush and square the next edge and continue all the way around. Keep pushing the 2 x 4's in or out as needed to flush all edges. It is always a good idea to use a laminating bit on a router and trim the outer edges to completely flush the plywood with the 2 x 4 frame.

Covering Platforms.—Many scenic shops glue a covering of muslin over the entire surface and sides of each platform. If you do this, make sure that the glue covers the entire surface of the platform before applying the muslin. If your budget allows, a nice (but not necessary) topping is ¼-inch masonite. A 4 x 8 sheet will fit perfectly on your 4 x 8 platforms. Glue and staple (using brads) the masonite smooth side up; then, if necessary, router the edges smooth with a flush trim bit. The masonite reduces noise considerably and gives a good, smooth surface to paint on. After painting the joined platforms, the seams disappear. Be sure not to schedule a rehearsal on the platform until the masonite is at least base coated. It is very slippery. On raked stages you may want to apply the masonite rough side up for better traction.

An excellent way to soundproof your platforms is to sandwich a layer of thin (industrial) carpet

Example platform legs. Interior view

between the platform and the masonite. This is especially helpful when doing a musical with a lot of choreography. When you join the platforms together, make sure that all platforms are topped the same way. If not, you may need to adjust the heights of various legs to create a level surface.

Legs.—Once the platforms are built, they will probably need to be legged up with 2 x 4's. If placed directly on the floor without legs, the platform height would be a little over 4 inches.

The leg heights should be made to fit your specific needs. However, we suggest that you make them in standard increments of feet (1ft., 2ft., 3ft., ect.). If necessary, make them at the half-foot, such as 18 inches high.

When you cut the legs, it is very important that all legs be cut exactly the same, to prevent wobble. The best way to do this is to measure from the chop-saw blade, along the saw

An exterior view of platform legs.

table, and mark the exact measurement. Nail a small block at that point. Each time you lay the end of a 2 x 4 against the block, the chop-saw blade will come down and cut at the same measurement.

For each platform, cut six legs—one for each of four corners and two for the long sides.

Make a metal template approximately 3½ inches square. With a metal bit, drill two holes in the square, each offset left/right and top/bottom.

Turn the platform upside down on the floor. Place a leg in one corner, flush against the 2 x 4 frame. Place the template in the corner against the leg and flush it with the platform bottom and side. With a half-inch wood bit, drill through the template holes, through the leg and the 2 x 4 frame. On the outside holes of the frame, countersink for a half-inch bolt and washer. From the outside of the frame, insert a 3½ in. long (half inch) bolt through the 2 x 4 frame and through the legs. On the inside, place washers and nuts and tighten. Repeat this for all six legs on the platform. *Note:* It is important to flush the bolt head into the outer 2 x 4 so that two platforms can join tightly together.

Once these legs are braced they will support an enormous amount of weight. However, if your budget allows, there is a stronger, safer, but more expensive leg. The first part of the leg is made exactly as above. However, each leg will now be doubled with a second 2 x 4 cut 3½ in. shorter than the first. This leg will flush against the one bolted to the platform, but will sit under the platform 2 x 4. Glue and screw the outer leg to the inner leg. The support will be on the shorter leg, but secured by bolts in the inner leg.

Leg bracing.—Turn the platform over and stand it on the legs. 1 x 3's are the ideal for leg bracing, but if you have a tight budget, any scrap wood material can be used as long as it is the proper length. Using two drywall screws, attach with brace in the upper inside corner of a leg and angle the brace down to the opposite leg and use two screws on the lower inside. Cut off any excess lumber flush with the leg. On the opposite side of the platform repeat the process but reverse the angle, so that you end up with an X. Do this on the sides and ends.

Jacks.—Jacks are a stronger replacement for legs; however, the cost is nearly double. Cut two 2 x 4's (top & bottom plates) at four feet (the width of a platform). Cut three 2 x 4's (legs) at the desired height. Nail the top plate and bottom plate to the legs, two legs at the ends and one splitting the middle. This will create one jack. Three jacks are required for each platform, one at each end and one in the center. The platform rests on top of the jacks and is secured underneath with drywall screws. Jacks also require leg bracing.

Note: Remember when cutting the height of the legs to consider the top and bottom plates and the platform for your overall height.

Joining platforms.—When two-legged platforms are to be joined, you can use drywall screws or half-inch bolts through pre-drilled holes. This will require crawling underneath. When several platforms are joined, they should be joined at the ends and sides so that all platforms become a whole. If the legs are too short to reach underneath, turn the platforms on their tops, secure, then flip them over. This is difficult when several platforms are joined.

Wagons.—Platforms placed on wheels or casters are called wagons. They have been in use since the Greek theater. They carry scenery, flats, props, or set pieces. Wagons are usually low units providing single-direction run through the use of wheels or casters whose swivel mechanism is locked, or multiple-direction run when provided with swivel casters. The type of caster or wheel must be carefully chosen after a study of the total design load of the frame.

Flats.—These are solid structures usually made of 1 x 3 framing and covered with material or plywood. The material is usually unbleached muslin that is stretched onto the frame and sized with sizing glue (a long process). The use of muslin flats is an outdated theater method. This method is not as practical, as simple, or as cost effective as studio flats. We believe that studio flats are the best choice for church productions.

A standard flat is 4 feet by 8 feet. Construct the frame much the same as the platforms, but with 1 x 3's instead of 2 x 4's. Nail and glue. The cross pieces inside are nailed at the 2-foot, 4-foot, and 6-foot marks. Three more cross pieces come down the center in between the other three cross pieces. Cover the frame with eighth-inch or quarter-inch doorskin (luan). Make sure that the edges are flush and squared all the way around. Glue and staple, or nail. Use a laminating bit on a router to make sure that all outer edges are flush.

The flats can be painted, are light weight, and last for years. It is a good idea to create a large inventory of flats at various sizes, such as 4 x 4, 2 x 8, and so forth. They can be stacked for easy storage.

To join the flats, lay them on face-down on a flat surface. Align the tops and the bottoms, then drywall screw through the sides in

Once the individual flats are constructed, they can be joined together with drywall screws. For more repeated use, drill uniform holes with a template and fasten with bolts, washers and nuts. This will make all flats interchangeable.

79

In this example, two 4 x 8 flats are joined together and a 4 x 4 flat is joined to the side.

several places. Make sure that the screws alternate on the 1 x 3 edges. In other words, if you always place screws in the middle of the 1 x 3, the two flats will have a tendency to snap when you raise them up.

Several of these flats can be joined together to create a wall of any length or height. The seams can be covered with tape and the whole background painted to look solid. Flats will also be used for interior walls of a set. They can be joined together with other flats that have doors or windows to create an entire three-walled room.

Bracing flats.—When you stand flats up, they can be screwed into the floor of the stage and/or held up with braces.

With 1 x 3's, construct a triangle brace. Cut a 1 x 3 anywhere from 4 to 6 feet and lay it on the floor. Cut another anywhere from 2 to 4 feet and lay it on the floor at 90 degrees from the other, forming an L shape. Lay another 1 x 3 on top of these from corner to corner and trace where they meet. Cut the angles at each end of the third board, then lay it on the floor, forming a triangle. Cut small triangle shapes of luan or plywood. Glue and screw these triangles at all three joints. Turn the brace over and do the same on the other side.

Place a hinge on the long edge of the brace near the top and one near the bottom and attach with appropriate screws. When the flats are standing, you can screw the other side of the hinges into the back framing of the flats. The brace should swing left or right to adjust. It is always wise to place weights or sandbags over the bottom of each brace to help secure the flats.

Ground/Floor Coverings

Floor covering serves two purposes, one aesthetic and the other technical. Any special floor covering helps to unify the stage composition by bringing colors and forms of the set into the floor. A painted ground cloth can simulate wood planking, marble, cement, or just about anything you need to complete the realism of your set.

Because regular scene paint will dust off when walked on, ground cloths are usually painted with dyes. The cloth can be folded for storage easily when it has been dye-painted. Occasionally ground cloths are painted with oil paints, to obtain a harder, water-repellent surface for scenes where water is spilled on the floor in the course of the action. Oil paints, however, tend to shorten the life and effective reuse of the cloth.

The main technical reason for using a ground cloth is to deaden the sound of the actor's movements. For deep, soundproof padding, ordinary rug padding is used. It is expensive, but it can be reused indefinitely. The cloth can be the actual pad or it can be used to cover additional padding.

Ground-cloth construction.—Ground cloths are made of heavy canvas to withstand the wear of action and scenery. The seams, which run parallel to the footlights, are double-stitched, flat-felt seams for strength. The edges and corners are reinforced with webbing to take the tacks that fasten the cloth to the floor. A functional size is usually two or three feet wider than the stage. For a play with action taking place in front of the stage, the cloth can be extended to the front row of pews.

Securing floor cloths.—On wood or vinyl floors, the cloth can be secured with wall-paper paste. The paste is water-soluble and after the production can be mopped up.

Wood floors.—Once you have prepared the cloth, artists can paint any type of flooring needed. For instance, a wood plank floor can be painted to show lines, grains, and nail pegs. The process is simple and very effective. Paint a solid wood-tone base color on the entire canvas. Then dip a thick-bristled broom into a darker wood-tone color and drag it in one direction across the canvas until you have grain lines on the entire canvas. Then, using a straight edge and an even darker (brown or black) wood-tone color, draw lines, evenly spaced at wood-plank widths in one direction on the entire cloth. Next, lay the straight edge across those lines and draw lines across every other plank. Move down approximately six feet and repeat on the opposite planks. Then paint two nail heads at the beginning and end of each plank. Notice the example below

Another method of simulating a wood plank floor is to build a floor frame with 2 x 4's, then nail half-inch plywood to the frame. Next cut strips of eighth-inch doorskin, or *luan*, the size of your planks and nail them on top of the plywood in the same direction, staggering them as in the example above. The grain is already there; you need only to stain and/or varnish with your desired color. This is a little more expensive, but creates greater realism.

Vinyl flooring.—Touring or stock floor of vinyl 12 feet wide in huge rolls is available at theatrical supply companies. It has durability, shift-ability, dance-ability, and acceptability as a canvas for the scenic artist. Vinyl flooring has many advantages over canvas or other similar fabrics. Obviously, it is both thicker and more resilient. It also accepts pads and seams beneath—while hiding more of the cracks and unevenness—and does not require stretching or sizing. In addition, vinyl floors need a minimum of taping or adhesive, and even then, usually only around the periphery. Wooden decking in luan or plywood may be laid under it as a base. But obviously in laying a "seamless" vinyl floor, the smoother and flatter the surface beneath, the neater the result.

The vinyl flooring you would purchase at theatrical supply companies is a great product; however it is very expensive. You can get basically the same effect with common linoleum found at any hardware store. Usually, you can find excellent sale prices. This also comes in 12-foot-wide rolls, but by "mending" seams you can create surfaces 24 feet wide or more.

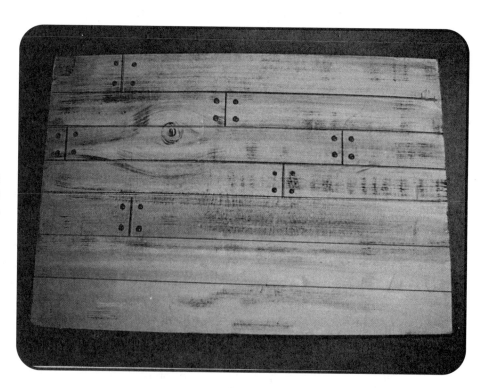

WOOD GRAINING: A wood grain effect is easily created with paint and brushing techniques.

The vinyl flooring you would purchase at theatrical supply companies is a great product; however it is very expensive. You can get basically the same effect with common linoleum found at any hardware store. Usually, you can find excellent sale prices. This also comes in 12-foot-wide rolls, but by "mending" seams you can create surfaces 24 feet wide or more.

You can use the flip-side, which is an absorbent composite of vinyl and flexible fibrous substances, or even retain the option of flopping it over to the finished side for use as the real interior flooring it is. The linoleum can be painted in a variety of textures, earthen, marble, stone, and so forth. With the proper lighting, these textures are capable of evoking a variety of different locales and settings. After production, the floors can be rolled up and saved in their entirety or in large pieces.

Joining vinyl seams.—The tools you will need are the usual for measuring and squaring, like a tape measure and carpenter's square. A long, metal straight edge will be invaluable. A watercolor marker is also useful, but indelible felt-tipped pen would bleed up through most paints later. For cutting—depending on the shapes and your preference— you need a pair of electric rotary shears, a utility or linoleum knife, and a putty knife. You will also need a caulking gun. Good-quality vinyl caulk works well. However, acrylic and silicone caulks might bond even better and maintain plasticity when dry. Next, be sure to have a highly adhesive, strong duct or gaffer's tape. And finally, have a roll of heavy-duty aluminum foil. An old electric iron is the only other tool you will require. It has been suggested that an iron with a Teflon™-coated face—or, alternatively, a Teflon coating sprayed on the usual stainless steel—might eliminate the need for the foil. Avoid the temptation to borrow the costumer's iron.

Avoid tearing or creasing the vinyl flooring. Handle it gently when moving it. When it is rolled, you will find it best to keep it intact and straight.

Lay the flooring seam to seam with its finished commercial side up, then tape the seams. Make sure the surfaces are flat and the edges are aligned with a thin but consistent gap. The tape should be pressed down smoothly and firmly. Now carefully re-roll the partially-joined flooring in preparation for turning it over without damaging it. You may want to roll it under and away from yourself as you go. This allows you to quickly unroll the piece with the commercial bottom-side up.

Take your choice of caulk, and using the appropriate gun, lay a thin, even bead on the seam. Smooth this with the putty knife. For the cleanest, most presentable results, do not spread the caulk out from the seam. Instead pick up the excess by cleaning the surface with a firm drag of the knife. After a few minutes of dry-time, smoothly lay the aluminum foil, shiny side down, on the flooring seam. Set your iron on its highest non-steam temperature. Then carefully, somewhat slowly, iron the seam. Allow it to cool for a least five minutes before peeling the aluminum foil slowly back—not up.

You now not only have a floor, but a canvas you can proceed to prepare for painting. Do so by preparing a latex, vinyl, or acrylic undercoat of approximately the same color as the flooring. You may find it useful to add a small amount of Rosco-Bond™ or other strong acrylic adhesive. Add no more than one part adhesive to ten parts paint. This will aid in bonding and generally strengthen the surface. Whenever possible, use a fairly thick consistency of paint, and more paint rather than more layers. This will cause less buckling of the surface. The flooring responds a great deal like some watercolor papers when it is too saturated with water—it absorbs extraordinarily well, and becomes smooth again only as the water evaporates.

When you've painted the effect you desire, you may wish to seal the surface. Depending on the finished look you want, there are many products available, but we prefer Johnson's Future™ acrylic floor wax. The wax has a tendency to bubble and froth if worked too vigorously by brush, and care should be taken to apply the substance evenly. After the wax dries, your floor will withstand damp-mopping when necessary during the show's run. If necessary, a new application of the sealant will revitalize its finish.

To secure the vinyl to the stage floor, use strips of two-sided carpet tape around the periphery of the area. The more you protect the vinyl from staples and tears, the longer it will function. The tape can be used on carpet, wood, linoleum, or just about any stage surfaces found in churches.

Ground.—Most realistic period Easter and Christmas plays will have an exterior setting that requires dirt or rock for the ground covering. A realistic method would be to lay the canvas on the stage and dump wheel-barrels of dirt on top of it. This is a possible but of course not practical method, due to clean-up and maintenance inside the sanctuary.

Upside-down carpet.—You can achieve near realistic results from much simpler and cheaper methods. Old "mohair" carpet padding that could be found in the dumpsters at most carpet stores is realistic but rare. Used carpet also works well and carpet stores are usually amenable to your taking it free of charge, if you ask them first.

The upside-down carpet, when molded on the stage floor, looks amazingly like dirt or mountain terrain. For further distances, crevices and valleys can be molded with the material and then painted with highlights and shadows.

When laying the carpet or padding out on the stage, start at the back (the upstage end) first and work toward the front (downstage), so that the overlapping seams aren't exposed to the audience. Seams running upstage-downstage should be cut to butt against each other and then be taped with a thin, but strong, tape. When painted properly, the tape lines should not show.

An example of how upside-down carpet can be molded, shaped, and painted to look like mountains, hills, or any type of terrain. The shadows and highlights can be brushed on or spray painted.

In most areas of the stage, the floor covering will not need to be secured to the floor. However where it folds over steps or where there is a great deal of activity, it is probably wise to secure the covering to the stage floor. This can be done with double-sided carpet tape between the covering and floor, or with nails, staples or tacks, or a combination of them. Don't be concerned with nails or tacks going into the floor. Most church stages are covered with carpet and the nails will not damage it. When they are pulled up, no one will ever know they were there.

When using a canvas floor covering that has been sewn together, the painting can be done in a large auditorium or parking lot. However, if you are molding upside-down carpet or padding directly onto the stage, it will need to be painted on the set itself. "Mohair" padding will only need highlights and shadows and can be done with spray paints. Carpet may need a light base color on the whole carpet; then highlights and shadows can be added.

The base color should be at least two tones of brown ground color to give dimension and depth. One time-consuming but effective way of doing this is to apply first a dark brown base coat. Then drop several other colors (dark brown, dark green, light green, black, light brown) into a paint tray. Allow the colors to run together but do not mix them. Then lightly touch a large sponge into the paint and dab all over the carpet.

When painting the base coat, roller brushes tend to apply an excessive amount of paint which seeps into the carpet. Sometimes the carpet will be so saturated with paint that it will not dry. We suggest that you use hand brushes (which can be tedious) or an airless paint sprayer. If no church member has one, it can be rented very reasonably.

It is advisable to mask off all walls, furniture, carpets, and such before any painting is done. Plastic should be spread over the entire stage prior to laying the ground covering. A box of 1 ml. plastic sheeting comes 12 feet wide and 400 feet in length and can be purchased at most paint stores. This will probably last through several productions.

Many other types of floors can be painted onto the ground cloth such as marble, stone, tile, and brick. Instructions for creating most of these effects can be found at most paint stores. Painting brick is discussed later in this chapter.

Sand on stage.—Sand is a very inexpensive way to create a realistic ground cover. Cover the entire stage with thick plastic. Sand is very cheap if ordered by the ton. One dump truck will hold 10 tons of sand and should cost around $10 a ton plus a small fee for delivery. When it is delivered it should arrive wet. This is a good thing since it will help prevent dust. It should remain wet for approximately two weeks. If it starts to dry, spray it with water whenever necessary. The strike should be fairly simple if the plastic was laid out properly. What do you do with it when the show is over? Give it to anyone who will take it away. You won't have any problem finding people who want it. The disadvantages of this process are obvious. The main one is the constant tracking of sand from the stage to other parts of the auditorium, requiring constant clean-up.

Backdrop/Cyclorama

Too often church productions have elaborate sets that are placed against a backdrop of paneling, baptistry, pipe organs, choir pews, and so forth. The set cannot be complete in its purpose without a backdrop that is consistent with the set design, location, and period of the play.

Backdrops can be in the form of walls, buildings, sky, etcetera. Sometimes the background is painted onto a large drop cloth. We will first discuss cycloramas.

Cyc.—A cyclorama, or "Cyc," is a large backdrop hung from floor to ceiling and wing to wing behind the set. A "soft Cyc" is generally made of cloth (muslin or canvas) and "hard Cyc" is made of wood and plaster. The most effective Cycs are curved at the ends, partially encircling the stage. They can be lit with various colors but most often are lit to simulate the sky.

Most Easter/Christmas period productions require an exterior and would benefit from a cyc. These can be relatively expensive for smaller churches. You can, however, make one that is inexpensive and effective.

To construct: Measure the distance from the front side wall of the stage to the back wall and its length to the opposite wall and again to the front. The measurement will be a large semi-circle. In an average-sized church this would be approximately 80 feet. Then

Muslin cyclorama with clouds projected from gobos.

measure the distance from the floor to the ceiling or to the highest straight line if the ceiling is sloped.

The material used can be the widest unbleached muslin on long bolts or rolls, or any other cheap and dyeable material. Please note: consistency of materials used should not vary. If you choose muslin, it must all be muslin.

Cut the material at the longest measurement. Then continue cutting these lengths until, when sewn together, they will adequately cover the height of the background.

If the material proves to be too costly, donated white bed sheets without hems or seams can be sewn together very effectively. There will be more seams to hide, but this can be taken care of with paint, which will be discussed later.

Once the material is sewn together, it must be dyed a sky blue. Dyeing is difficult under the best circumstances and extremely difficult when dying something this large. We offer one method below; however, you may discover an easier and more effective method.

To dye: Obtain a large, inflatable child's swimming/wading pool. Fill the pool with warm water and "many" packages of the desired color dye. Add several packages of fireproofing powder. Several crew members, wearing rubber gloves, will dip the Cyc into the pool, making sure that it is all covered and there are no folds causing the tye-dye effect.

Some of this will be unavoidable, but you will notice how it gives a three-dimensional look to the sky. When thoroughly saturated with dye, use several crew members to spread (do not drag) the Cyc on the church parking lot to dry. Secure the edges with bricks or suitable heavy objects.

To mount or hang the Cyc: A two-inch hem or "sleeve" should be made at the top of the cyc. PVC pipe, or thin wood that bends easily such as molding, is joined together to equal the length of the backdrop, then slipped through the sleeve.

Screw "eye hooks" into the ceiling at approximately six-foot intervals, in the shape of the intended backdrop. Then, screw eye hooks at the same intervals into the top of the Cyc, through the material and into the wood. Where the curves are located on each side,

Hanging a soft cyclorama.

several eye hooks should be placed in the wall at the level of the top of the Cyc. Tie heavy-duty fishing line or thin wire in lengths cut to reach from the top of the Cyc to the ceiling with ample length for tying. Then, tie each line from the eye hooks in the ceiling and tape the bottom ends of your tie-line straight down onto the wall.

On a bare stage, place several tall ladders at equal distances across the back of the stage near the wall, with the Cyc on the floor between the ladders and the wall. Several crew members, holding the top of the Cyc, climb the ladders, lifting the Cyc in an even motion, reaching the fishing lines taped to the wall. Each ties the line into the corresponding eye hooks. The eye hooks from the wall at the curve should be tied first to make handling easier. They may need adjusting after the others are tied. Someone should be in the back of the sanctuary "eyeballing" the level and "shouting out" directions. The bottom of the Cyc should also reach the floor.

Once the Cyc is suspended securely, the bottom should be stretched downward and stapled to the floor or back wall to cover all sight lines. Two crew members should start in the middle and work toward the ends at the same time. Pay attention to the wrinkles and waves in the material as you stretch it tight. When the Cyc is lit these wrinkles will show, breaking the illusion of reality.

Painting the Cyc.—Next you need to add some dimension to the sky so that it doesn't look like "sheets dyed blue." First, make a drawing of the Cyc on paper and sketch a cloud formation, using perspective that draws the eye to center stage, but is balanced on the sides.

Then, using white spray paint, spray the outline of the clouds onto the actual Cyc, using rolling, circular motions. Next, go back and fill them in, again with circular motions. Using grey or silver spray paint, add shadows to define and separate the clouds. This gives them a more three-dimensional and realistic look.

Another option is to take sheets of white batting or pillow stuffing and mold them into cloud shapes and attach them sporadically to the Cyc on top of the painted clouds. Spray the grey or silver on these the same as you did on the Cyc. This gives an even greater three-dimensional effect. You can go one step further and suspend clouds from fishing line at various heights and positions, a foot or so in front of the Cyc, to create several three-dimensional layers.

Clouds and other effects can be projected onto the Cyc from the lights. This would keep the Cyc free of paint and allow greater futures uses.

The more you create, the more you will be inspired to create. The ideas will begin to flow and the artistry will snowball. Don't be afraid to experiment and try new ideas.

A soft Cyc made of sheets sewn together and dyed blue. In this example, clouds are sprayed on with spry cans. Once this is done however, the Cyc can only be used as an exterior backdrop.

Backdrops.—Most churches have limited stage space for sets and props. Productions requiring scene changes are difficult. You may want to consider using drops as a way of maximizing space. There are several ways to construct and rig a drop. The quickest but most expensive way is to purchase one from a major theatrical supply company. There are several that do excellent work and are fairly reasonable. A large selection of pre-painted scenes are available. If you choose this method, be sure you go to the source to save money. Many of the companies purchase from the same sources available to you, then "up" the price. Most of the companies we know of order through Rosebrands in New York.

A less-expensive way to create a backdrop is to find an expert from a local theatrical supply house to work on a freelance basis. The least expensive and of course the most time-consuming method is to make the drop yourself. If done right a homemade Cyc or backdrop can be just as effective as the expensive professional ones. You will need a clean room, a good sewing machine (an industrial is helpful but not mandatory), and all the proper supplies. Drops hang from a strip of webbing at the top through which grommets are inset to seat the tie lines. Scenic muslin is sewn in strips (horizontally) to the dimensions desired, as was described above for the Cyc.

The sides of the drop are hemmed and the bottom is finished with a sleeve hem (usually about six inches deep) if a pipe or chain is to be inserted, or left raw if a sandwich

90

batten is to be used. If you don't have sufficient fly space over your stage, you may have to rig the drop on a roller or some kind of trip system to raise and lower during the production.

Painted drops.—Any good artist can paint the desired scene on the cloth. A sketch on paper should be done first; then a scale grid pattern created. When the drop is laid out on the floor, a larger scale of the pattern should be chalked out on the drop. The sketch could then be transferred to the cloth. The colors should be painted on last.

To some extent the number of repaints on a backdrop depends on the type and thickness of the paint each time a drop is redone. If latex is used, there will be only one or at the most two repaints, as it seals the fibers faster than scenic paint. If you use latex, four paintings are max, and you had better have plenty of touch-up after it's hung on that fourth one. Old drops can be reversed and used to cover platforms or floors which can then be painted—but only once.

The drops are quick to hang, rapid to change for scenes in a good fly house, and low cost compared to three-dimensional construction. However, drops are an "old-fashioned" look and not interactive with performance, except cut drops which will be discussed later. Drops are a single-plane orientation with a need for a fly space if there will be scene changes. They also take a lot of time for at least one scenic artist.

If you decide to do drops, Lynn Pektal's *Designing and Painting for the Theatre* is a must. It's a painter's cookbook. To draw the outline on a Cyc or drop, you will need to create a handle extension to hold your brush, chalk, or pencil. Here is how to make such a handle. Get some bamboo cane fat enough to hold as the handle of the tool. Cut the bamboo to length, making sure to lop it off behind a section. Whittle a bevel on the end and split it on four sides to the next section. If necessary, carve out some bamboo in each cut so the open end will close tightly around a piece of chalk or a pencil. Once the tool is wedged into the bamboo, wrap a hefty rubber band around it several times. You cannot work on the floor without one of these.

Storage of painted drops.—Drops should be rolled on their top and/or bottom battens or pipes. Folding in reduces the reuse life drastically and will crease or crack the paint. It probably will be necessary to fold the drop at least in half and maybe once again. The drops can be rolled on large carpet tubes. These tubes can be obtained from carpet stores, again at no cost.

Scrims.—A scrim is a theatrical cloth similar to cheese cloth in texture and density. When light is projected on the front of the scrim, it appears solid. When there is light behind the scrim, it becomes transparent. If a scene is painted on the front of the scrim, it will also disappear. A scrims is very expensive and very fragile. However, with its many applications it might be well worth it.

Scrim painting.—It is always better to spray a scrim than to use a brush. If you must use a brush, thin the paint. You must always be careful not to fill in the weave with paint as this will diminish the transparency.

There is a scrim painting technique which allows for two completely separate images to be displayed, one when light is shined on the front and another when the light is projected from the rear. This technique was used in the original production of *South Pacific,* for Bali Hai. The image on the front of the scrim was the island in a normal, sunny light. On the back of the scrim, an aurora and fantastic cloud formations were painted. During the song, light was brought up on the rear of the scrim and the island transformed completely, returning to "normal" slowly during the applause following the number.

Legs and teasers.—Designers in churches must be concerned as much with the cost of having their designs realized as with the integrity of the designs themselves. Of course, as a rule, soft goods like painted drops have generally been less expensive to construct than hard goods like platforms and three-dimensional scenery. It makes sense, then,

When scrim is lit from the exterior, it appears solid, hiding the interior scene.

When the light source is from the interior, the scrim becomes transparent, revealing the scene behind it.

92

for a designer to be aware of the scenic effects that can be created with soft goods.

A leg is a soft curtain that usually hangs well above the set to the floor and is hung in the wings as a mask. It is usually made from duvateen. Legs are usually two, four or six feet wide. A teaser is the same type of material, but it goes across and above the set. Teasers are usually used to mask things such as stage lights, fly space, and wiring. A teaser can run across the top front of the set, and when it is combined with legs on the front sides, a proscenium will be created.

Besides muslin and duvateen, certain fiber materials found in building supplies can be effective. Probably the best known fiber material with considerable texture and seemingly infinite uses for scenic design is erosion netting. The material comes in large rolls that are approximately four feet wide in natural taupe or dyed green.

Constructing an erosion net drop.—(1) Calculate the number of widths of material needed which would have to be placed side by side and sewn with vertical seams to create the full size of the cut drop.

(2) Lash together these widths at their edges with thin jute twine, using very large needles generally employed in sewing through thick canvas or leather.

(3) Instead of using the usual webbing for the top of drops to attach them to the pipes, it would be easier to roll the tops of the erosion net drops until you have about a four-inches-in-diameter roll, then run the tie lines through this roll, thus securing its tightness and allowing the tie lines to have proper placement. The tie lines should be placed six feet apart because of the weight of the erosion net.

(4) The work on the uneven cut-edge portions of the drops will take time. All loose and irregular edges should be knotted and hand-tied to adjacent loose strands. If this is not done, the erosion net drops will start to unravel. Although this procedure is time consuming, it may be the best way to preserve the frequently irregular outside shape of the drops.

(5) After each erosion net drop is constructed, add tonalities to its basic green color, using thinned down mixtures of latex paint and aniline dyes applied by an air-compression paint gun.

(6) Once the paint is dry, begin to attach additional materials to the basic drop to create greater density and diversity in each piece. Other irregularly shaped pieces of erosion net are attached to the basic drop using the same lashing procedure mentioned above. Jute ropings, which should be pre-dyed in a series of earth colors and fireproofed, are attached to the tops of the drops at six- to eight-inch intervals, and various suggestive macramé-like designs should be created by tying and weaving different strands of the rope

together. You might want to attempt to create actual patterns using the rope on erosion net, such as a spider web pattern. Again, at the specific points where you need precise angles marked or created with the rope, the rope should be secured to the erosion net using bits of thin jute cord. In all cases, the macramé-like rope patterns will be attached at various places to the erosion net drop with bits of jute cord so that the rope patterns will not become inextricably tangled up when the drops are folded or rolled and transported from scene shop to theatre.

(7) Additional dyed and ripped rags will be added for other effects on some cut drops. For a number of erosion net drops in the final scene of an opera, skeletal outlines of tree branches cut out of burlap were glued to the back side of the erosion net. When back-lit, the shapes of these branches could be seen through the erosion net.

Things to remember: Generally, erosion netting is not fireproofed when purchased from a distributor. Like all other fiber materials, it is extremely flammable. Hence, it is important to soak the finished drops thoroughly with a fireproofing agent before using them on stage. Erosion net and jute roping can shed small particles of lint and fiber into the air when moved or brushed against, and such particles occasionally may make it more difficult for singers or actors to perform. One solution is to spray the stage area with a fine mist of water before each act or scene, since this will help settle many of the particles. Each roll is four feet wide and contains 100 running yards.

Cut drop.—Many churches do not have the budgets for new mechanical wonder effects or the space to accommodate them. And when they do decide to rent or buy, the problem of finding knowledgeable operators arises. As a result, a return to older, more simple methods is taking place. One of the many ideas that has seen a rebirth is the *cut drop*.

The cut drop is one of the most versatile and least talked about pieces of scenery. In its pure form, it can recreate the turn-of-the-century gaslight theater, when the cut drop was in its heyday. Used in conjunction with contemporary staging methods, it can help produce even more exciting and spectacular effects. It can be used with all kinds of projections, three dimensional scenery, revolving and moving stages, and other advanced technical scenery. Ideal for stages with limitations of depth, wing storage or limited fly space, and more versatile than a hard profile piece, the cut drop can be flown with minimum effort. Parts of it can appear to be free floating. The actual construction of a cut drop is almost easier than building a simple flat. Virtually no carpentry is involved, which makes it ideal for churches with few skilled technicians.

The most difficult problem is in finding the proper materials. Net is used to reinforce a solid canvas or muslin drop, allowing parts of it to be cut away, creating a profile or silhouette effect. The net covers the entire area of the drop including the solid portions.

Fish net is the basic material for the usual cut drop, but no theatrical supply house carries it. Scrim, bobbinnet, theatrical gauze, or even cheese cloth can also be used, but they cause a hazy effect. A visible net responds to light the same way as a scrim. Fish net, or an extremely open-weave net is transparent with only a slight grid visible. The most important thing to look for in buying fish net for a cut drop is the "weave." The proper net for cut drops is made with the edges of the square holes in a straight line so the sides hang vertically and horizontally when held by the knots on any one edge. Some fish net is made on the bias with the corners of the squares forming the sides of the net. This will hang on the bias and is useless as supportive backing on a cut drop.

The kind of drop being made and its intended use determine the size of the opening of the net. One-inch-square-hole fish net is most often used. A rule of thumb is that the more delicate and detailed the edges of the solid portion of the drop, the closer the net weave should be. If the cut edges are extremely delicate and involved, scrim or bobbinnet might be required. Cotton fish net is the most practical type. It is much cheaper than nylon and it takes dye and glue well. Its dull finish usually disappears under proper stage lighting. Small pieces of cotton fish net can be purchased at some marine stores or novelty or gift stores. Decorator fish net can be found in sizes approximately 6 feet by 15 feet. Larger pieces for a full stage drop can be purchased at major theatrical supplies companies.

The solid part of the drop can be any flexible material that might otherwise be used for soft scenery. Scenic canvas, muslin, scrim, felt, and foam rubber can be used with great success. The material applied to the net must be lightweight so it does not stretch the net, or bulge and sag.

Construction of the basic cut drop.—A muslin drop several feet larger than the design is stapled to the floor face up and base painted. If the drop is base painted after the design is cut out, the edges of the cuts will curl.

When the paint is dry, the design should be drawn on the face of the drop in chalk, allowing approximately one foot of extra drop on each of the four sides. The staples are then removed and the appropriate portions of the drop cut away. When all the cutaway areas have been removed, the entire drop is flipped over onto its face and fastened again to the floor at the remaining outside edges. Wire nails are tacked around the perimeter of the drop every three inches or so, in order to stretch the fish net square and hold it in place for glueing.

When all the remaining cut muslin pieces have been placed carefully in the proper position on the floor, a large piece of net, cut to size and dyed to match the background, is placed over the design back and hooked onto the nails around the edge—like an old-fashioned curtain stretcher. After the muslin pieces are checked for position, the stretched net is snapped from the center of the drop to equalize tension in all directions. The muslin underneath is checked again for positioning and the net snapped again. Then, the muslin portions are glued to the net. White glue (in a one-to-one mixture with water) is painted over the parts of the net that touch the muslin. The glue is allowed to dry overnight.

The next day battens are placed on the top and bottom of the drop. Some battens can be fastened to net and muslin while the top batten holds only net. Cut drops are always held in place by at least one batten. Full-stage drops that touch the floor across the entire stage usually have two battens.

A full-stage proscenium cut drop can be made with legs that reach to the floor on each side and a large opening in the center. These need a separate batten on the bottom of each leg. Free-hanging drops that do not reach to the floor, such as leaf borders or signs, need only one batten at the top, as the bottom edge is often irregular and cut to show as little of the net as possible. Seldom is it left in a straight line, as that would be more noticeable to the audience.

Any net that is not needed to hold up portions of the drop or to hold the shape of the drop can be cut away. But the more use and travel for which a drop is intended, the less net should be cut away.

Construction of silhouette drops.—A much different construction is used for a silhouette drop (where the front surface does not show) or on a drop which would be enhanced by piecing, such as a leaf border.

Because this kind of drop has more cut-away portions than solid ones, it can be constructed from muslin scraps rather than from solid cloth. For a silhouette drop, white butcher paper a few feet larger than the drop is taped to the floor. This paper is blocked off in grid sections onto which a rear view of the design is sketched with a marking pen. Scraps of muslin are placed on the sketch, traced through, and cut out.

When all the muslin pieces have been cut out to complete the design, they are placed in position on the sketch master and the net applied.

The small church is just as capable of producing magnificent effects as large theaters through the use of the versatile cut drop.

Foliage

One of the best ways to complete an "outdoor" set and make it appear natural, is to add greenery. The strategic placement of bushes, trees, flowers, and such brings the set to life and psychologically takes the audience outdoors.

Research the correct foliage that is native to the location you are recreating. For instance, if the scene is to take place in the Holy Land, you might want to add some fig and palm trees.

The easiest way is to use "live" plants and trees that have been planted in pots. These can be placed about the stage and the pots masked with the floor covering, rocks or anything that blends into the set. Often times, you can make a deal with a local nursery to supply all of the needed plants in exchange for advertising in your program. Church members may be able to supply some of the plants.

You also can make your own trees, bushes, plants, and flowers. A quick method is to find dead limbs and branches and join them together to create the type of plant you need. Then, if you need to add any greenery such as leaves, these can be made from crepe paper or papier-maché, painted and attached with thin wire.

A palm tree can be constructed of carpet tubing wrapped with slit carboard and topped with real palm branches.

To make palm trees, slip a long carpet tube over a wooden X-brace. Then fray four-inch-wide strips of cardboard on the top edge and spiral them around the tube from bottom to top so that they overlap. Lightly spray the whole trunk with brown spray paint.

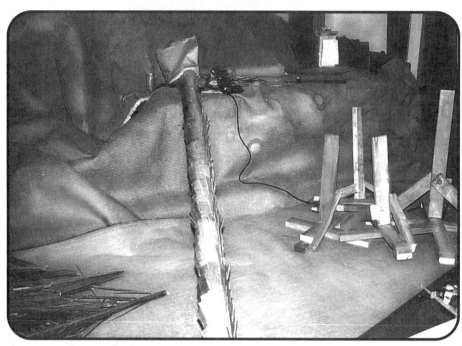

Drill several holes around the top of the trunk down to approximately one foot. Jam real palm branches into these holes and shape them to the desired shape.

Tree trunks and large branches can be made by constructing a frame made of furring strips and chicken wire and covering it with papier-maché. The papier-maché can be molded to simulate any species of tree bark and then painted the appropriate colors.

Leaves.—You can making leaves out of a very inexpensive filled cheesecloth. Stretch the cheesecloth in strips between two sawhorses and then secure the ends with weights or fasteners. Paint the entire section with Rosco-Gloss tinted green and/or mixtures of various colors for texture. When the paint is completely dry, cut the cheesecloth into leaf shapes. You will end up with a translucent, somewhat shiny material that will hold a shape. It

is waterproof and can be made flame retardant.

Flame-proof leaves.—Leaves can be made from Estes model rockety recovery wadding. It is essentially self-extinguishing toilet paper. It has a rather bland color that could handle a light misting of dye. It can be picked up at Toys-R-Us (or a hobby shop) for about three dollars for one hundred sheets. It does smell pretty bad when burned, though.

Rocks.—Rocks are used for two purposes: (1) to dress the set and (2) to provide seating for chorus or "crowd" members. The latter, of course, should be determined and blocked by the director and should appear natural. Both should be constructed with durability and appearance in mind.

First draw shapes on 4 x 8 quarter-inch plywood. These shapes can be any size or shape. Cut out the shapes with a saber saw. Half of these shapes will be for tops of rocks and the other half for bottoms. Next cut 1 x 3 boards into approximately six equal lengths of the desired rock height. Nail or screw the 1 x 3 pieces around the perimeter and the middle of one of the plywood shapes. The boards should be evenly spaced around the outer edges with at least two in the middle for support. Screw in a couple of diagonal braces inside for sturdiness. Next, cut cardboard or chicken wire several inches taller than the rock frame and long enough to go around the base. Roll the cardboard and crunch it to make it pliable. Staple it around the top and base, shaping it as you go. Cover the cardboard or chicken wire with papier-maché. After several coats, allow it to dry thoroughly in the sun before painting. Paint a solid base coat of color, the splatter-texture colors. Varnish

99

Papier-Maché Tree

1. Construct a wooden frame using firring strips.

2. Shape chicken wire around the frame. Wire together.

3. Apply papier-maché around the chicken wire. Muslin or sheets dipped in glue and starch are also very effective.

4. When the glue/starch has dried, paint the tree with appropriate colors.

5. If you need a full tree, you can attach real branches and leaves around the top.

PALM TREE. Constructed of carpet tubing wrapped with slit board and topped with real palm branches.

or liquid plastic will help seal the paint.

Rock-face mountain.—There are several methods of creating a rock-face mountain. The following is among the least expensive and it is light-weight and portable. Most of the materials involved can be found or donated. You will need:

- 2 bundles (12 in a bundle) of 1 x 2 furring strips, or as many as your project requires
- Plastic milk cartons
- Muslin
- Staple gun
- Staples
- Screws
- Screw gun
- Elmer's glue

100

- Water
- Paint.

Using the 1 x 2's, construct a wood frame with the vertical "studs" spaced randomly at approximately one foot apart and "spacers" nailed between. Next, smash some plastic milk cartons and other plastic bottles into various shapes as you staple/screw them to your frame. Next, make a one-part glue and one-part water mixture in a fairly large bucket and dip the muslin before applying on top of your plastic masterpiece. Be sure to mold the muslin around the bottles until you are satisfied with the look. Do not dip larger pieces of muslin than you can handle! Give about six to eight hours to dry. Next, paint varying shades of grey and splatter paint with greens and blues for extra texture. You can add organic materials (moss, bushes, branches, etc.) to give it a more 3-D and realistic look. Instead of milk cartons you can use laminated layers of cardboard.

The most effective yet by far the most expensive method for a rock-face mountain is the use of Styrofoam. Construct your wall by joining several flats together. Apply large blocks (4' x 8' x 2') against the wall and secure them with large rods and washers, or wire. Using an electric Styrofoam cutter (heated wire), you can carve your various rock shapes on the entire face. Next, paint with the appropriate textures and tones.

There is a very realistic method for a more permanent mountain. Build your frame with a 3-D look or build up your 3-D on flats with various wood shapes. Mix several buckets

A rock-face mountain built with platforms, ramps, and legs, and faced with carved styrofoam.

of plaster and cover the entire face, swirling and creating various textures as you trowel the plaster. While the plaster is still wet, take handfuls of dirt and sand and throw them with force against the plaster. Do this on the entire surface. When the plaster is dry, mix several different tones of sepias and umbers in various buckets and water them down. Spray them one at a time (drying in between coats) by spraying at the top and allowing them to run down. Do not try to cover. The final coat should be a moss-green color applied randomly and in a few places allowed to run. For a final touch squirt a rust color in a couple of places and allow it to run from top to bottom to represent a water path.

Contoured hills and paths.—While the easiest and least expensive method of creating contoured hills and paths is to haul in truck-loads of earth and sod, most churches will not approve this. Urethane foam could be sprayed and sculpted, but it is messy and expensive. Sculpted Styrofoam is another great look but it also has excessive material costs. A series of ramps built next to platforms and covered with materials suggested above works nicely and is durable.

The following design is an inexpensive method of creating contoured paths on a relatively low (two to four feet) hill or mountain. It could be built higher with platforms underneath. This method allows the director to block the actors actually riding chariots, wagons, bikes, and so forth or walking around the paths and grassy hills.

First, design a scale model of the set with many sections joined like a puzzle. The set should be built in units small enough to transport from the construction site into the

Stones made from papier-maché. This is constructed on a sheet of luan, then attached to the front of a flat.

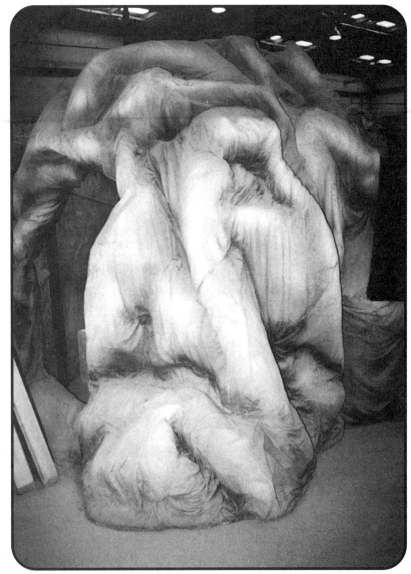

A tomb constructed of wood, chicken wire and covered with muslin dipped in plaster.

church. Construct frames of 1 x 3 lumber to contain each cardboard hillside section. The frames do not serve to strengthen but merely to contain the cardboard. Build the frames as perimeter frames with one internal support and without tops or bottoms. The frames should be built to match the model sections with all the contours and shapes.

Glue each layer together side-by-side on their ends (do not stack flat) and fit them into the frames. The cardboard is cut to fit within the frames and pre-contoured on a bandsaw. Once the frames are filled, lay them out in their final configuration and continue to sculpt them with a hand grinder so that the contours meld nicely together from one framed unit to the next.

After final sculpting, the result is a strong, lightweight hillside ready to be set up and covered. The set-up should go quickly with a minimum of labor as the separate contoured-cardboard hill units fit together with ease and simplicity.

The next step, to cover, is a little more difficult. To simulate real grass, the surface should be covered with a layer of artificial grass carpet. Be aware that the carpet may have a definite weave pattern. Forcing the carpet to follow the contour's form will not easy. The carpet may need to be cut away in several places so that it will dip into a hole or run over a bump. The carpet should be glued and then stapled to the cardboard. A final painting will add texture and life to the otherwise flat, artificially green carpet. If you prefer a dirt look to grass, use upside-down carpet or combinations of both. Muslin or canvas can also be used.

Stones and Bricks

Fireplace (stone or brick).—Build a frame of furring strips to the style you need and include the hearth and mantle. Complete the hearth and mantle with plywood. Cover the rest of the frame that is to be rock with cardboard (it doesn't matter how neat). Now, cut dozens of cardboard pieces in various sizes and shapes. Make one cut to the middle of each shape and overlap the cut, to make it a three-dimensional cone-shape. This piece can be stapled to the frame. Continue arranging these pieces to fit side by side as on a rock fireplace, until you have covered the entire frame with these pieces. Cover them with papier-maché, giving each piece several layers. Paint all the stones with a solid base color, probably a light grey or off-white. Then, using a brush dipped in a darker grey, splatter speckles over the whole piece. An effective but messy way of doing this is to saturate a roller brush and spin it over the area. Then go to a black paint and do the same thing. Try various colors to give the effect of stone. Look at some stone fireplaces to find all of these colors. Then, use fast-drying plaster or spackle to thickly dab in the mortar lines between all stones. It won't be necessary to paint the plaster.

To make a brick fireplace, build the frame the same way but cover it with doorskin or luan and try to avoid making seams. Then, draw your pattern of bricks onto the doorskin, remembering to stagger the rows and leave a half-inch gap between the bricks for plaster. Then follow the steps outlined below under "bricks."

Smoke.—One thing that most people forget when doing a fireplace that can really make a big difference is smoke. If you can get even a small stream of smoke coming up lit by some reds and yellows it is *very* effective.

Constructing the fireplace.—Construct a frame with plywood. For a lighter and less durable fireplace, construct an outer frame with furring strips and cover the body with cardboard or luan. Cut cardboard pieces in assorted sizes and shapes or crush empty plastic milk cartons. Cut one split in each cardboard shape, fold them into three-dimensional shapes, then staple them onto the fireplace face. The plastic cartons can also be stapled on. Cover the entire fireplace with papier-maché. Paint a solid-grey basecoat; then, speckle with black, dark grey, white, and gold. Experiment with the colors. A mantle and hearth can be

104

A scene from *Nathan,* produced by Morning Star Entertainment at the Jess Moody Theater, Van Nuys, CA. The rock fireplace in the background was constructed of papier-maché.

Example of a fireplace built into a flat.

constructed of plywood or furring strips.

Bricks.—There are many ways to create theatrical bricks for fireplaces, walls and floors. We will discuss two of them.

One: Measure the width of a large, industrial-sized sponge (approx. 5" x 7"). Draw a series of horizontal lines across your working surface (wall, fireplace, floor, etc.), at five-and-one-half-inch intervals. The extra half-inch is to allow for the mortar.

In a paint tray, pour brick-red paint, plus a little

105

black and a little white. Swirl but do not mix. Dip the sponge into the paint and dab off the excess. Starting at the top line, press the sponge against the surface on the far left. Move to the right a half inch and press again. Continue until you need to dip paint again. When you begin the second row, remember to stagger the bricks as in the illustration below. This will probably mean a half brick starts the second row. When the bricks are completed, mortar can be painted between the bricks or plastered in.

Two: Bricks can be cut from sheets of very thin Styrofoam. They can be glued onto the surface in the same pattern described above and then painted with the appropriate colors. The Styrofoam has a texture similar to real brick and is extremely effective from a short distance.

Glass

Inexpensive plexiglass has made creating glass windows on stage fairly simple. A clear plastic lighting panel two feet by three feet is very inexpensive and is a realistic substitute for most window glass.

The old concern with glare and reflection from theater lights is easily solved with

Example of bricks created with a sponge and a mixture of paints.

106

anti-glare sprays or even hair spray and/or slightly tilting the windows down toward the stage. Frosted and textured ceiling panels also help with this problem.

Leaded or stained glass.—To create a leaded glass, select the desired design and transfer it to a full-scale drawing. Place a sheet of acrylic or plexiglass over the design, and then duplicate the drawing with the hot glue gun, using a wide, interchangeable tip. Once it is dry, apply gray latex paint to the texture. Paint in appropriate colors on the glass.

Pillars and columns.—Most biblical-period sets will require pillars and columns. The styles will vary greatly and should be researched. The basics of set construction for these are the same. The painting and dressing are what give them unique character.

The bases and moldings can be constructed from any materials solid enough to support the column. We suggest that these be fairly lightweight, especially the crown pieces which should be carved foam. Even the molding on the bottom base could be Styrofoam.

The columns are fairly lightweight and simple to construct. A reasonably priced material is sonotube. Sonotube is the round cardboard form used as a cement mold for columns. It can be purchased at construction supplies in various circumferences and lengths. Cut two circles of plywood to fit inside each end of the sonotube and screw through the outside cardboard to secure the plywood in place. The plywood ends will help mount the column to the base and crown. The textures, colors, and styles are now up to the scenic artists. They can be stone or marble or whatever medium your designer has chosen.

Below is another method of creating a column of scraps and inexpensive materials. It works as well but takes time.

Stairs

There are three categories of stairs used in the theater: (1) stairs that are designed and built as part of the set; (2) stairs that are existing for the stage and incorporated into the set; (3) stairs that are functional for an actor's backstage escape and are not part of the set. All three should be built with strength and safety in mind.

The set stairs will carry the same amount of weight as the stage stairs and should support the same amount of weight without creaking. All stairs should be properly secured to a foundation and braced in all directions.

For bracing, use 2 x 4's across the bottom and top and 1 x 3's criss-crossed at the back and middle. When bracing, two screws or nails should be in each end of each brace to prevent movement of the brace.

Ramps

Ramps are built much like platforms but with a slope. The slope can be at whatever grade is required for the set and adjustments may be necessary as you customize each ramp. As with stairs and platforms, proper bracing is essential. Plywood would be attached to the top and bracing would be secured at the back, middle, and bottom.

Crosses and Bases

Most Christian churches have performed a passion play at some point, in which they have used crosses. As many churches have made as many different kinds of crosses. It is difficult to say which is correct because, in this case, authenticity may not be practical in the theater.

Historians don't completely agree on the dimensions, technique, and materials used in the Roman crucifixions. There were several kinds, and we could probably estimate pretty accurately which was used at the crucifixion of Christ.

The designer and construction coordinator should work together to design the right structure and materials for the crosses and bases. However, there are many things to consider that may influence the way you construct the cross.

The most important concern is safety. There have been far too many accidents on passion play crosses. The results of these accidents range from breaking the illusion of reality to severe injury to the actor. During one well-known passion play, a cross piece broke and since the actor's hand was wrapped in a spike, the resulting jerk dislocated his arm. Another safety concern is location of the cross near any high places. The actor must be secured properly. If the actor is to be raised on the cross by the Roman soldiers, the movements must be precisely choreographed and well rehearsed.

If the cross is made of a solid piece of wood, carved from an actual tree, or built too large, it may be too heavy and awkward for the actor to move about the stage. The resolution then is to create a lightweight cross with strength for safety. One way to achieve this is to construct an inner frame of aluminum and "dress" it to look solid with plywood. This can be done by filling all gaps with wood putty, sanding and staining. The corners and edges should be carved and gouged to appear to be cut from a tree.

Aging or Distressing Sets

Dirt buildup.—Use an airbrush (not a large spray gun) and diluted sepia inks, paints, and such to spray dirt into corners, around light switch covers, along baseboards, and wherever else as needed. The right tones of flat spray paint can also be effective.

Wall hangings.—Take newspaper or scrap of an appropriate size, secure to wall with tape, airbrush around it, and remove (suggesting pictures which used to hang there for years and have now been removed, and that the wall is less dirty and faded behind where they used to be). Build up dirty areas, continuing to step back and take a look—under stage lights if possible, so that you get a real look. Keep spraying even and soft, not spotty and patchy.

Aging walls.—Figure out where, logically with the architecture, the roof might have leaked. Take sepia inks or diluted umbers and keep pressing a wet brush into corner or along cornice mold, allowing paint to run naturally and dribble as the leak would. If using a wallpaper pattern, carefully set up a couple of peeled corners (use brown paper glued to painted set, and painted as your wallpaper if you painted a pattern on walls themselves). Figure out what color and type of mildew would characterize the area; sponge some on with a stippling sponge. For the old-paint look, use a "dirty water wash" of a little paint and a lot of water, with a soft bristle lay-in brush. Experiment with the base paint tones. Make some hand spatter along the bottom of an exterior wall for ground spatter and low weathering. For interior, use same kind of wash, and some light spattering in the corners. Sponge the wash in around light switches, door jambs, other hand-worn areas, wherever your research photos and observations suggest.

Scenery Painting

There are many standard scenery paints that can be purchased at theatrical supply companies. The best known is Rosco scene paint. These can be found in liquids and powders. Many churches cannot afford these paints in their set budgets and may need to find a cheaper alternative. Any water-base paint can be effective for base coating sets and scenery. It can also be used for scenic artwork providing the proper colors and pigments can be mixed.

Most paint and hardware stores have cans of "mistake" mixes on sale for as low as $2.00. You are limited to colors, but often you may find whites that can mix with pigments. We have found that most paint can be donated by church members who happen to have old cans sitting in their garages. The problem with using old paint is that sometimes it smells pretty bad—like a million dirty sneakers are decomposing in the locker room. Once opened, and once any kind of water or other substance is added to the paint, it faces the danger of developing the odor. Many scenery paints are casein paints. Casein is a soy-milk based paint. The smell, if you have mixed it with water, is unavoidable. All paints will eventually rot if mixed with tap water. Prior to sealing the used cans for long periods of time, add some liquid Lysol to help prolong the shelf life. It won't hurt the paint and will kill the bacteria that is causing the smell. When you're done for the day with a can, float a thin layer of Lysol or Simple Green on top of the paint. Beyond the disinfectant qualities, it provides an air barrier which retards spoilage. The layer can be carefully poured off at next usage, or theoretically, stirred in, although this does add a certain amount of water to the mix.

Painting textures.—Scenic art in the theater is literally a specialized art form. The only limits are in the creative mind of the artist. New techniques in scenic art are discovered and created with each new production. We will name a few standard painting techniques.

Splattering: This is generally used for creating stone effects. It usually requires a base coat of one solid color. Dip a stiff-bristled brush in another color paint and dab off the excess. Flick the brush with a snapping motion, splattering dots of paint over the solid color. The speckles will have random sizes and shapes. Repeat this with other colors until you have reached the desired effect. For splattering large areas such as floors, use a roller brush. Saturate the brush in the paint. With your hand, spin the brush with a rapid motion and hold it over the surface to be painted. This will create speckles and dots in a large area. You can get several spins of the roller before reapplying paint. This is a messy process. Wear paint clothes, old clothes, goggles, and a hat or hood. Make sure the surrounding areas are masked off.

Stippling: This is used for creating various textures and marbleizing on floors, walls and set pieces. Use a sponge, preferably a sea-sponge. Dip the sponge in the paint and dab off the excess. Dab the sponge in random patterns around the surface area. Depending on your desired goal, use one or more colors. This effect can also be done with crumpled newspaper.

Graining: There is an excellent graining tool with instruction that can be found at craft and paint stores. Another method is to use a kitchen or garden broom. Dip the bristles in the paint, dab off the excess, and drag the bristles the length of the surface. Practice your graining techniques before trying it on the set. The details such as knots and large grain gaps can be completed with a small paint brush.

Glues and Adhesives

The knowledge of appropriate glues is a must while constructing scenery and costumes. Following is a list of various kinds of adhesives you may need during your production. It is not all-inclusive but it will certainly suit your needs.

Wood construction.—Several varieties of glues are used in wood construction. The most popular synthetic glue used in scenery construction, commonly referred to as white glue, is polyvinyl resin glue. Available brands include: Elmer's Glue-all, Wilhold White Glue, and Swift's. Another popular synthetic adhesive is a yellow- or cream-colored glue made specifically for wood joints—aliphatic resin glue. When applied according to directions, it creates a bond that is stronger than wood. Air-exposure causes this glue to dry to the touch in 10 minutes and to dry completely in 45 minutes. The quick set-up time may cause problems when gluing large objects or surfaces. Aliphatic resin glue has a low water resistance and is more expensive than white glue, but it has a higher heat resistance than white glue. Available brands include Elmer's Professional Carpenter's Glue and The Bond Glue from Franklin Industries. *Note:* Aliphatic resin glue is sometimes called carpenter's glue.

Casein glue is another adhesive often used in scenery construction. Made from milk curd, it is available in powder form and must be mixed with water for each use. Casein glue is a good gap filler, dries in two to three hours, and is water resistant (but not waterproof for outdoor use).

When a very strong, waterproof joint is needed—such as for properties construction—Resorcinol resin glue is the adhesive to use. The heat caused by the chemical reaction produced by mixing the liquid (resin) with the powder (catalyst) sets this two-part glue. After mixing, the glue must be used within one to two hours. Resorcinol resin glue takes a long time to dry, leaves a dark stain where it soaks into the wood, and is very expensive. However, it is very strong and holds well when exposed to extreme heat or extreme cold.

The glues we have discussed so far are the "work horses" of theatrical scene shops. Most wood lamination—the gluing of layers of wood—is done with one of these glues. There are, however, many new synthetic adhesives available that are good for special jobs. Plastic resin glue is a strong, water-resistant glue useful for close-fitting joints (it is not a good gap filler). This adhesive is available in powder form and must be mixed with water and used within four hours. Plastic resin glue dries in approximately 16 hours and does not stain.

Another adhesive used primarily for very close-fitting joints is urea resin glue. It is used mostly in furniture assembly shops or other high-output wood shops. Application is by electric or high-frequency glue machines. A third special application glue is Scotch Grip Brand Wood Adhesive, used to glue plywood floors to joists. It can be used for other wood joints, too. This adhesive is available in tube form and is applied with a caulking gun. Several other glues, also available in tube form, are used to hold paneling in place or to glue wood to other surfaces such as concrete and brick. Many types of contact cement are available for theatrical application. Some types are better for joining certain materials than others, but woods, metals, plastics, wood laminates, and hardboards can all be glued with contact cement. To use, both surfaces of the material to be joined are coated with the adhesive. When the cement becomes tacky, the pieces are joined in an instant bond. Proper alignment is very important, because some contact cements cannot be moved once the surfaces touch. A special contact adhesive for plastics and theatrical use is Rosco Bond (see "Plastic construction" below). *Note:* Almost all contact cements emit some form of toxic vapor. Read and follow all directions carefully.

Epoxy glue is especially valuable for small gluing jobs such as props. This two-part adhesive consists of resin and a catalyst adhesive. Epoxy glue, although expensive, can be used on a wide range of materials and dries quickly (30 seconds to 5 minutes). It forms a waterproof, high-strength bond and is a good gap filler.

Plastic construction.—Different types of plastics are being used increasingly in scenic construction. Many adhesives are already available for plastic applications and new materials and new techniques are being introduced constantly. Rigid foams such as Styrofoam, polystyrene, urethane, and Ethafoam are used for textured walls, carved moldings, and other set detailing. Several types of adhesives for foam have recently been developed to replace polyvinyl glue. (White glue needs air to dry, and drying time for rigid foam glued with polyvinyl adhesive takes several days, if it dries at all.) Special adhesives for rigid foam should be applied to both surfaces to be joined, allowed to dry for several minutes, then clamped together if possible.

Sheet plastics, such as Plexiglass and sheet acrylic, require special glues. These adhesives are actually solvents that cause the plastic to dissolve and weld together as the solvent dries. Consult your plastic supplier for the best adhesive for your particular plastic. Vacuum-formed plastics can be joined together by two types of adhesives: the solvents used for sheet plastics and bodied adhesive. Bodied adhesive contains a filler material made of the same material as the plastic and is particularly useful with very thin plastics. For more information on vacuum-formed plastics and their adhesives, see *Thermoplastic Scenery for the Theatre*, volume 1 by Nicholas L. Bryson (currently out-of-print; try your library).

Two glues work well with plastic films such as Mylar, foil, and vinyl. Sobo's Quick glues plastic to porous surfaces such as cloth and wood, and is flexible when dry. Rosco Bond glues plastic to porous and non-porous surfaces. Both adhesives must be thinned with water prior to this kind of use and do not give off any harmful vapors.

Scene painting.—Adhesives are used often in scene painting, but they are best understood in the context of painting rather than adhesives. Gelatine glue, also known as ground carpenter's glue, is available in flaked or granular form. It must be soaked in water and then heated in a double boiler before use as size water. The size water is then mixed with dry pigment and acts as a binder. (Although this method is no longer widely used, some scene painters still prefer it to other methods.) Polyvinyl glue can be thinned with water and used as a binder for priming and painting. It can also be used to glue canvas to flat frames and to glue other fabrics to various surfaces. Polyvinyl adhesives are particularly useful on fabrics that must move, such as curtains and drops.

Several other adhesives work well for specific applications. Rubber-based clear latex can be used as a binder for paints to be used on drops and scrims. Wheat paste and various kinds of wallpaper pastes are useful for attaching wallpaper and photo enlargements to other surfaces.

Spray adhesives are good for prop work and for attaching certain kinds of paper to various surfaces. These adhesives, such as Scotch Spra-Ment and 3M Spray Adhesive #77, are available in aerosol form.

Water soluble contact cement.—Water soluble contact cement purchased in large quantities is an extremely versatile adhesive. It can be used to cover all foam and ethafoam props to make paint stick and to slightly stiffen the surface. You can also use it as a texture paint, building up rock, brick, and cobblestone texture on a ground cloth. The texture can be between a quarter-inch and a half-inch thick without chipping or peeling off. DesignLab sells a product called "Sculpt or Coat" that has amazing properties. Give them (or your local theatrical supply house) a call and ask for a sample.

Hot glue gun.—The hot glue gun is another indispensable prop shop tool in that it glues by cooling rather than drying. It is invaluable for use during construction but should also be available during the performance. Keep one plugged in and hot backstage. It can also be an emergency middle-of-performance repair tool. Almost everything in the theater, from props to costumes, can be instantly repaired.

Summary on Sets

Constructing sets can be a very rewarding experience. Construction time can be a great opportunity for fellowship and meeting new friends in your church. As with anything else in your production, take it seriously without taking it too seriously. In other words, the process of creating quality can and should be fun.

CHAPTER EIGHT

PROPS

Stage props are actually the design details of the over-all visual composition and, many times, the accent or artistic touch that makes or breaks the effectiveness of a stage setting.

All moveable objects except lighting equipment, scenery, and costumes that are essential to the production of the play are classified as props. The person in charge of these props is called the propmaster. This is one of the most specialized jobs in the theater. It requires the utmost of creativity. Since most period prop or set pieces need to be built in a shop, it is wise to enlist as a propmaster—or at least as a prop crew member—a woodworking hobbyist who has a home workshop.

The position of propmaster can be one of the most challenging and rewarding jobs in the theater. He has the opportunity to use his creative talents and imagination to the fullest. Once he knows what the director and the designer want or what the script calls for in a certain prop, he can rent it, borrow it, buy it, or make it from scratch. His job can be fun.

The propmaster's duties include the care and maintenance of the set and hand props, rugs, mechanical sound effects, and any trick device handled by the actors too small to be classified as scenery. He supervises the handling of props during rehearsals and performances with the help of "grips" assigned to the property department.

To begin, the propmaster should compile a prop list, beginning at the first "read through," and update it continuously (and make sure that the stage manager has all current copies). The stage manager should be in constant communication with the propmaster to ensure that the props will be delivered as soon as possible. Throughout the rehearsal process, he should be compiling four separate lists, as follows:

- *Set or scene props:* large items such as furniture, rugs, draperies, garden furniture, grass matting, and three-dimensional set pieces such as rocks, trees, shrubbery, and so on.

- *Hand or action props (character props):* small objects handled by the actors such as food, drinks, vases, baskets, books, magazines, newspapers, guns, etc.
- *Trim props:* smaller, decorative refinements such as window curtains, lamps, pictures, vases, hanging shelves, clocks, flowers, fruit, etc.
- *Rehearsal props (working props):* substitutes that may be required during early rehearsals to accustom the actors to the use of the actual props.

In the theater, there are many grey areas of responsibility that seem to "cross-over." The boundaries and responsibilities must be determined at the beginning of every production. In planning the properties, the designer's chief concern is to correlate the needs of the director with his own ideas. The production designer is responsible for the selection of properties, for the design of specially built pieces of furniture, and for the furniture plot or general arrangement of properties in the setting. Most other props will be left to the propmaster.

Sometimes electrical props cause what may seem to be double handling. A living room lamp, for example, is placed on the set by a member of the prop crew, but it is connected and made functional by the lighting crew. The offstage storage and visual appearance of the lamp is the responsibility of property men, while all electrical maintenance is done by the electrician. This division of responsibility should be clearly and logically defined in the early stages of the production.

There may also appear to be a "cross-over" of some props that appear to be costumes or visa versa. A sword that is part of the Roman soldier's uniform will probably be made by the prop department, but cared for by the costume department as a costume accessory. Again, the division of responsibility should be clearly defined.

Properties on the set should be planned and built simultaneously with the rest of the scenic elements. Their importance to the design and production scheme is sometimes overlooked in the planning period. The construction of built properties is often started too late, or too many decisions in their selections are started too late, or postponed until the final hectic rehearsals. This often happens when the designer, overworked and pressed for time, places the responsibility of organizing the props on the shoulders of a willing but not-too-reliable volunteer. The designer and propmaster must work together and share the load.

Making Props

The purpose of a prop, like any other part of the design process, is to create the illusion of reality. The audience must believe that what they see on stage is real. The best way to do this, of course, is to use real items to represent real items. But many times these items are not practical on stage or too expensive or simply do not exist. When props need to be created, this can be both a challenge and a joy.

On the original *Star Trek* series, the pieces of futuristic medical equipment in "Sick Bay" were made from old salt shakers, turned upside down and painted. They were convincing. With the use of imagination, the propmaster can create any prop necessary by exploring his environment.

Following is a list of the most commonly used props for church productions. The instructions can be followed exactly, adapted to your particular needs, and/or enhanced with your own creative talents.

They can be designed to be relatively inexpensive and can be stored for reuse for years. Like most of the other sets and props you will be creating, the one-time cost can drastically reduce the budgets of future productions.

Many of the same techniques found in the previous chapter on sets will be used in prop making. The most important technique will be papier-maché. Most of the props that would be used in a church production can be found in the "Set" and "Special Effects" chapters. Below are a few tips for some common and not-so-common props.

Books.—Of course, old books can be purchased at thrift stores and used as is, or cut in half. Another inexpensive method is to use cardboard tubes from paper towels or toilet paper rolls. Slice the tubes down one side and fold them back, forming a long "M." Glue several of these (of various heights) side by side on a board and paint them. Paint appropriate colors such as gold or black for the lettering on the binding. The lettering doesn't need to be detailed and from the audience will look realistic enough. When this board of books is placed in a bookshelf, it is light and takes up very little space.

Stage smoking.—It is not very often that a church production requires an actor to smoke on stage. However, we have seen instances where a sketch or illustration requires this in order to prove the point or moral of the story. Since most churches, rightfully, would not allow the actor actually to smoke, following is a realistic method to simulate it. Take an index card or other plain white paper that is fairly tough, and roll it to cigarette size with the middle being hollow (which means you'll have to trim the card some). Then take a Band-Aid and wrap it around one end and in the same end put a small piece of cotton—this is your "filter." Then fill the rest of the tube with baby powder and put a small piece of red-and-black colored paper in the end. When the actor lightly blows through the "filter," the baby powder will come out looking like smoke. From a distance it should create the illusion.

Vases.—Cheap plastic vases can be purchased at thrift stores or flea markets. To

Example of props (vases and baskets) and methods of storage. Notice the baskets tied with rope and suspended from the ceiling.

give them the appropriate period look, sculpt a layer of quick-drying plaster over the entire vase. When it is, dry paint it the appropriate color.

Pottery.—The same method is used for the vases. Plastic bowls, cups, and such can be purchased and covered with a layer of plaster.

Baskets.—Baskets are readily accessible. Most of the church members will have old baskets lying around. Most of these however are too clean and perfect. They can be soaked in water and left in the sun for several weeks to age. Bleaching helps give a different look and vinegar yet another. For a more distressed look, use sand paper on handles and edges.

Jewelry.—Costume jewelry works well unless you are doing a period play. You may need to research the period style and reproduce it yourself. Most of the time you can adapt existing jewelry and chains. To create stones, you can use silicone or hot glue in molds to give a round shape with a flat back. Paint these the desired gem color and spray with a high-gloss finish. Gold or silver metallic spray paints are very realistic.

Food.—In most cases, use papier-maché to create the look. For meat, cut gingerbread to the shape. For fowl, carve a stale loaf of brown bread to the proper shape. Eggs can look real and edible by using a canned half peach or apricot on white bread cut to shape. Bread can be made of papier-maché; if it must be edible, use real bread. When food is artificial but needs to appear hot, place a small piece of dry ice inside to create steam.

Recipe for candy-glass bottles.—The basic recipe for the candy is simple. By weight mix 70 parts sugar, 30 parts corn syrup, and 20 parts water. Use brown sugar for brown glass, and use white sugar for clear glass. Color the white sugar with food dye for green or yellow glass. Heat the mixture until it dissolves, approximately 225° F/107° C. Let the mixture stand until it begins to harden, and then pour it into the mold. You'll have to tilt the mold to make sure it is evenly covered. *Caution:* Wear gloves, being careful not to burn your hands.

There are several ways to make molds. For bottles, simply cover a bottle with multiple layers of aluminum foil. The outer layers need to be smooth, but the intermediate layers can be crumpled to help build thickness and strength to the mold. Before you pour the hot sugar into the mold, spray the interior with "kitchen spray" for easier release later. When you pour the candy, keep turning the mold so that it covers a thin layer without "filling up." The mold is removed by carefully cutting it and then taping to close it again.

You can also make the mold from papier-maché and again spray with kitchen spray. The best materials for the molds are plaster, using the methods as above.

Borrowing or Renting Sets and Props

Most set props can be borrowed. We have found that an insert in the church bulletin listing all needed supplies, money, and personnel usually brings fruitful results. Church memberships are made up of such a variety of people and occupations. The odds are in your favor that someone just may have that rare prop you are looking for.

The prop crew must submit to the production manager an accurate list of the sources from which they are obtained, and assist him in seeing that they are returned promptly after the run of the play. The usual sources are members of the cast and their friends or local stores that can often be compensated with a program credit and/or a special invitation.

When beginning a theater or production department in your church, it is important to make an effort to establish a credible reputation for the future. When borrowing sets and props from the community, you must make an effort to maintain good will if you want to continue to do business within the community.

Unfortunately, many a prop room has been furnished with unreturned props, which is obviously not the way to build good will. A few simple rules for borrowing help to create a friendly, businesslike way of handling the loan.

1. Establish a method of recording each article borrowed, listing: name and address of owner; date borrowed and date to be returned; estimated value; description of article, noting its condition (scratches, cracks, or parts missing); remuneration (cash, complimentary tickets, or program credit); and a signed receipt from the owner upon return of the article.

2. Centralize the responsibility. Handle all borrowing transactions through one person rather than selecting a different person to be responsible for each item. If possible, the same person or PM may also be available to pick up this task on a future production and already have a rapport with the community at large.

3. Never borrow priceless heirlooms or irreplaceable antiques.

4. Take preferential care of borrowed properties on the stage, using dust covers and padding to prevent undue damage from movement of the scenery.

5. Return borrowed pieces promptly and on the date promised.

6. Secure a receipt and file it. If a record of all transactions is kept, it can become an excellent source for a future production.

Props and Set Storage

If your church plans on doing productions or drama on a regular basis, a secured prop room is an absolute must. By taking care of reusable props and sets you save thousands of dollars on future productions. Large prop set pieces should be stored in a separate warehouse or shed used only for that purpose. Most churches do not have any storage space that they are willing to designate for a "new" production department. However there are many creative ways of finding storage space. Of course, the most ideal would be to use donated materials and labor and build one. One church we know of bought an old cargo container from a shipping yard. Another church bought an old truck trailer and moved it

Examples
of storage of flats
in racks and
floorings on
suspended racks.

their property. Or a small warehouse can be rented. It can be done.

Once the storage area has been created, a smaller, locked cage with shelves should be built inside for securing the smaller props. Then give out keys to certain people: just the TD and properties master, for example. Use "checkout forms" that are filled out and signed by the propmaster and borrower. Note on the form when the item is to be returned. On that date, the propmaster will receive all items and put them away. If something is broken, missing, or misplaced, it is easy to find out who is responsible. At the strike of each show, one supervisor controls the return, to make sure both that everything gets back and that the props room is left in good condition. It really doesn't take up a lot of time, and if strictly followed and enforced this system will cut down the number of things that might "disappear."

CHAPTER NINE

LIGHTING

Ideally, a single person should design the entire production—scenery, costumes, and lighting—thus assuring a unified concept. But all too often, a highly gifted designer will disclaim sufficient knowledge of the technical aspects of stage lighting or is too busy to devote enough time to it. Whether the scene designer is one of the notable exceptions who lights his own set(s) or is one who depends upon a specialist (often his assistant) to do it for him, he will certainly broaden his design concepts if he makes a study of stage lighting.

The Design

Before the lighting designer (LD) can begin, he must understand the director's concept and be familiar with the proposed set design. In his design he will make sure that all areas of the stage are covered with a general and even fill. Using the director's charts on general blocking, he will see that all "special" areas the actors are to use are covered with a key light.

Like the director, the LD has many different choices to underscore dramatic effect and help the audience to tap into the mood of the play. A figure left in silhouette can create a dark and sinister mood; one performer left in a single pool of light can convey a feeling of total separation from the others. Lighter and brighter colors can tell the audience that the play will have a comedic or upbeat tone.

Lighting also can convey information. It can indicate the time of day, distinguish the difference between indoors and outdoors, and even imply geographic locations. Colors and intensities are the LD's tools for creating and sustaining this information. Straight white light is seldom used in theater, unless it is for a specific effect. Even spotlights would be "gelled" (colored material over the lights) with some color to prevent the harsh washout of white light upon the subject. Colored gels in each light will create the hues and values necessary to elicit the desired mood. Cool colors, such as blue and green, can create the mood of morning or evening; warm colors, such as amber and red, can create the mood of day. These colors can also indicate seasons. Intensity, the degree of light projected through the color, further enhances the effect.

The design.—The design of lighting usually begins with the set designer's sketch. Here he presents a suggestion of the light that will illuminate the scene. It may appear to be coming from such natural sources as the sun, the moon, or a fire; or from such artificial sources as table lamps or ceiling fixtures. In contrast, the sources may be arbitrary and depend on the position and color of the instruments used to build the composition. If the sketch is carefully done, the direction and color of the light will be apparent. To indicate any changes in brightness, color, or direction, the LD should prepare several sketches to show such altered compositions and moods.

These sketches, however, are only a start in the planning of stage lighting. Although a sketch represents an artistic concept, it must be technically sound to be realized properly. The floor plan that accompanies the sketch gives the first clues as to the credibility of the designer's lighting ideas. Many a beautiful sketch has been based on a floor plan that revealed, on closer study, impossible lighting angles and insufficient space for the lighting instruments.

In order to begin the design, the LD must create what is known as the light plot. The plot is basically a ground plan of the set on which is superimposed locations of each of the various lighting fixtures and the stage areas they are intended to light and the gel colors. The simplest method is to place a sheet of plastic transparency over the ground and draw the light plot with a fine permanent marker. Write the name of each scene on a separate piece of transparency.

The LD must keep in mind details such as the capacity of electrical sources and placement of existing light fixtures. Sometimes additional power can be drawn from adjacent buildings. This, and all other electrical procedures, should be performed by a qualified electrician.

Using light.—The two principal types of stage lighting are general illumination (wash) and specific illumination (specials). When the stage is lit only by a general wash, the lighting lacks definition and becomes dull, flat, and uninteresting. Specific illumination, if not blended into the general, tends to be harsh and unreal. In many stylized plays this may be the intent; however, in realistic plays it may distract and break the illusion of realism. In most productions neither one is used exclusively; rather, a combination of the two is used. The type of lighting that will predominate will usually be determined by the type of play and by the director's concept.

Area lighting.—In a stylized play, the area lighting should be exaggerated to the same extent as all other design elements of the play. Strongly accented lighting would be necessary to reinforce the stylization and underline the esthetic and dramatic values. In some cases, lighting can be used to create almost the entire environment in which the action of the play develops.

In a realistic play, the LD will not be as free with his imagination. When the director's concept requires all possible means to create and sustain the illusion of reality, the lighting will be one of the most effective. To be effective the lighting will require depth, motivation, and proper use of colors.

Depth.—Depth or dimension in lighting is achieved through creative combinations of lights and shadows. Light on an object makes it "pop out" while a shadow makes it recede. Combined, light and shadow create three-dimensional composition to the set or set pieces. Since we live in a three-dimensional world, this type of lighting creates the most realistic illusion.

Depth of lighting on stage is usually created by at least two light sources aimed at each stage area. These sources, usually spots, should be located so that their light source comes in at approximately a 45-degree angle from two different directions; in other words, each stage area should be cross-lighted in order to give depth to any person or object in that area. The light from one side should be brighter and usually of a different color to produce the effect of light and shadow.

Realism.—When it is possible to achieve the effect, all light on stage should appear to emanate from some natural source, especially in a realistic play. In an interior set the light in the room during a daytime scene should seem to come largely from a window or some other opening in the set. In an evening scene, the light should seem to come from sources inside the room such as a chandelier, floor lamp, table lamp, or even a fireplace. In both cases however, the light hitting any given area will actually come from the theatrical lights covering that area, but it should appear to come from the source. Often times *source lighting* can actually come from the source. This helps heighten the illusion of reality.

Color.—Color is achieved by the fixture lighting projected through a plastic sheeting called gelatin (gel). Appropriate-size squares are cut and placed in gel frames which are mounted to the front of the lighting fixture. Gels come in paper-thin sheets in a wide variety of colors. They can be cut easily to fit the frame of any instrument. The colors do fade over a period of time and tend to crack and tear from the heat, but replacement is simple and inexpensive.

Colored light naturally has an effect on everything it touches—scenery, costumes, and even faces. Sometimes the effect is easily predictable, and other times it comes as a surprise. Red light on a red costume will tend to deepen the red. Green light will turn the costume black. Yellow light on a nice blue wall will turn it an ugly gray. Magenta light, which has blue in it, will keep the wall blue. In other words, the light striking a colored surface must contain some of the primary of the pigment used in the costume or scenery if it is to bring out the intended color.

The same rule applies to makeup. Since most theatrical makeups have some red in them, there must be some red in the stage lights. Otherwise the actors will turn gray. This is the reason that one of the two spots used to light an area should almost always have some in its color medium.

Color also has an emotional effect on an audience. Generally speaking, warm, bright colors make an audience feel happy and friendly and more apt to laugh. It stands to reason that these colors would be used in a comedy. Cold or dark colors induce a feeling of solemnity or foreboding and are often used in more serious dramas.

Equipment

Most lighting instruments, or lamps, fall into two main groups: floods and spots. Floods project light over a wide area, ideal for general lighting. Spots concentrate light on a controlled area which is used for key lighting. The most commonly used spots for theater are *Fresnel* and *ellipsoidal*.

The *Fresnel* projects a soft-edged beam of light, which can be varied by moving the lamp and reflector in relation to the lens. When the lamp-reflector unit is moved towards the lens, the size of the projected beam of light increases. When the beam of light is at its maximum size, the instrument is in flood position. If the lamp-reflector unit is moved away from the lens, the size of the beam decreases. When the beam of light is at its minimum size, the instrument is in spot position. As is the case with the floodlights, the beams of light can be somewhat controlled and shaped with "barn doors," or made into smaller circles by the use of "top hats."

Due to the large amount of spillage, or peripheral light, from the Fresnel lens, barn doors should be used behind the proscenium arch, where the set itself can control the spill of the light. In most churches that would be the bottom of the stage steps, approximately eight feet from the front pew. Fresnels are impractical in most house positions, for the spill would be excessive on the proscenium arch, and using barn doors would be of little help.

126

Fresnel spotlights come in a variety of sizes, beginning with a 3-inch lens. The next size, the 6-inch lens, is the most commonly used Fresnel size in theater today. Fresnels can also be found with lens sizes varying from 8 to 20 inches and even greater; however, the larger sizes are rarely found on the conventional stage.

The *ellipsoidal* spotlight, unlike the Fresnel, uses a lens to focus a variable shaped gate through which the light is directed by a mirror system. While the Fresnel throws a very soft-edged beam, the ellipsoidal throws a sharp-edged beam. This beam may be softened somewhat by moving the lens barrel in or out, but it can never reach the softness of the Fresnel. Another major difference between the two instruments is the method of shaping the beam. In the Fresnel, this is accomplished by the use of barn doors, while in the ellipsoidal, it is done by moving shutters located at the gate, which provides far better control of the shape of the beam. The ellipsoidal therefore proves invaluable in front-of-house positions where it is important to prevent the light from illuminating the proscenium arch, or even worse, the audience.

Fresnel (above) and Elipsoidal (left) lighting unts.

Another feature of the ellipsoidal that is not found in the Fresnel is the ability to use gobos. These are templates made from a heat-resistant material and cut with a desired pattern such as leaves or a lightning bolt, or clouds. When the instrument is properly focused, it will project this image onto the stage or background.

Like the Fresnel, the ellipsoidal comes in a variety of sizes, starting with a 4 ½-inch lens (very useful for covering a large area with a short throw) and going as high as 12 inches (excellent for extremely long throws). The exact ratio of length-of-throw to the diameter of the circle of light for each size of ellipsoidal (or Fresnel) can be found in any complete catalogue from the various lighting manufacturers.

Follow spots are generally used in musicals to follow the soloists, but also can be used for "specials" and special effects.

Batten and border lights can provide fill to eliminate unnecessary or unnatural shadows. Both are strips of 8–12 lamps in joined compartments. Battens are suspended from above, while border lights shine from the front edge of the stage floor.

Control equipment to control various lamps; it is preferable that each should be on a separate circuit for independent control. In the case of the batten floods, three circuits will control three sets of primary colors; in larger battens, four circuits will control the primaries and white.

A gradual transition from full brightness to a black-out requires a *dimmer* connected to the switch controlling the circuit.

Ideally each circuit should be controlled by a dimmer, but it is seldom economically possible to give one dimmer to each circuit. It is not uncommon to connect two units to one circuit.

It is, however, rare that all the circuits require dimming at the same time. It is therefore possible to connect one dimmer to one circuit, up to the number of dimmers fitted, while the rest of the circuits are controlled by switches only. Switches and dimmers can be interchanged by plug/socket changes during performance to give greater flexibility, provided that this has been well thought out and noted during the lighting rehearsal.

Trees are tall, extendible metal poles supported by collapsible spider legs. Light units can be attached up the length and across the top arms. Trees are usually positioned at the sides and front of the stage and provide low-angle light across the stage.

Acquisition of Equipment

It is understandable that your church may not own such sophisticated lighting equipment. At the same time, the existing lighting, more than adequate for worship services, will not be sufficient for a major production. You might want to consider the purchase or rental of the needed equipment from a nearby theatrical supply company. If your budget will not allow for this, you can solve the problem by tapping into your available resources.

We have found that schools, civic organizations, community theaters, and other churches are often willing to loan the needed materials, especially if the schools are out of session at the time. Someone in your congregation may have direct contact with any of these groups; you have nothing to lose by asking. Another new and exciting resource is the

Internet. By typing in such combinations as "theatrical lighting" or "stage lighting" you can find lighting companies that sell used equipment. There are times when you can purchase elipsoidals and Fresnels from pennies on the dollar.

If for some reason you are still in need of lighting equipment, there is yet another alternative. You can make your own lighting units inexpensively but effectively. Don't let this scare you, as it is easier than most people realize.

If the money is unavailable in the budget to rent the necessary and proper lighting equipment, it can be made relatively inexpensively by an electrician. We suggest buying or renting good equipment, but if you have the equipment made properly, you then own it and will save future costs.

Following is a step-by-step guide to making what are known as "coffee-can" lights.

You will need a five-pound coffee can or the equivalent, a porcelain electrical receptacle, a heavy-duty extension cord, tin foil, and a standard 250-watt exterior spot or flood. Using a church key or drill, make several ventilation holes around the bottom sides of the can. Cut a half-inch hole in the bottom of the coffee can. Paint the can with heat-resistant stove-black flat spray paint. Cut off the female end of the extension cord and insert the exposed wires up through the bottom hole, into the can. Connect the two wires to the porcelain receptacle and

The various components of a coffee-can light.

129

Above: Short coffee-can light.

Right: Tall coffee-can light made with a paint-can base and a coffee-can telescope.

secure it to the inside bottom of the

can with metal screws. Line the inside of the can with tin foil and screw in the bulb. The light unit is now complete and ready to be mounted.

A variation of the above unit gives a more focused or spot beam. Use the same process as above, but use a one-gallon paint can instead. Cut both ends out of a five-pound coffee can and slide it inside the paint can approximately one inch. Join the two cans together with short metal screws.

A homemade control unit.—A portable control unit can be tailor-made by a lighting/electrical technician to suit most church productions. A control, in a basic form, can be made from a single 1-kw box dimmer running from a 13-amp wall

130

socket and clipped to a stand supplying four 250-watt bulbs, two 500-watt bulbs, or one 1,000-watt bulb. Two, three, or more of these units (up to the number of sockets available) could provide sufficient lighting for any combination required.

All lighting units must be patched-in to a power pack and dimmer board. Before you can begin installation of your lights, it is necessary to know the limits of your electrical supply. The LD should take into consideration the maximum wattage capacity of each dimmer unit. Self-made dimmer boards, having a standard household dimmer, will obviously accommodate a fewer number of lights per channel. Be sure to obtain the advice of an electrical expert to avoid overloading your system.

Batten and border lights.—You can make your own batten or border lights using a similar method. The base of the strip can be constructed from half-inch plywood cut to eight inches wide by six feet long. Drill eight, half-inch holes at eight-inch intervals into the center line of the board. Using half-inch plywood, frame this base board to create a box one-foot deep. As described above with the coffee-can lights, connect your extension cords to the porcelain receptacles and attach them to the base board.

Tin-foil or mirrors could be lined inside each compartment to increase the intensity of the light and its throw.

The Hang Up

Whatever type of lighting units you have to work with, you are faced with the task of how and where to hang them. In a theater or studio, you will find a lighting grid: a series of 1½-inch steel bars evenly suspended above the stage. A standard Fresnel or ellipsoidal has a C-clamp that is easily mounted on the grid. With coffee-can lights, it will be necessary to create your own mounting device, using metal strapping, bolts, and wing-

nuts, or something of your own creation. In the photos on page 130, two L-brackets were bolted to each side of a coffee-can light, then joined in the center.

Always make sure that safety chains are around each light unit and attached to the grid. Safety chains can be made of heavy cable with retractable latches.

Most churches do not have a lighting grid from which to hang the lights, making

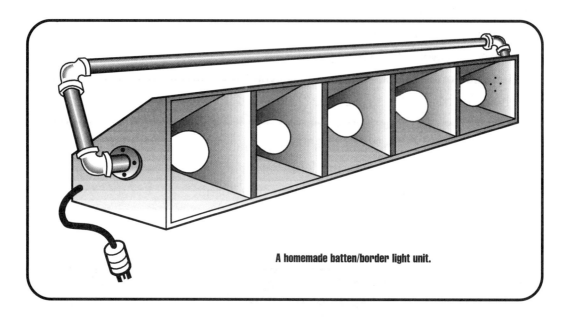

A homemade batten/border light unit.

it necessary to install one. Once again this is much easier than it would seem. You will need several sections of 1½-inch steel pipe, heavy duty chain, bolts, washers, and nuts. Drill a hole through the ends of each pipe. Wrap one end of the chain around the pipe and bolt it securely through the holes in the pipe.

These bars will be suspended from the ceiling (by eye-bolts and chains) fifteen to twenty feet above the stage floor and approximately twenty feet out from the front edge of the stage (see illustration). If you are using coffee-can lights, you will probably need to suspend them closer to the front edge of the stage.

An additional means of hanging lights is to mount them on Trees. As discussed earlier in this chapter, these are vertical poles on a tripod which are positioned on each side of the proscenium. Also, many churches have volleyball stands cemented into old tires, which can be easily adapted to accommodate the C-clamps.

Special Lighting

While mounting any play production, you will undoubtedly use other forms of lighting besides key and general. These are lights that require special placement and special instruments, and are used to create a mood or highlight a specific moment. Quite often, these may cross over into the special effects department. For instance, we once used a high-powered strobe light to create the illusion of lightning during the earthquake at the crucifixion. When mixed with the proper sound effects, the strobe was very effective in creating the illusion of the approaching storm. Another special

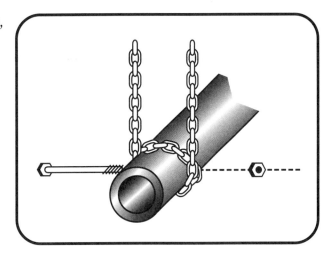

Use 1" pipe. Drill holes at each end of the pipe. Wrap heavy gauge chain as shown and bolt securely with nuts and lock-washers. Depending on the length of the pipe, a center chain may be necessary.

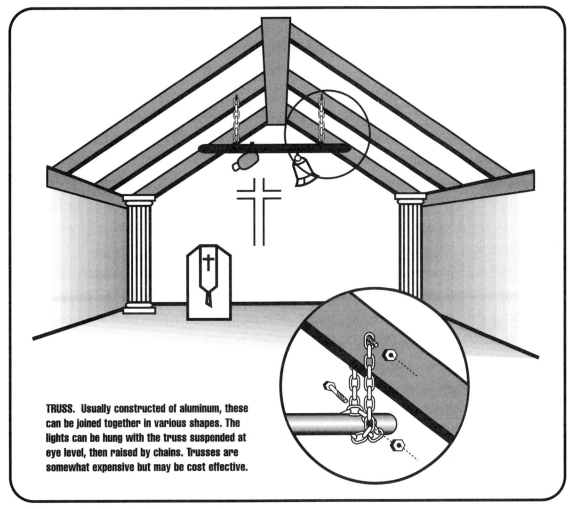

TRUSS. Usually constructed of aluminum, these can be joined together in various shapes. The lights can be hung with the truss suspended at eye level, then raised by chains. Trusses are somewhat expensive but may be cost effective.

instrument is a mirror ball, suspended above the set, with a penlight or spot focused on it. This can be used to create a variety of atmospheres such as snow-flakes, miracles, celebrations, and angels. Again, your creative imagination is the only limit to the possibilities.

Black light can be extremely effective in creating certain illusions and moods. Christ, after the resurrection, can be given a ghost-like appearance as His white robe glows softly from the black light. By putting the rest of the cast in darker colors, the sharp contrast gives an ominous effect. Black light also can be used as a general fill to give the dark-purple hue of evening. Use your imagination.

Sometimes there will be a need to place a light under, off, or (hidden) on the stage. Some productions use a softer white light, glowing from the manger, to give the heavenly appearance of the baby Jesus. A powerful beam of light coming from the tomb enhances the majesty of the resurrection. In contrast, a bright red light from an open pit in the set invokes chilling images of hell.

Backlighting.—Although it is not absolutely necessary in church productions, backlighting can be very helpful for general fill or for creating special moods. Backlighting separates the actor from his background and adds another dimension to stage composition. It is accomplished by lighting the actor from overhead and behind. By intensifying this light on the head and shoulders of an actor, you can create a halo effect. Anyone familiar with the original *Star Trek* series has seen this glow on Captain Kirk's head. If you are staging a living painting of Da Vinci's *The Last Supper,* backlighting would give the twelve apostles the appearance of painted figures.

Backlighting must be executed with great care. If the instruments are not properly mounted, they may shine into the audience, creating discomfort and distraction. These lights should almost always be "masked" by "teasers" made of duvetyne or an appropriate, inconspicuous material.

So far we have been discussing light sources hidden from the audience's view, but there may be times when a light source is incorporated into the set design, such as a living room lamp. Any lights on the set should be functional, but they may need to be reinforced by key or general lighting. For wall units, chandeliers, and other electrical fixtures, suitable spots with warm color filters must be directed to the area of supposed light. The actual light or lights in the setting should be fitted with low-wattage bulbs. Candles, fireplaces, torches, and gas lanterns can be fitted with batteries and small bulbs, unless special fire precautions are taken for using real flame. (See chapter 13, "Special Effects.")

Most sets designed for outdoor scenes will require some type of backdrop or cyclorama (cyc). (See chapter 7, "The Set.") The placement of cyc lighting plays an important role in creating dramatic effect and requires special attention. A cyc is usually lit with battens from the top, borders or ground rows from the bottom, and floods from the side. Any variety of colors can be applied to achieve the desired effect.

Other effects can be achieved through selective lighting of the cyc. A moon or star or even storm clouds can be projected on the backdrop through a metal "pattern" or gobo. There are hundreds of patterns available at theatrical supply companies. A bolt of lighting can be projected onto the cyc during the earthquake at the crucifixion.

The LD will have a few other responsibilities besides directly lighting the set. Before the first rehearsal on the stage, the LD must provide "work lights" to the rehearsal area. These can be any instruments that provide adequate light to the rehearsal area.

At the same time, backstage and wing lights should be installed to provide visibility and safety lighting to the actors and crew members. These should be low-wattage bulbs with very little spill. Christmas lights are often practical and effective. During performances this is critical.

One of the problems with using a live orchestra is providing lights for their music stands. These also should be low-wattage bulbs, and they should be covered with a dark gel, preferably blue. They should be easily controlled, either by the orchestra or from the technical booth.

House lights.—The LD is also responsible for the house lights. These are the lights that are normally in the auditorium and are "on" upon the arrival of the audience. They remain on until the show begins. Ideally, the house lights are controlled from the tech booth. They should be dimmed to "off" a few moments before the stage lights are brought up. The order should be reversed at intermission and at the end of the performance. Sometimes, to help set the mood, the house lights are pre-set to half power.

An electric flame.—Live candles on stage can be a hassle. The fire marshall may require additional personnel as a fire watch—if you are allowed to have live flame at all. And even if you get permission, the danger of the fire is still there. Live flame, as simple, honest, and beautiful as it is, may not be worth the bother. There are several electric candles with simulated flames that flicker now available on the market.

Tech booth.—In most theaters, professional or amateur, the play is controlled from a small room located in the back of the theater called "the tech booth." The lighting operator, the sound operator, backstage cues, and many effects, are controlled from the tech booth. Ideally, this booth would be behind and above the audience. The technical booth(s) must also be properly lit. Again, using low-wattage bulbs covered with a blue gel is the best way to light the booth. Light should not spill out from the booth onto the audience.

Most churches do not have the luxury of a tech booth and must find a suitable alternative. Some use a balcony, others set up a platform in the back of the auditorium or even over the pews. And some actually construct a tech booth into the upper back wall. The location may differ but the setup is much the same: a long table for the lighting and sound boards; a clear view to the stage; headsets for communication between the operators in the booth and backstage. The booth is lit with a tech table lamp that allows the operators to follow cue scripts and work the boards without light spilling on the audience. A variety of lights are used for this purpose—stand lights, clip-ons, gooseneck lamps, and others. Most of these light the scripts and do not shine in the operator's eyes, making it tough to see the stage. One suggestion is to use a banker's lamp—the type of lamp with a green glass shade over the horizontally mounted bulb. With a few modifications it can be a very practical and inexpensive fix to the tech lamp problem. First, cover the outside of the green glass shade with black duct tape. Having a colored light lighting the script may alter perception of the color on stage. Install a 25-watt lamp, and put a dimmer in the power cord about 8 inches from the base of the lamp. With the dimmer at full there will be more than enough light with the 25-watt lamp, and you will be able to lower the level as needed.

Running Crew

The lighting designer may not necessarily be the same person who controls the lights during rehearsals and performances. There may be several lighting "stations" that need operators and the main control board is only one of them. There may be several spot lights with operators, houselights, special lights not controlled by the board, and so forth. All of these stations should have communication among them.

Lighting should be well rehearsed long before dress rehearsals so that each member of the team understands and is familiar with all lighting cues. During rehearsals and performances, the production manager will be "calling" the show. Though each member of the crew will have a script and score marked with cues, the tech director, stage manager, or production coordinator will be giving commands to execute those cues over the communication system.

We have given you some general guidelines for lighting, but by no means are you limited to this information. Like any other designer, the LD's greatest tool is his imagination. Be creative, experiment, and study, and you will contribute the professional quality your church deserves.

CRESCENT MOON   EVENING STAR   LARGE STARS   LIGHTNING   SEASON'S GREETINGS

CLOUD #5   CLOUD #6   CLOUD #7   CLOUD #8   CLOUD #9

BARE BRANCHES   TREES   PALM TREES   MUSIC   RAINBOW

FLAME   SUNBURST   CHURCH WINDOW   CROSS   STEEPLE

Various light gobos or patterns.

CHAPTER 10

SOUND

In the theater of earlier times, sound meant only a consideration of the space acoustics and the ability of the actor to project his voice. However, in the modern theater, sound has become one of the most difficult and misunderstood areas of theater. The difficulties are often exaggerated in church productions. This is true in part because churches aren't designed with theatrical acoustics in mind. But the greater reason is usually the lack of knowledge of the one in charge of sound.

It is extremely important to employ the expertise of someone with professional knowledge of sound. Hopefully, this "sound man" would be the one who is normally in charge of the church sound system. Too often, though, that person is not properly qualified to the degree needed for a major production. Modern sound technology and equipment are so advanced that not many people could be considered experts. We do not claim to be, either. That is why this chapter is the shortest in this book. The systems and equipment must be individually designed for each church and each production. Your sound "expert" must be the one who does that. We will only discuss here the thought process behind sound in the production.

The major reason for the sound man's problems is that the director's and set designer's needs and wants must be accommodated. For example: usually the director and designer do not want the speakers visible, yet they must be effective. Under normal circumstances it is difficult to place speakers in a church auditorium. If they must be placed on the set somewhere, they must be incorporated into the set or camouflaged. Even though the speakers may be necessary, they must not, after all other efforts, break the illusion of reality.

The most common confrontation happens in the discussion of microphone placement. When vocal amplification with microphones is necessary and the set is in a realistic-period play, microphones must not be held or placed on the set in full view of the audience. The sound man should work with the set construction foreman and the set designer to find the best means of placing and hiding the microphones. We have hidden them in bushes, behind rocks, in palm trees, in crosses, and in many other out-of-sight places.

Most often the choir director would rather compromise the realism and place the microphones in plain view of the audience so that his choir members and soloists can be heard better. This is not done in professional theater and should be avoided in the church. You can find a way without compromising the quality of the overall production.

If your budget allows it, soloists and lead characters can wear wireless micro-phones. These can be purchased, borrowed, or rented; regardless, the cost expended could be well worth it.

The sound man is also responsible for all inter-communication devices for the technical departments and stage crews. During the run of the show, the technical director or production coordinator will be calling the show—giving cues to the appropriate crews on communication lines. Sometimes the devices used are wireless with headphones, and sometimes an intricate wire network needs to be assembled between all stations.

The sound man maintains all sound equipment during rehearsals and throughout the run of the show. This means a sound check must be conducted at least two hours prior to each performance. We once "held" our opening night for 45 minutes when the sound system went down right at curtain time. Over 2,000 paying audience members waited and watched as the sound man finally traced the problem to a connector that an orchestra member had kicked loose. The equipment should be secured at the end of each perfor-mance and rechecked prior to the next.

Research and Prep

The sound department is responsible for recording and editing each show tape, as well as the operation of sound equipment for sound cues. They are responsible for researching and collecting all digital, CD, tape, and live-recorded sound effects. These sound effects should be properly labeled and categorized for future use. The sound department might organize and service a sound-recording library.

The director will have final word on the choice of sound effects so the sound man should get a good idea of what he's looking for at the first meeting. Whatever the choice, these effects should always sound realistic to the point that the audience does not ever think "recording." Whenever possible, the sound should come from the source. For instance, a doorbell should be an actual bell wired on the stage. It is irritating to an audience to hear a telephone ring behind them and watch an actor on stage pick up the receiver. Try to make the telephone functional, ringing from the source. The sound man may want to control this from the booth; however, the stage manager could also perform this function from backstage.

Even recorded sound effects should come from the source. A canary in a window would have a speaker nearby; a radio or record player should be functional or have speakers built in to amplify prerecordings.

The director and music director may decide to prerecord the choir numbers to supplement the live singing. The sound man should supervise the recording to ensure a top-quality recording. Again, the speakers should be placed at the source where the chorus will be singing, to support the voices. The performers will be actually singing along with the track and not simply silently moving lips. Bellevue Baptist Church in Memphis, Tennessee, uses a costly but very effective method they call "the pit." In an isolated room they place another choir of their best voices. Each member wears a headset. They are well covered with appropriate microphones. They watch a large screen image of the choir director as he is shot from a live camera in the at the edge of the stage. These voices are played live, in real time, supplementing the voices on stage.

The sound man should also research and secure "pre-show" music. This is the music that is played as the audience arrives and will continue until curtain. It is meant to help set the mood and prepare the audience for the upcoming play. The proper selection of music is critical, since it helps to establish what the play is about. The director will have an idea of what he wants and will, of course, give final approval on the selections.

Rehearsal

During the rehearsal process, the sound man should be concerned with three things: rehearsing the performers with microphones, rehearsing his control board, and developing the sound system. This is the time that decisions are made: types of microphones, placement of microphones, volume levels, and so on. It is a learning process, and things will change many times before the actual performance.

It is important for the volume levels to be set properly during rehearsals, since the director will be moving about the empty auditorium, listening for weak voices. Volume levels will also change for each actor and each musical number. The sound man will need to be alert and quick with his hands. Rehearsals are a time to develop this quickness.

As the sound man listens and develops his system, he will be moving and shifting the speakers to gain an optimum balance. Speakers may need to be added or moved and masked, or moved and incorporated into the set, etcetera. This is what is meant by "developing the sound system."

During rehearsals, the director will need a microphone (preferably wireless) to communicate with the actors on stage and the tech crews. As he moves about the auditorium giving both acting and tech commands, he will quickly lose his voice without a microphone. Ideally, he would have a headset and a com-line to communicate with the tech crew without disturbing the actors in their scene, and a separate microphone to communicate with the actors.

Running Crew

The sound running crew for performances should be the same crew as the rehearsal crew. The sound designer might not be a part of this crew, but he would be wise to oversee it. As stated above, the operators should be on their toes to execute cues at the precise moments. Miscue of a sound is one of the biggest offenders when it comes to breaking the illusion of reality. An actor picks up a phone and it keeps ringing, or pulls the trigger on a gun and three seconds later the "blast" is sounded—the illusion is shattered.

The sound man also must be prepared to resolve problems instantly, such as feedback (which destroys the illusion) or bringing up microphones after the first few words of a solo. These incidents should never happen if crews are well rehearsed and alert.

CHAPTER ELEVEN

COSTUMES

When an actor first steps onto the stage, the audience gets its first impression of the character he is portraying (even before he speaks a line) from the way he is dressed and the way he looks. It is important that this impression be the correct one.

An actor should not only feel the character he is portraying; he should also look like the character. While makeup will certainly be a factor in his success, his costume will probably play an even more decisive role in conveying the correct impression of his character.

A costume should convey to the audience certain important information about the character who is being portrayed. It should show the period in which he is supposed to be living as well as his age, his wealth, and his social position. It should indicate the type of work he does. It should indicate his mood or even the dominant mood of the play. And finally, it should give some clue as to his basic character, his goals and ambitions, his likes and dislikes, his phobias and prejudices, his nature and disposition.

The costume designer should be aware of all the possibilities to be found in costuming, not only so that he can take advantage of them to create a good costume, but also so that in observing them, he can avoid creating a bad one.

Period Costumes

Clothes are one of the best means available for setting the period of a play. The audience may not recognize the exact date of the costume or the social position of the costume, but it will be aware of the general period in history. Establishing this in the mind of the audience will begin to establish or to reinforce and support the illusion of the time period.

The term *bathrobe drama* is used to describe a very amateur and unrealistic church play for a very good reason. If the audience is supposed to believe that these characters are in the established time period, but the actor is wearing a department store bathrobe for a costume, the illusion is shattered when the audience notices a "J.C. Penney" tag sticking out the back. Unfortunately, many church productions feel that bathrobes are "good enough" for church.

The costume designer and the director should be thorough in the research of styles, colors, fabrics, accessories, and such to create authenticity. Each character, including each of the chorus members (village people), should be researched and an appropriate costume assigned. For example, if the character is a beggar, the clothes may be torn and dirty and not as colorful. If the character is a wealthy politician, his clothes will probably be colorful, clean, and adorned with accessories and jewelry. One common mistake in church productions is to have all the costumes cleaned and pressed for the production. They should look worn and should be used to show real life characters involved in everyday activities.

Acquiring Costumes

With a period play, there is the question of whether to rent or make the costumes. There are advantages and disadvantages to both.

In renting, the costumes are likely to be more elaborate and better made than they would be if made by local, volunteer help. They are also likely to be historically more accurate. But they are expensive, often do not fit, and often do not arrive in time to make alterations.

If possible, it is better to make the costumes than to rent them. The one-time cost of making them is much more practical than renting for each production.

There should be a competent and imaginative designer available who is capable of designing and supervising the construction of the costumes. There must be enough experienced and willing volunteers to make whatever number of costumes are required. And there must be enough time and enough work space to accomplish the job.

We usually schedule several work days when dozens of volunteer church members fill the fellowship hall with sewing machines and material and "crank out" the costumes as designed and supervised by the costume designer. This can go rather quickly, and it helps create an environment of comradery.

There are many other advantages to making the costumes. They can be designed to serve a specific dramatic purpose, or to fit a specific actor or actress. The colors can be selected correctly for the character, or mood, or compatibility of the other costumes and scenery. And, most importantly, the church can build a collection of costumes to be used again and again from year to year. If a choir or cast member is asked to pay for his or her own costume, these costumes could be donated afterward to the collection, thereby saving on the budget yet still building the theatrical supply for the future.

Making Costumes

The basic costume of the biblical period is a gown or tunic, sometimes with a waist tie, or a cloth coat, or cloth wrap, or any combination of these. Sometimes head coverings of wrapped material are worn.

Patterns could be created by the costume designer from looking at pictures. Books can be found in libraries or religious book stores. The human frame has not changed through the centuries, and clothing is only a variation on a theme. You won't find a pattern for a disciple in a modern pattern book, but with two basic modern patterns and a good supply of newspapers, you will be able to construct patterns to costume any character from the past.

For men's costumes, use a pajama pattern. This is more useful than a shirt pattern, which has the unnecessary complication of a yoke. It can be lengthened to accommodate any size man. For women's costumes, the very simplest dress pattern will work. Most of the well-known pattern books have a "basic" pattern, consisting of a plain bodice and sleeve, a 4-piece flared skirt, and a straight "shift." These also can be used for men's costumes.

The tunic of Roman times.—The tunic was a Roman innovation. It was comprised of a single piece of cloth, with a slit for the head at its center point. Although now this garment was hanging from the shoulders, it was also woven in one piece on a frame-shaped loom. The tunic began to develop when the cloth was first woven in the shape of a cross: when folded in two, the cloth itself formed a pair of sleeves. Long and short cloaks or mantles were worn over the tunic; just as people had earlier worn the "himation," so the Romans now wore the "stole" and "toga." In early Christian times, with the spread of the narrow horizontal loom, a new garment appeared: the "dalmatic." It is fashioned from more than one piece of cloth; its shape is that of a narrow tunic with sleeves sewn onto it and gussets inserted in the side seams. This is the garment that survived as an element of local Greek costumes in the form of the basic undergarment, the chemise. From that point on, once the single piece of cloth was cut to make a composite sewn dress, the way opened to the development of cutting and tailoring skills that led in time to the designing of clothes.

Basic T-tunic.—The T-tunic is so called because of its resemblance to that letter when opened and laid flat, and it has been worn by just about every culture at some time. It's good for a starter costume, as it may be converted easily into a garment fitting the era you finally do choose to portray. The pattern can be adapted to be short, long, or anywhere in between, as full or narrow as you desire, with sleeves that are long, short, medium, full, narrow, or even sleeveless, and with open or closed sides, as you wish.

To construct:

1. Find and record these measurements:
   - Neck to desired length plus at least 2 inches
   - Neck to crown of bust (2–3 inches below center of armpit where bust is fullest)
   - Bust or chest at fullest plus 3 inches for ease of movement.
2. Fold your fabric in half width-wise.
3. Fold it again length-wise, creating four layers.
4. Find the length from the neck to the crown of the bust and mark on the fabric with tailor's chalk all the way across.
5. Find the chest measurement and divide by four. Mark this point on the line you have just drawn with the chalk, measuring from the center fold out.
6. Find the point from the neck to the desired length of the garment and mark it. Now note the length from the line you drew in #4 to the line you just drew. Draw a diagonal line, according to your own desired fullness, issuing from the armpit and ending at the edge of the fabric. Mark the distance from the bust line to the hem on this line, and round off the bottom edge.
7. Parallel the lines you have just drawn (which are your seam lines) a half inch out—these will be your cutting lines.
8. Draw a line issuing from the bust-line/armpit intersection across the fabric at 90 degrees or at an angle which will provide you the desired fullness in your sleeves. Parallel this line as well with cutting line a half inch out.
9. Mark the point along the center fold which is 3 inches from the top. Find the point on your shoulder where your head, if not for your neck, would meet your shoulders, and mark this point on your fabric. Connect these two pints with an arced line. This is your seam line. Parallel this seam line a half inch closer to the edge of the fabric, as before, for a cutting line. This will give a neck hole which is a little wide, but which should slip right over your head.
10. Cut out pattern, cutting along all cutting lines, open the fabric—you now have only two layers—and stitch along side seam and sleeve-seam lines.
11. Turn neck, face edges, hem and wear. For longer sleeves, simply add fabric to sleeve edges before sewing side seams.

Hint: Turn raw edges of neck, cuffs, and hem to the outside. Press down and cover over with ribbon or trim. This is a period practice and it secures the edges, increasing the life span of your new garment while adding a measure of grace at the same time.

Whether you are working from a set of designs worked out by a designer or simply reproducing from a portrait or a picture in a book, study the costume and break it down into basic sections. However complicated and elaborate a costume may seem at first, a preliminary dissection will give you a rough idea of where to begin to adapt your pattern. Keep in mind, especially since you intend to preserve these costumes for future use, that apparent authenticity with respect to design and texture is part of what you are striving to achieve, and not actual replication. Experience will show that an overall impression may be given with far less actual cutting and sewing than the picture demands.

Dyeing

In any period production involving a large cast, the question of dyeing is likely to arise. For someone inexperienced in the art of dyeing, it can be a complicated, technical process. There are many types of dye. Some work well with certain materials and badly with others. It is advisable to enlist at least one dedicated and knowledgeable individual who is willing to devote himself to the undertaking.

Sometimes it is cheaper to buy quantities of unbleached muslin and dye it the various colors needed. It is advisable, though, to start the process as soon as possible after the production plan and the costume sketches have been approved. Otherwise the seamstresses will still be trying desperately to finish the last costumes on the afternoon of the first performance.

Tea-dying.—To give a natural aging look to your newly constructed costumes, soaking them in a strong tea solution is an effective and inexpensive trick. This is also a great way to mask stains. When tea-dying you may be concerned about the longevity of your finished project. The tannic acid from the tea will eventually destroy the fabrics. This, of course, will take years and will probably add to the realism. To simulate actual antique and make the costume darker in some places, push tea bags harder into certain areas and leave them longer.

Simply make some strong tea and bring it to a boil. Orange Pekoe-Pekoe Black is best (herbal tea is too light). Put the costume into a big pot, pour in the tea, and let your fabric soak. How much tea you used and how long you soak will determine the amount that is soaked into the cloth. Dye the costume in stages; take it out and let it dry; check how you like the shade.

To tea-dye lace, use the same recipe for tea-dying fabric. To make the tea solution, boil a gallon of water with four tea bags in it for 15 minutes. Strain the solution and return it to simmer. Wet the lace in plain water, then put it into simmering tea. When the lace has simmered for 15 minutes, take it out and put it in a setting solution of one-half cup white vinegar in one gallon of water. Let it set for 15 minutes, then rinse it thoroughly and press.

Another method is to tea-dye material in a washing machine. Make a heavy brew, using about 4 cups of boiling water and a box of cheap tea bags, allowing them to brew for some time. While the tea is brewing, fill the machine to the low or medium load line with warm water, depending on how much material you have. Then add the brewed tea. If you want, you can add the tea bags in a mesh bag. Let the warm water and tea agitate for a minute or so before adding the material. After adding the material, let the machine agitate for a long while. Turn the machine off and let the material sit in the water for a while or until you like the shade of the material. Next, turn the machine back on to rinse and spin (using cold water).

Using tea again to drip into a fabric to age it and give it a dirty and worn look is often done. If a character is supposed to look unkept and unlaundered, this effect can be achieved by letting the tea solution drip down at strategic points, bearing in mind how and why the character came to look this way. Coffee and other such solutions (juices to dyes) can be used to achieve the same effect.

For a better permanent dye, buy a red beet at the supermarket and chop it and boil it in water and vinegar. Strain and then dye your goodie. Another method that has been around for centuries is to take filings of rusty iron in boiling water and soak the material. Adding vinegar will help it to set.

Store-bought dyes such as manufactured by RIT Dye can also be used to give fabrics an aged look. This may be simpler, but a lot less fun and sometimes more costly.

Gluing costumes.—Adhesives are used basically two ways in the costume shop: to attach decoration to a portion of a costume and to create designs out of the glue itself. Sobo, a polyvinyl, is the most widely used adhesive for costume work. Its advantages are clear drying, flexibility after drying, and a capacity for dry cleaning. These attributes are especially important in costume construction. Hot melt glue is a popular adhesive for costume work. It can be used in the same way as the polyvinyl and, in addition, dries very quickly. One drawback is that some costumes decorated using hot melt glue cannot be dry cleaned or laundered because the heat employed causes the glue to remelt. New adhesive products and new applications of adhesives for theatrical use become available regularly. If you are interested in new glues and how to use them, write to the manufacturers and ask to be placed on their new products mailing list.

Footwear

Footwear is almost always a problem with period costumes. Costume houses cannot afford to stock the wide range of styles and sizes required to serve all periods and fit all feet. Here again, a group will probably do better by trying to solve the problem by itself.

For Greek or Roman footwear, sometimes simple store-bought sandals are appropriate. However, these should not appear to be modern, department-store shoes. Try to stay with leather sandals. Following is a simple design for constructing your own:

Armor

Armor is a necessity in most passion plays where Greek and Roman soldiers are involved. Armor is usually a severe headache to the costume designer and costume crew. While a few of the best costume houses have first-class armor to rent, it can be very expensive, and the armor available from the lesser costume houses is hardly worth renting at any price. So unless a group can afford to rent good armor, it had better resign itself to the necessity of fabricating its own.

There are two main types of armor: plate armor and chain mail. Plate armor usually provided the most effective protection and was the predominant type, at least until the fifteenth century. Chain mail gave the wearer much more freedom of action, and gradually it gained favor during the fifteenth and sixteenth centuries. Knights and foot soldiers frequently used a combination of plate and chain mail—plate for the legs and torso, mail for the arms.

Although chain mail is much easier to simulate for stage purposes, it is advisable to go with plate armor if it is in keeping with historical accuracy.

Plate armor.—This can best be made with papier-mâché. (See chapter 7, "The Set," for details of this process.) The plates can then be fastened to the body with leather straps or cloth straps made to look like leather. The plates should be painted with a mixture of powdered graphite (available at most paint stores) and liquid glue in order to simulate the dull-gray look of steel. They can be highlighted with silver to give a well-worn and

burnished look. But, armor should never be made to look like the chrome-plated metal of a modern car. Gray or silver spray paint, sprinkled with a little black and gold spray paint, can also be effective. Avoid the shiny or glossy look.

Chain mail.—This can best be simulated by securing the heaviest, knobbiest fabric available (usually found in the curtain or drapery department) and dyeing it to a medium-dark gray. The material should be of natural rather than man-made fiber (burlap opposed to nylon) in order to take the dye readily. After being dyed, the knobs of the material can be highlighted with silver paint to give the impression of well-worn links of mail. Any seams should be covered or camouflaged if possible, since mail was made in one piece.

Whatever type of armor is made, the designer should make careful study of the subject in a museum, an encyclopedia, or a good book of costume illustrations to see how each piece served a specific protective function and how each joint of plate armor was articulated to provide the wearer with as much freedom of movement as possible.

Helmets.—When worn with armor, helmets can offer the designer a little more scope for his imagination than the armor itself. There was great variety in the shape and design of helmets during the many centuries when armor was worn. The purpose of the helmet was to ward off or deflect the blows of a sword, a mace, a battle axe, or a lance; and each individual armorer had his own idea of which design would best serve the purpose. Some made their helmets round, some flat, some peaked. As a result, the modern designer has considerable latitude in selecting his designs for helmets. It is better to remain uniform when there are a number of soldiers in the scene, however, they may vary according to rank. For instance, the Centurion may have a feather plume running down the top of his helmet.

Like plate armor, helmets are best made out of papier-maché. The form of the hard

150

batter's helmet can be used as a mold for the papier-maché over and over again. A few of these and you are on your way. The glue and paper, of course, should be allowed to dry thoroughly before the visor, crest, or other decoration is attached. The visor should be cut from cardboard and reinforced with papier-maché if desired; it also can be wired to maintain its shape. The helmet can then be painted with graphite to give it a dull, burnished-steel appearance; if Roman, it might be bronzed. In any case, the helmet should be shellacked heavily on the inside to protect it from perspiration.

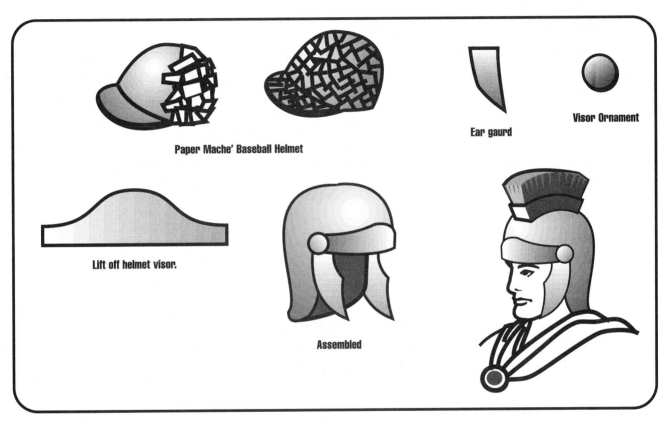

Constructing a Roman soldier helmet with papier-maché.

Leather vambrace construction.—This is one of the simplest projects I can think of to get started in armor construction. Over the course of a couple of hours a pair of vambraces (forearm armor) can be constructed. Looking at figure 1, the shape of the pattern can be determined. Cut the pattern shapes and sizes to fit the actor's arms accordingly. Choose anywhere from 9- to 14-ounce leather. Stiffer vambraces may be uncomfortable with extended wear.

Once the pattern has been cut out of the leather, you should then dye the leather whatever color you wish the vambraces to be. Brown or black is the normal color, but more exotic colors are possible. Dyeing leather should not be an intimidating task. Nothing more is involved than dipping a sponge with the dye and rubbing it on the leather. Several coats may be needed depending on the shade you want and the quality of the coats. Also, the choice to dye the inside of the vambrace is up to you, but don't be surprised if the dye colors your arm during wear. Next, apply a finisher to the leather. Two basic options are available—a high-gloss finish and a neutral finish. The choice is up to you, though the high gloss has usually stiffened the leather more than the neutral finish. We prefer the neutral finish since it leaves the leather looking more combat-ready. The holes may be punched with any leather punch. The size of the holes should be appropriate for whatever lacing you wish to use. Leather lacing is probably your best choice. After you have punched the holes, roll the leather into a roll and break in the leather so it will tend to retain a curved shape. Lace it up and you will have a wearable vambrace. You may find that after wearing it you want to trim the edges for a better fit. Many alterations are possible to the vambrace. You could insert eyelets into the holes to allow the lacing to slide through more easily.

Leather-Working

Tools: • Ruler or pen for marking out
• Sharp knife for cutting (scissors are pretty useless for cutting leather)
• Needles
• Leather

Leather can be obtained in a number of ways. One of the cheapest ways of buying leather is to get old leather coats from charity shops. Shops and cobblers that make and sell leather goods might sell "off-cuts." If you want a large quantity of leather, go to a tanner and buy from them directly as they will often give you better prices. Sometimes taking cash helps when it comes to negotiating prices.

Leather is sold by the square foot. The leather will be priced by the square foot. The cost per square foot depends on the thickness or "weight" of the leather. Retail suppliers of leather sell it by the skin/side using an ounce range (an ounce being 1/64 inch in thickness), so 8–9 oz would be 8/64 to 9/64 inches in thickness.

Full leather skins and sides are measured by intricate machines and the size is marked on the back in square feet. The first figure is the square footage, and the smaller following numbers refer to quarters of a square foot; or if a decimal point is used, then it means a tenth of a square foot.

Joining Leather.

Stapling.—This is only useful for medium to thin leather. It is very quick but it can be difficult to get the stapler in the right position, and it is not recommended. The staples leave sharp edges, so they need to be covered or placed on the inside of the item; the outside also needs to be covered, as they look awful. Stapling doesn't produce a very durable join and tends to give way if it is placed under a lot of stress.

Gluing.—This is a quick and easy way of joining leather. Use Evo Stick Impact adhesive. When gluing leather, make sure that no glue gets on the areas that will show, as it is virtually impossible to shift it afterwards. It also is a good idea to lightly glue things before punching holes for lacing/thonging. Not only will the glue make the join stronger, but it will ensure that the holes line up; then you can punch the pieces together rather than marking each one out individually and running the risk of the holes not lining up.

Riveting.—This is quick and easy for medium and heavyweight leathers and gives a good finish. Rivets also can be used as a form of decoration in themselves. In order to rivet leather you will need a hole punch, a riveting tool, and a hammer, as well as the rivets and leather. Rivets come in a variety of sizes and metals and give a good durable join.

Sewing.—Sewing can be used for all weights of leather. You can use cotton for sewing leather, but if you plan to do a lot of leather work it is worth getting some waxed linen thread which is thicker and stronger than cotton and gives a nice finish. For lightweight leather you can just sew using normal needles; for heavier-weight leathers you will need to use a hole punch to punch holes in the leather before stitching. There are several sewing styles, but one of the best is saddle stitch. Use two needles at once, passing them both through the hole at the same time in opposite directions and then pulling the thread tight. (You will need a length of thread about three times longer than the seam-length you plan to sew.)

Lacing/Thonging.—Lacing and thonging are done in much the same style as stitching described above. You will need to punch larger holes than for stitching, and a thonging needle can be a great help in getting the thong through the holes.

Wearing Period Costumes

Much of the effect of period costumes will be lost if the actors do not know how to wear them. The actors must believe that these are their daily wear or they will end up looking comical. They must be made to realize what costumes can do for them and why it is so important that they wear them properly. A costume is not intended simply to dress up a character; it is intended to be incorporated into the characterization.

Wearing clothes of any period is something of an art. Some people have it, almost by instinct. They can put on almost any dress or suit and give it distinction. Other people are not so fortunate. They are said to "lack a clothes sense." However, almost anyone who is able to handle himself acceptably on the stage is capable of learning how to wear a costume.

The costume designer should know how each costume should be worn and pass that information on to each actor. He should make notes during rehearsal and pass those notes on to the director. He knows how he wants his clothes to look; and he should know how the actor or actress will have to move in them to make them look the way he intends.

Learning to move with a costume is largely a matter of practice. The object is to see that the actors have their costumes (or acceptable substitute costumes) far enough in advance of dress rehearsal so that they will have plenty of time to get thoroughly accustomed to moving and performing the necessary "business" in them. In this way, they will gradually lose their self-consciousness about the costume and learn how to incorporate the clothes into the role. The costumes will also become appropriately "worn" and lose their newness.

Restrictions are to be found in the costumes of many periods. One of the most difficult for amateur actors to overcome is the costume of the Roman soldier. Large men wearing skirts have a difficult time adjusting to movements such as kneeling and lifting. During one of our productions, two Roman soldiers fainted near the tomb at the resurrection. As they lay on the ground for several minutes, giggles began to ripple through the audience. One of the actors had fallen with his legs apart, facing the audience, who had a complete and graphic view of his jockey shorts. Needless to say, the illusion of reality was broken. This is another good example of why authenticity should be exercised in strict detail. A loin cloth should have been worn to complete the costume. You never know what an audience might have the opportunity to notice!

Costumes are only one element of the production. Like scenery, properties, make-up, and lighting, they serve a necessary function. But they must be kept in the proper perspective. They are a contributing art, and their contribution must not be allowed to overshadow other elements of the production. Most especially, costumes must never be allowed to speak so loudly that they obscure, distort, or negate the message of the play.

Accessories

Costume accessories fall into one of those grey areas as far as responsibility. However, the boundaries can be clearly defined logically. Accessories are those items that add to or enhance the appearance of the costume, such as purses, hats, and jewelry.

Here is how to tie a turban using two contrasting tassel scarves:

1. Begin by tying your hair back into a pony tail. (If your hair is short, skip to step 2.) This will be tucked up into the snood (sack portion) of the turban at the back of the neck.

2. Open the scarves and drape them over your head, one on top of the other. Make sure the tassels hang down evenly on each side. Allow a half inch of the bottom color to show at your forehead.

3. Hold the tassels on the right side in one hand. Smooth the extra fabric up toward your ear so the extra fabric drapes (sacklike) over your shoulders. Repeat on the other side. Tie the scarves behind your neck using the first pattern of a square knot (right over left and pull). If someone else is tying the knot for you, hold the two scarves firmly in the front while the other person ties the knot.

4. Make the snood part by tucking the extra material and your pony-tail back up and over the top of the knot along with the loose material in the back. Arrange till the snood looks nice. (Take your time with this step.) Tighten the knot till it feels slightly snug on your head. The tassels should hang straight down before you start the next step. Any billowing around the tassel needs to be worked up into the knot at the back of the neck.

5. On both sides, twist the two colors together toward your ears. Bring the right twist over your head. Take the left twist over the tassels of the right twist that now hangs by your left ear. The left twist will go in front of the right twist until you reach your right ear. Take the tassels behind and under the twist by your right ear. Arrange tassels so they look like the left side.

6. This step takes a little practice. You will need to arrange the tassels so the turban doesn't come undone. Play with it until it stays firmly on your head. Tighten by pulling the knot at the back of your neck.

Ok, now take it all off and try it again. Practice it several more times until you feel comfortable with all of the steps. Always allow plenty of time to tie your turban before a performance. There's nothing like trying to dance when you're worried if your hat is going to fall off! A few well-placed safety pins will give you a little insurance.

Please remember that these scarves bleed their color. Washing them in cold water with a quarter cup of salt helps but doesn't always eliminate the problem.

The costume for the High Priest requires a large, necklace-type breastplate displaying the twelve jewels of the tribes of Israel. This may be made by the prop department and maintained by the costume department.

If a weapon such as a sword or knife is part of a uniform, it is the responsibility of the costume department to maintain it. However, if the costume designer decides that it

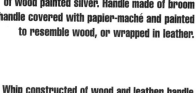

VARIOUS WEAPONS: SWORD.—From wood strips, 1 x 2, 1 x 3, etc., cut shape, rout and sand to the desired shape. Wrap leather around the handle. Paint with metallic silver and mist with black. SHEATH.—Made of leather or naugahyde sewn with leather straps. SPEAR.—Blade made of wood painted silver. Handle made of broom handle covered with papier-maché and painted to resemble wood, or wrapped in leather.

Whip constructed of wood and leather handle with strips of foam pipe insulation.

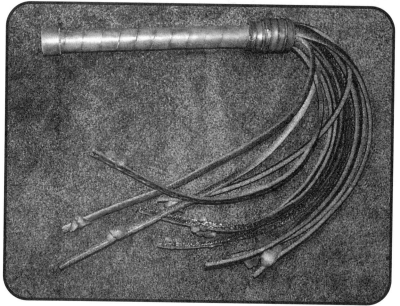

would be best to have them made, he may enlist the prop department.

A spear is not necessarily a part of a uniform and would be considered a prop. A shield may or may not be considered part of the uniform. These are all grey areas that should be defined at the onset of production. Though the making of weapons is the responsibility of the prop department, we have decided to show them here, since the ultimate responsibility will rest with the Costume Department.

Special Costumes

In addition to the costumes of principal actors and chorus members, you may need to design and make special costumes for special characters. Sometimes these may be so elaborate and intricate that they would require several departments working together. Special effects (FX) and props departments and the production designer may collaborate with the costume designer to create the exact effect required.

An angel costume may require the FX and prop departments to provide the wings which must be incorporated into the costume. The costume might be fitted with lights underneath to provide a glow. A glowing-halo effect might be created by the FX department. If the angel is to be flown, a special harness and wires must be fitted under the costume and designed to be unseen.

In one of our Christmas productions, we had a man dressed in a giant rooster costume covered with feathers. When the rooster crowed, a farmer fired a shotgun at the chicken, causing the outer feather costume to blow off the actors body and fly off stage. The actor was left standing in long johns, sparsely covered with feathers. The breakaway costume had velcro at the seams and thin wires were pulled by the prop crew off stage.

Loin cloths might be "rigged" with a hook in the back to support an actor on a cross. For battles, breastplates might be "rigged" with exploding blood packets or made to tear away.

Any effect will elicit the opposite reaction if it goes wrong or looks phony. With the combined knowledge, creativity, and efforts of each department, the possibilities are limitless. Think big and work together to create the most impressive effects while maintaining always the illusion of reality already established.

Costuming Care Tips
Resource books.—Singer puts out a series of sewing books that are an excellent resource for costumers. The stain removal chart in the middle of *Clothing Care and Repair* is worth its weight in gold. Another book, *Sewing Specialty Fabrics*, discusses sequin fabrics, velvet, metallic, and so forth.

Deodorizing costumes.—Put a tablespoon or so of baking soda in a square of fabric, tie off the fabric into a pouch, and place the pouch in the smelliest part of the costume when ready to store. Remove before re-wearing, of course. Certain undergarments or smaller costumes can be placed in a large gunny sack (for air circulation) and the baking soda will absorb the sweat and odor. Another method is to hang them with plenty of space to air, and lightly spritz them (especially the insides) with Lysol. There is also a new product from Arm & Hammer which is a baking soda designed particularly to remove litter box odors. It could be hung in a costume room. The product that most professional costumers use is called End Bac. It sanitizes and deodorizes and is not harmful on fabric. Try your costume shops or sports shops to find it.

Storage

The costume department is responsible for the acquisition and making of costumes and accessories. When rehearsals begin, the costume department becomes the wardrobe department. Wardrobe is responsible for the storage, care and cleaning of all costumes during the performance run and through the strike. The wardrobe and costume departments could be manned by the same persons, some of the same persons, or a completely different crew.

There should be a special room large enough to hold racks for all costumes and accessories. These racks should be portable and separated as follows: "male principals," "female principals," "male chorus," "female chorus," "armor," "fx," and any other specialty items. They should be separated by characters and name-tagged with the character's and/or actor's names. There should be plenty of aisle space for key wardrobe personnel.

Portable racks are not difficult to make and are relatively inexpensive. You can design them to fit your needs. Following is just one design:

Storage boxes with lids can be purchased in large quantities for a few dollars each. Complete character costumes and accessories can fold nicely into a labeled box. Snapshots of the character wearing the costume can be taped to the front of the box. These boxes can be stacked and then moved to accompany the wardrobe racks or lined in the halls or set in a designated area during the show for easy access by the actor and wardrobe crews.

Short-term storage between performances will be determined by your particular needs and facilities. If the room where the racks are kept during performances is one that is not otherwise occupied by classes or groups during the dark days or in-between, then there is no concern for this issue. However, if you must remove the items to another location, then it is imperative that a short inventory or check list be created to go with each rack or cart so that all appropriate items are accounted for prior to and after their temporary relocation.

Upon closing the performance run, when the long-term storage process is to be implemented, please take steps to appropriately clean or deodorize all garments and accessories. Placing like items into cabinets, lockers, garment bags, boxes, and such is a good idea. Coding and marking the placement of such items is further detailed in chapter 18, "Opening, Closing, and Strike."

CHAPTER 12

MAKEUP

One of the quickest ways to break the illusion of reality and give the production an amateur quality is the incorrect use of makeup. Makeup is a very delicate and necessary area of the theater and must be approached with as much care and preparation as any other part of the production.

The head makeup artist will be responsible for the design and execution of the makeup, beginning at the pre-production phase. Even if the actors will be applying their own, or if makeup assistants are used, the head artist is responsible for what is seen on stage.

As the head makeup artist, you must know the script and its characters as thoroughly as the director. You must also become familiar with the actors portraying each character. Research each scene that each actor is in and develop a file for each character and each actor, containing notes on changes during the story development. For instance, the character may be slowly aging from scene to scene or act to act. Or, there may be an injury to the face or a disease that might affect the makeup.

When designing the makeup, always have a purpose for everything or don't do it. There are three main reasons for the use of stage makeup, and remembering them will help you in the initial design process.

First and possibly most important, makeup can be used by the actor to give the audience immediately the correct impression of the character's age, health, and basic nature. In other words, makeup is an effective means of conveying certain types of information to the audience, without any waste of words or time.

Second, makeup serves to counteract the bleaching, or "washed out," effect produced by the strong light concentrated on the stage. The intense light that makes actors visible to everyone in the auditorium tends to wash the color out of the actors' faces and hands and to flatten their features. Makeup, by adding more color, counteracts this tendency. This usually applies only to people with lighter skin tones; black actors and others with dark skin tones will seldom require as much additional color.

Third, makeup serves to accentuate certain expressive features, such as the eyes and mouth, which are necessary for the actor to convey his feelings to the audience. By accentuating these features, makeup enables the actor to do this accurately for those people in the most distant seats of the auditorium.

In order to ensure that makeup will fulfill the above functions, certain basic principles should be observed. Never use makeup "in general." An actor should always have a purpose for everything he does. If you decide he needs an olive color rather than a ruddy one, there should be a valid reason to justify the choice, such as the character's health or age or a combination of that with the color of lights being used. If the decision is made to lengthen the nose with putty or to put a large wart on the cheek, you should know exactly why and what effect this alteration will produce on the audience.

Never fight the face. You cannot change the actor's face; you can only modify how it appears to be. You must learn to work with what the actor has and learn how to modify it in order to achieve the effects desired. If he has a large nose, learn how to minimize it when necessary. If he has a receding chin, learn how to bring it forward with a beard or a highlight and counter-shading technique. If he has large and protruding ears, learn how to make them less noticeable.

The basic rule in using shadows and highlights is: darken those portions of the face you wish to recede, and lighten those portions you wish to bring forward. Shadows alone are usually insufficient; you need to highlight the adjacent areas as well. This rule applies to lines as well as shadows.

Adjust your makeup to fit the light actually being used on the stage. While strong light tends to wash out all colors and the facial features, different colored lights produce sometimes strikingly different effects. Light that contains some of the same color as that used in the makeup will usually tend to brighten and enhance the makeup. Light that contains none of the color used in the makeup will tend to darken the makeup. Because of this, it is best to try out the makeup under the actual lights before finally deciding on the base and shadowing colors.

Apply makeup to all the exposed parts of the body. Do not simply make up the face and neglect the hands or the back of the neck. It is very distracting for an audience to discover that the heavily suntanned "shepherd" has somehow managed to keep the sun from reaching his neck and ears or even his hands.

Always use makeup sparingly. Do not spread it on like butter on bread. Use it to cover the skin and no more. A heavy makeup not only appears unnatural; it is also uncomfortable, especially if it consists of greasepaint. Heavy greasepaint tends to cake and rub off easily, and may cause heavy sweating underneath it.

Start experimenting with your makeup long before dress rehearsal; then make the necessary adjustments throughout dress rehearsal. Remember, there is nothing so dispiriting to a cast as a dress rehearsal scheduled to start at 8:00 that actually gets under way at 10:00 because of makeup problems.

Application of Makeup

There are two basic types of makeup currently in general use: oil-base (or greasepaint) and pancake (or cake). Since the first has an oil-base and the other is water-soluble, the methods of applying them differ considerably. In either case, there are certain items of equipment essential to proper application. If it is self-applied, there must be a mirror to permit the actor to view his progress. This mirror should be framed in lights to prevent shadows on the face and body, which might lead to some distortion or uneven application of the makeup. There should be a shelf under the mirror on which to set out the makeup materials.

There should be facial tissues and towels for cleaning the face. These items, plus a large wastebasket, access to water, cotton swabs, brushes, sponges, and puffs are really the essential tools for applying most makeup.

Greasepaint

Greasepaint is generally available in two different forms. There is the old-fashioned stick greasepaint, and there is the so-called "soft" greasepaint, which comes in tubes or bottles and which, because of its ease of application, has largely replaced stick greasepaint. Both forms may not be available at all stores selling makeup supplies, but they are available directly from the manufacturer or from a larger supplier.

Foundation.—The first step in the application of stage makeup is the foundation or base. With stick makeup, it is necessary to prepare the face first with a little cold cream, moisturizer, or remover, which is then wiped off with facial tissues or a sponge. With soft makeup, this cleansing preparation should be applied evenly and sparingly. Since the greasepaint itself is of just the right consistency to spread easily, any additional cream on the skin will probably leave the makeup too greasy.

The foundation is applied with dots of paint directly from the tube or from a pat that has been squeezed out into the palm of the hand. If two or more foundation colors are to be mixed, the colors should be applied in separate dots and then blended together on the face. Here again, only enough paint should be used to cover the skin. Too much base will give a mask-like appearance and cause profuse sweating under the makeup.

Though the makeup needs to be applied to look natural (it should not distract the audience or generate more interest than the drama itself), it must also serve its purpose throughout the length of the performance. The type of makeup, the closeness of the lights to the actors, the intensity of the lights versus the heaviness of the wardrobe, the action taking place on stage, the season in which the play takes place are all factors that will need to be considered. The makeup application will need to appear exaggerated to the person applying it, yet acceptable to the audience. Makeup should serve to enhance the production, not upstage it.

If you continue to use oil-base shadows and highlight colors or blush, then you do *not* powder down the foundation at this stage. *The powder is not to be applied until all oil-base colors have been applied and properly blended.*

Rouge.—After the foundation has been blended, it is time for the rouge, commonly applied only to the cheeks and lips. Its purpose is to supply color that will otherwise be washed out by the strong lights. Since rouge is usually darker than the base, it will also tend to make the portion of the face that is rouged appear to recede. For this reason, rouge normally should be kept relatively high on the cheeks, and it should be blended so that there is no clear line of demarcation where it ends. On a man, the rouge should not be more noticeable to the audience than the natural color of a man's cheeks. Thick red cheeks on men is a major offender of quality makeup in amateur productions.

On the lips, of course, lip color or rouge can be used not only to color and emphasize them, but also to modify or reshape them, if that is desirable. The line of demarcation here should be sharp. In order to get it, the lip color should be applied with a lip brush or pencil. While most women will use some lip color, some men may find it unnecessary to use any. Those who do need some will probably use a lesser amount than women.

Blush or rouge color is very effective when lightly applied at the temple and along the neck. It can be done so by using the sponge or fingers after having blended the areas of stronger application. At the temples it can be blended up towards the forehead to brighten those areas. The same should be done on the neck, starting under the jaw line near the lobe of the ears and making a "V" towards the center of its base under the chin.

Lining.—To be effective, lines should follow the natural creases of the face. Take the nasolabial folds, for instance—those creases that run from the curvature of the nostrils down towards the corners of the mouth. With these folds emphasized, the face can be given added sternness, or firmness, as well as increasing age. Now consider the pouches under the eyes. By emphasizing the lines that mark the pouches, it is possible to increase the age of a face (see illustration at end of chapter). Of course, to be really effective, lines must always be highlighted on both sides. This highlighting is done with a white or lighter lining color or with a lighter shade of base color. The lines themselves should usually be of a brown or gray tone, and they can be applied with a pencil, a brush, a sharp edge of the white sponge, or a pointed cotton swab. The lines will be blended very slightly, but the highlights should be blended rather carefully into the base. The highlights applied slightly above the line of shading should be feathered out broadly and evenly. The one directly below the shading line should be blended in a smaller area of coverage, from the lowest portion of the shadow, down.

Highlights and shadows.—For most purposes, shadowing is usually more effective than lining. Shadows also should follow the natural contours of the face. For example, the bone structure of the face tends to become more apparent as people age. The cheekbones stand out and the hollows beneath them tend to recede. To heighten this effect, the areas beneath the cheekbones can be darkened. Or to make the cheeks appear rounded, these areas can be lightened and made to stand out. This will make the face appear more youthful.

In any case, shadowing should be done so as to make that character appear as natural as possible. The shadow normally should be the same as the base color, only several shades darker. The highlights should be a lighter base color or white. Both shadows and highlights should be applied by whatever means is easiest, usually the fingers, brushes, or sponges; and they should be blended so that there is no line where they join the base.

Other highlight colors are used to override or negate other features. If the area to be highlighted is blue in its undertone, then an orange highlight should be used. If the area is brown or grey in appearance, then a pink highlight color should be applied. Keep in mind also that yellow tends to neutralize red. A base with more olive may be all you need to neutralize a red scratch or other such blemish. Don't create a problem by overcompensating in this important phase. The color of the highlight should match the intensity of the base color and not that of the feature to be diminished.

Eyes.—The eyes, being one of the most expressive features of the face, need special attention to realize their full potential. The object should be to make them visible to the entire audience, but to avoid making them look unnatural. This requires considerable care. For emphasis, a fine dark line should be applied with a fine brush, cotton swab, or pencil to the lash line of both the upper and lower eyelids. To make the eyes appear larger, these lines can be extended past the outer corners, then brought together. To provide still more emphasis for eyes, the lashes can be darkened with mascara, false eyelashes can be applied or painted on, or a combination of these options may be desired. To give the eyes an added sparkle, a small red dot can be applied at the inner corner of each eye.

If you want to make the eyes stand out from the face, highlights can be applied to the upper and lower lids, the brow bones can be shadowed, and the mascara and eye liner omitted. If you want to make the eyes appear sunken, the brow and upper edges of the cheekbones can be highlighted and the eyelids and under brows shadowed.

In any case, women normally will use some eye shadow on the eyelids. Unless the nature of the character demands it, the shadows should always have a matte finish and not possess any iridescent qualities. Colors that are more natural (taupe and other browns, peaches, plums) are best suited to a character whose makeup serves to enhance the feature without drawing attention to it. If the character is clearly not defined in this way, then more gaudy or pearlized colors may be required. This exception would not be as frequent in a biblical period piece as it would in something more contemporary.

In using eye shadow, however, it is important to avoid extending the shadow onto the sides of the nose, unless it is intended to add age to the face. Shadows on the sides of the nose tend to sharpen it and make the face seem older.

The eyebrows, which serve to frame the eyes, can enhance or injure the total effect of the eyes, depending on the way they are treated. If the brows are too narrow or too light, they can be widened or darkened with a brown or black eyebrow pencil. This pencil can also be used to reshape them to some extent. If the brows are too wide or too dark, they can be narrowed with base paint or lightened with white liner or a lighter base color. If they are too low, they can be blocked out entirely with wax covered by a good application of foundation paint; then new brows can be drawn in at the desired location with an eyebrow pencil, a fine-liner or a dark shading color. (If using wax to cover the existing brow line, then pencil is not the first tool of choice). Perhaps a water-base liner applied with a very fine brush would be your best option. But eyebrows should not be raised too high on the forehead. In addition to paint, crepe hair can be used to enlarge or thicken the brows. We will discuss the use of crepe hair later in this chapter.

Powder.—Once the oil-base makeup is completed to satisfaction, you are ready to set it by the application of powder. Powder is usually applied by a powder puff, and is blended with a soft, clean blush brush. Theatrical powder comes in a variety of shades intended to match various base colors. As a general rule, the powder applied should be somewhat lighter than the base used in the makeup. Still better, a neutral powder is available and can be used with any color base. This powder will neither lighten nor darken the makeup. Talc is a finer-milled powder than are the standard translucent powders. It is a lifesaver in keeping the makeup color from bleeding onto the wardrobe in the areas where the two come together. Therefore, regardless of the facial powder you choose, try to utilize the talc along the places where it is blended down to go beyond the line of the costume itself, such as the collar or neck line. It is also critical to use it when someone is to rest their head on the shoulder or lap of another character. It often happens that makeup will rub onto another costume after even slight perspiration. This can be avoided if it is adequately powdered after the initial application or if touched up whenever possible throughout the play.

You can "load" your puff with powder now, and then use it for touch ups and blending as you continue through the final application and throughout the performance. Re-load as necessary. This is especially useful when you are mixing different powders together to arrive at a specific color or consistency.

Once the oil-based makeup has been well blended and powdered, then additional color or contouring can be done with pencils and powder shadows or dry rouge. It is suggested that when applying eyeliner over oil-base foundation and shadows, powder should be brushed onto those areas to set them before applying the liner. If all cream makeups that are to be applied have been done so (with the possible exception of lip color or lashes), when you are ready to apply the eyeliner, you can go ahead and set the entire makeup application with powder before proceeding.

Dry rouge.—If, by chance, the powder used has darkened or cut the intensity of the makeup more than anticipated, dry rouge (blush) can be applied over the powder to restore the color. It should, of course, be used with great discretion. Dry rouge can be used between acts to touch up makeup, if necessary. It can suffice as eye shadow and even can be applied as lip color to wet lips with a brush, sponge applicator, or damp fingertip. It can also be applied to the neck and temple areas as indicated earlier.

Pancake Makeup

Since cake makeup is water-soluble, it is usually applied to the face with a dampened sponge. A natural silk sponge is best for this purpose, although rubber or cellulose sponges can be used. The foundation color is applied by rubbing the damp sponge over the cake of makeup and then transferring the color to the face. The makeup should be stroked on evenly so that it produces a smooth, thin coat. The foundation should also be applied to all exposed areas of skin, such as the neck, legs and hands—only the back of the hands (not the palms).

Once the foundation is in place, another small sponge should be used to apply the rouge. The same general rules apply to the application of cake rouge as to the application of grease rouge; both should be used sparingly and blended in carefully. The same rules also apply to the application of lines and shadows and their highlights. With lines, however, it is often easier to use a brush instead of a sponge to apply both the line and the highlights. For the lines around the eyes, it may be necessary to use a very fine brush. Once the rouge, the lines, the shadows, and highlights have been blended into the foundation, the makeup is complete. Again, once you have set the makeup with powder, all other applied makeup must be in the form of powders or other water-based product. (Exceptions would be to lips and lashes.)

Body Makeup

In most religious, period plays, men wear loincloths or soldier skirts, and so they require body makeup. It can be comical to see an actor in a white loincloth with dark makeup on his face and a glowing white body. As stated above, every exposed area of the body should be evenly covered with the proper color.

Liquid body makeup is available at most makeup supply houses. Body makeup comes in various shades, and it can be applied directly to the legs, arms, or torso with a sponge. Once applied, it too should be set with powder. It washes off easily with soap and water. Alcohol or other makeup removers may also be used, though they are not as economical nor as quick as the conventional bath or shower.

Painting bodies.—Applying liquid body makeup with a sponge is time-consuming and messy. The appearance is usually blotchy. A formula of liquid makeup can be sprayed with an air-brush sprayer, and the colors will go on the skin smoothly and evenly. Only a thin coat will be necessary in most instances for complete coverage of the skin. It is important to have an air compressor that is adequate for the job. Most small air compressors do not have storage tanks. When overworked the compressors may shut down in the middle of a project. If you have a lot of bodies to paint, it is a good idea to use a larger compressor with a storage tank. Very little pressure is required to spray makeup. About five pounds of pressure is sufficient. Stronger pressure is uncomfortable in the eye area, but the rest of the body can tolerate a bit more. If you use a small compressor without a tank, use the "bleeder" setting so some of the air pressure is allowed to escape. Care must be taken so that the makeup is applied safely. It is extremely important that the spraying be done where there is a strong exhaust fan so that the alcohol fumes and pigment particles are withdrawn from the area. The makeup artist must also explain to the person being sprayed exactly what the procedure will be and the safety precautions involved, especially the coordination of spraying and breathing. The formula is as follows:

        3.5 oz cake of Aquacolor, Kryolan's glycerine-based makeup

        1/8 cup Fixier, Kryolan's makeup fixative

        1 cup 70% isopropyl alcohol.

Remove the Aquacolor from the container, cut it into large chunks, and place in a blender. Add isopropyl alcohol, cover, and blend on high for about 10 minutes to be certain there are no lumps. (Do not use old makeup for this purpose, as it takes longer to break down.) Lower the speed and add Fixier liquid. Continue blending for a few minutes. Test a small amount in your air brush or spray gun to see if the consistency is right for your equipment and if the coverage is right for your project. If the makeup is too opaque, try spraying a thinner coat rather than diluting the makeup.

Additional Materials

In addition to the basic makeup applied to the actor or actress under normal conditions, there are certain other effects they may wish to achieve under special circumstances. These effects usually require the use of other materials.

Spirit gum.—Spirit gum is not a glue that can be purchased at a hardware store. It is a makeup adhesive that can be found at makeup supply houses. It is used for securing any external appliance to the face or other areas of the body. It is very effective and must be removed with acetone, rubbing alcohol, or spirit gum remover. A good makeup supply kit would have a large quantity of spirit gum in stock.

Nose putty.—This material is the most widely used means of reshaping the nose or other parts of the face. Once you have a clear plan firmly in mind and know exactly what you intend to do, applying and shaping the nose putty is not difficult, but it does require patience.

Before application, the skin should be free of all grease or oil. The first step is to apply a coat of spirit gum to the area on which the putty will be used. Coat your fingertips lightly with K-Y Lubricating Jelly (not petroleum jelly) to keep the putty from sticking to them. If you have no lubricating jelly, you can substitute with hair gel. Then separate a small piece of putty from the mass and knead it with your fingers until it is very pliable. If the putty should be too stiff and the heat of the hand does not soften it sufficiently, immerse the container in hot water for a few minutes or place it near a heat source.

Stick the softened ball of putty on the part of the nose where the spirit gum has been applied and is now beginning to feel tacky. Press it into the skin for good adhesion. Carefully blend the edges of the putty into the skin, shaping the nose as you work. Use more lubricating jelly on your fingers if the putty sticks to them. Always confine the putty to as small an area as possible, being especially careful to keep it off areas surrounding the nose. If, in blending the edges, you tend to keep pulling the putty outward until it has spread well away from the area you want built up, blend in the opposite direction—toward the center of the nose.

When the blending is finished, you can make final adjustments to the shape. Cover your fingers with more lubricating jelly and keep pressing, prodding, and massaging the putty until you have precisely the shape you want, always keeping in mind the image of flesh and skin over bone and cartilage. A final light massaging with lubricating jelly will help to eliminate unintentional cracks and bumps and give a completely smooth surface.

When the surface of the putty is smooth, the edges perfectly blended, and the lubricating jelly dried, stipple the putty with a black or red stipple sponge to match the skin texture. Then, if the putty is lighter or less red than the skin, stipple it with rouge—dry rouge (applied with a damp sponge) or creme rouge (applied with either a stipple sponge or a flat red-rubber sponge). If creme rouge is used, powder it well, then brush off the excess powder.

A method of giving three-dimensional texture to putty by using a latex negative of a grapefruit, orange, or lemon peel is very effective and relatively simple. Paint liquid latex onto the grapefruit and allow to dry. Five or six coats may be necessary until you have a thick enough layer to use easily without tearing. Carefully peel the latex off, trim it, and apply it to the face with spirit gum. You may also use the same technique of painting latex onto the exterior of such citrus fruits, then inverting it and pressing it onto the wax or putty covered area and rolling over it to create skin texture. This works well if the stipple sponges are not available. Warning: be sure to powder the latex upon removal from the fruit. Dry latex sticks to itself upon contact.

After the wax makeup is complete, seal it with an appliance sealer. Powder the area dry, pressing gently with the puff or with a brush. Remove excess powder with a powder brush. Stipple the foundation color over the entire nose, using a natural sponge for cake makeup and a flat red-rubber sponge for creme or grease. (If you use a greasepaint or cream makeup, then apply before you powder the surface to set.) If this does not adequately cover the putty area, powder, then stipple on more of the foundation color. If you are using dry cake makeup, it will probably dry lighter than the same makeup applied directly to the skin. For that reason, it is not the best choice of makeup to use over nose putty. However, the problem can sometimes be corrected by coating the light area with more lubricating jelly. The water-soluble jelly will mix with the makeup and dry with a slightly waxy sheen. Powdering will counteract this.

For most characters, you will want to add rouge to the snares and other parts of the nose to give them a more natural appearance. This can be done after the foundation coat has been applied or when the various colors of stipple or other finishing touches are being added. If it is done afterward, most rouge can be stippled on, or dry rouge can be applied with a brush.

To remove the putty, a thread can be used. Starting at either the base or the bridge of the nose, run the thread along the nose under the putty, pulling the thread tight with both hands. This does not preserve the putty nosepiece intact for future use—it is simply a more efficient way of removing the putty than pulling it off with the fingers. Any bits of putty remaining on the nose after the bulk of it has been detached with the thread can be removed by massaging with makeup remover until the putty is soft enough to be wiped off with tissues. Always do this gently in order to avoid skin irritation.

This method of using nose putty can also be applied to the chin area or any other bony or cartilaginous area to shape and build them.

Derma wax.—Derma wax is softer than nose putty. It can be shaped and blended more easily, but it is also more easily damaged when touched than nose putty, and it can loosen and fall off unless it is very firmly attached to the skin. Like nose putty, it should be confined to bony parts of the face. For close work you may wish to blend the edges of the wax into the skin with alcohol and a soft brush.

Before using derma wax, apply a coat of spirit gum to the area of the skin to be covered in order to keep the wax from loosening. Let the spirit gum become tacky, then follow the same procedure as for applying nose putty.

For still greater security, cotton fibers can be added to the undercoat of spirit gum before applying the derma wax, as follows:

- Coat the area with spirit gum.
- Tap the spirit gum repeatedly with your finger or applicator instrument until it becomes very tacky.
- Place a layer of absorbent cotton over a slightly smaller area than that to be covered with derma wax, then press the cotton firmly into the spirit gum.
- When the spirit gum is dry, pull off all the loose cotton.
- Press a small amount of derma wax onto the cotton, and push it around firmly

with one finger to make sure the cotton fibers are embedded in the wax.

- Press a ball of derma wax into the center of the wax which has just been applied, and mold it with the fingers or sculpting tool into the precise shape you want. Be sure that the edges are well blended. Using lubricating jelly on the fingers makes the blending easier.

Makeup can be applied directly over the derma wax, or the wax can be coated first with sealer. If cake makeup is to be used, you may apply it directly to the wax without coating it with sealer.

For greater protection than sealer, latex can be used in the following procedure:

- Coat the wax construction with latex. This can be done with a stipple sponge or brush.
- When the latex is dry, powder it.
- Use a rubber-mask grease foundation over the latex. If the wax needs texture or wrinkles, they can be added at this point by pressing the wax with the latex negative of a grapefruit skin or with the tip of a brush handle to give a skin-texture effect or with an orangewood stick or a modeling tool to form wrinkles. In doing this, be careful not to puncture or tear the latex skin which protects the wax.
- Complete the makeup.

Latex.—Latex can be used for creating pieces, such as welts, that can be transferred to the skin after the latex has dried; and for applying directly to the skin to create three-dimensional wrinkles and skin texture. When using latex on the skin, use only the type that is intended for that purpose. If any latex feels as if it is burning the skin, *don't use it!* Try another brand or another technique that does not involve applying latex directly to the skin. *Note: Men should not shave just prior to the application of latex.* Several hours should pass between the time of shaving and that of applying latex. Later in this chapter we will discuss some of the uses of latex.

Blood.—Stage blood can be classified into two categories, depending on how it is to be used: external (outside the body) or internal (flowing from the mouth, nose, etc.). External blood should never be used internally. For internal blood, gelatin capsules, obtainable from your local pharmacist in various sizes, can be filled with blood formulated specifically for internal use, held in the mouth, then crushed at the appropriate time to release the blood.

In deciding which brand of blood to use, you should consider the ease with which the blood can be removed from the costumes or skin. Some brands of blood can be wiped off the skin easily without leaving a stain, whereas others leave a temporary stain which can be removed with soap and water.

Consider also the thickness of the blood and how believable it looks as it runs on the skin. The color, of course, should also be believable. Artificial blood is obtainable from the makeup companies and their distributors. Ben Nye's and Mehron's are both called "Stage Blood." Joe Blasco's and Bob Kelly's are called "Artificial Blood." Sometimes you will need to add a few drops of liquid soap to the blood to keep it from beading up unnaturally.

For blood coming from the mouth, red toothpaste can be used. Mixing it with adhesive powder for false teeth will produce an effect of dried blood.

If you cannot find or for some reason cannot purchase artificial blood, you can simply and effectively create your own artificial blood. Mix red food coloring with clear Karo Syrup at a ratio that produces the desired color. The consistency will already be realistic, but if you want it to be thinner, just add water. The effect is just as realistic as with the kind you can buy at professional makeup houses.

Tooth wax.—To simulate a missing tooth (or several teeth), black tooth wax is the most satisfactory material. If worked into the cracks between the teeth, there is little chance of its being dislodged. Tooth enamel can be used to whiten dark teeth or to discolor white teeth; it is available at most makeup supply houses. To darken or discolor white teeth (to achieve the appearance of age or decay), dark-yellow or black tooth enamel can be used. In either case, the teeth should be perfectly dry before application of the enamel.

Hair coloring.—If coloring natural hair or a wig or hairpiece, there are several workable methods. For natural hair, a liquid hair color or white cake mascara is probably best for graying or whitening hair. Powders and metallic substances are usually unsatisfactory. White greasepaint or a very light base can be used on occasion, especially if it is desirable to apply streaks of gray. For wigs and hairpieces, the best method is to use a specially prepared aerosol spray that comes in various colors. The silver is particularly effective. It is also easy to apply and easy to remove. You can find a variety of colors of hair spray at your local drug store or makeup supply house. Applying it with a brush or comb allows you to streak the hair, real or synthetic, especially in areas where control is essential (i.e., temples, sideburns, mustache, etc.). *Note: Darker hair tends to take on a bluish tint with white hair colors. Mixing it with a yellow, blond, or silver is advised.*

Special Makeup
Black Eye.—A black eye involving only swelling and bruising can be simulated with oil-based products. It may involve only the orbital area or the cheekbone as well. In either

case, it changes color as it ages. There is more red at first, but then the inflammation subsides, leaving a deep purple color (giving the "black" effect), followed by medium or dark gray, and then the greenish yellow color typical of bruises which are no longer inflamed.

The various stages of a black eye can be simulated by mixtures of red, purple, black, white, and greenish or lemon yellow. The purple can be deepened with black, and if the mixture is not red enough, red can be added. Application should be with a red or black stipple sponge. Once applied, hair gel should be used over the newer, redder colored bruise to give the skin a shiny appearance.

Bruises.—Even when accompanied by swelling, a bruise can usually be simulated with paint. For Caucasians, red, gray, purple, greenish-yellow, and light cream or ivory can be used. The fresher the bruise, the more red; the older it is, the more yellow. For darker-skinned characters, the colors should be adjusted to the color of the skin. The color being used can be either dabbed on the bruised area and then blended together with a brush, or stippled on. In either case, make sure that all edges are soft. If the bruised area is to be very swollen, you may want to build it up first with derma wax, latex, or a combination of both.

Here's one quick and easy method to make a bruise: Dab a purple color on the skin and blend it only as required. Then dip a finger or red stipple sponge in red and dab it on top of the purple. Experiment with it and you will be surprised at how realistic you can make the bruise appear.

Burns.—Minor burns can be simulated by stippling the skin with red makeup applied with a red sponge. For just-acquired, deeper burns, coat the skin with latex, which can be pulled loose and allowed to hang if you want it to. A single layer of cleansing tissue placed over the latex and then covered with another layer of latex will give more body to the hanging skin. Cotton can be used with the latex for burnt flesh. Makeup can be applied over the latex. For close work you might drop candle wax onto the latex to give the effect of blisters. Tuplast or latex also can be applied to the surrounding skin surface to show blisters as well.

Cuts.—Superficial cuts can be painted on, with or without the use of artificial blood. Deeper cuts usually require building up the area with wax or putty, then cutting into it with a dull instrument, such as a palette knife. Plastic sealer can be painted over the construction at this point if you wish.

The inside of the cut can be painted a dark red, purple or black, with greasepaint. For a cut that is still bleeding, a few drops or even a stream of artificial blood can be added to the cut with an eye dropper or fine brush and allowed to run out onto the skin. Before the blood is applied, it is imperative that the added skin be made up to match the actor's skin.

In some areas, such as the neck, where building up with putty or wax may not be practical, latex can be painted directly onto the skin and allowed to dry thoroughly. The skin can then be pushed together into a crease in the middle of the strip of latex. The latex will stick to itself, forming a deep crease that can be made to look like a cut with the addition of makeup. Blood may or may not be running from the cut. For a horizontal cut in the throat, be sure to use a natural crease in the skin if there is one. Pinching of the skin is not recommended, but is sometimes done.

Scars.—One simple but effective method is to use cleansing tissue or absorbent cotton with latex and spirit gum. The spirit gum is applied first, then a very thin piece of cotton or tissue, then latex. The scarred area can be roughened as much as you like by pulling up bits of cotton. Tuplast, Derma wax, and other materials can be used also. Special coloring for the scar may or may not be necessary.

If latex has not been used in making the scar, it's a good idea to coat the scar with sealer after the makeup has been completed. That will protect the scar as well as giving it a slight natural sheen.

Another method is to pour or brush latex onto glass and, with a palette knife or an orangewood stick, swirl it and shape it into the size and kind of scar you want. Then allow it to dry or force-dry it with a hair dryer, peel it off the glass, and apply it to the skin with spirit gum. When you complete the makeup, color the scar appropriately. For greater protection, combine the latex with cotton or tissue, as described earlier.

Similar techniques can be used to make scars with plastic sealer or liquid plastic film. The plastic is poured or smeared onto glass, then swirled with an orangewood stick to make bumps or ridges. This will give a semi-transparent scar that can be applied to the skin with spirit gum. The scar can be colored and given more body by adding tinted face powder as the plastic is being swirled with the orangewood stick. For stronger coloring, powdered rouge can be used. If you don't have powdered rouge, simply scrape the top of a cake of dry rouge to produce a powder.

When the plastic scars are pulled off the glass, both sides should be powdered, as with latex pieces. When the scars are applied to the skin with spirit gum, the edges of the plastic can be dissolved and blended into the skin by brushing them with acetone. The makeup can then be applied. The plastic scar can be left without makeup, or it can be partially or completely made up with appropriate colors. As with latex, materials such as cotton and string can be used in the plastic scar.

Once we had to create realistic looking scars on the back of an actor portraying Christ. The actor was carrying the cross down the aisle of the church and was within a few feet of the audience. We poured and shaped latex onto glass in long, narrow strips and allowed them to dry. We peeled them off and applied them to the actor's back with spirit gum in directions that would appear to be whip marks. Then we covered the latex in red and purple makeup. Next we brushed stage blood on in several layers, allowing each layer to dry. These were removed each night and reapplied for each performance, adding new blood each time.

Cream sunburn stipple.—Applied with a red stipple sponge, the sunburn stipple can be applied to the appropriate areas for the character and the story. As with the beard cream stipple, it must be powdered to keep from smearing off. Once powdered, gel can be dabbed on to give it the sheen usually acquired with the new sunburn.

Old age.—Use modeling rather than lines whenever possible. Lines are usually one of the least successful means of indicating age, because they are usually done improperly. Painting the face takes the same artistry as does an oil painting. Shadows and highlights used to model the face are much more effective.

Let's take, for instance, the deep folds on either side of the nose known as the nasolabial folds. Using a finely sharpened dark-brown or black makeup pencil, draw a thin line in the deepest part of the fold, the full length. With a dull, dark-brown pencil draw a thicker line parallel to the black. Then use a red pencil on its side to make a thicker line the full length parallel to the brown. Take a small brush and carefully blend the brown and red together, feathering inward. Then use white to highlight at the highest point of the fold and blend it inward to the red. This will take practice to use the right amount of color to make it appear natural.

The aspect of aging is to enhance, or play up, the less than perfect areas of the face, neck, hands, and any other exposed areas. Therefore, do not apply a base foundation before enhancing these areas. Shadows and bags under the eyes or hollows of the cheeks should be deepened with shadows. The orbital arch above the eyes should be exaggerated with highlights. The same applies to the hands. Study the skeletal structure: deepen the hollows, highlight the bones, yellow the nails. Liver spots can be added to the face, arms, and hands with a cream shadow. Use sunburn stipple or a red pencil to add broken capillaries around the bulbous end of the nose and under the orbital socket, if appropriate. Shade the eyelids to appear drooping with gravity or age. Use a lighter base shade (oil base only, no pancake) and with a sponge apply lightly to puckered lips. When the lips are relaxed to a normal position, the vertical lip lines are deepened and the paleness lends itself to the illusion of age or weathering.

Beards and Mustaches

Beards and mustaches are the most commonly used makeup applications in church productions, and they are often the most misused. If not done right, they not only break the illusion of reality, but become comical. How many of us, as audience members, have focused our attention on the rubber band pulling a fake beard up over the ears—and missed the scene itself?

The first step in constructing a beard or a mustache is to make a rough sketch of what you have in mind. Presumably you will have done this when designing the makeup. The style you choose will, of course, depend on the period and circumstances of the play and on the personality of the character.

You can make or buy beards or mustaches of real or synthetic hair ventilated on a lace foundation. This type of beard is the quickest to apply, the most comfortable to wear, and the most convincing. It is also the most expensive, but it will last for many performances. If you will be using a beard or a mustache for only a few performances and if your budget is limited, you will probably want to use crepe hair. In any case, you should become proficient in the technique of applying crepe hair.

Wool crepe is relatively inexpensive and, if skillfully manipulated, very effective. It can be used for beards, goatees, mustaches, sideburns, and eyebrows, and occasionally to add to the natural hair.

Various shades of hair are available, and for realistic beards or mustaches, several shades should be mixed. This can be done by partially straightening braids of both shades, then combing them together. This will give a far more realistic effect than would a flat color. It is especially important for realistic makeups that pure black or pure white crepe hair never be used without being mixed with at least two other colors. Black usually needs some gray, brown, or red; and white, some blond, gray, or light brown.

Preparation of crepe hair.—Crepe hair comes in braids of very kinky, woolly strands, which for straight- or wavy-haired actors should normally be straightened before the hair is applied. This is done by cutting the string that holds the braids together and wetting the amount of hair to be used. The portion of the hair that has been dampened can then be straightened by stretching it between two solid objects not too far apart, securing the ends, and allowing it to dry.

The crepe hair can be straightened much more quickly, however, with a steam iron, but be careful to avoid scorching the hair. Pressing under a damp cloth is preferable.

After the hair is dry, it should be carefully combed with a wide-toothed comb, then cut into lengths as needed. A great deal of the hair will probably be combed out of the braid. This extra hair should be removed from the comb, gathered in bunches, and re-combed as often as is necessary to make it useable for eyebrows, small mustaches, and the shorter lengths of hair needed in making beards. In combing, always begin near the end of the braid and work back, combing gently. Otherwise, you may tear the braid apart.

In cases where slightly wavy hair is desired, the crepe hair should be stretched less tightly while drying. Sometimes it needs only to be moistened and allowed to dry without stretching. It is also possible to use straightened hair and curl it with an electric curling iron after it has been properly trimmed. Crepe hair can also be curled by wrapping the straightened hair diagonally around a curling stick and allowing it to dry or force-drying it with an electric dryer. Spraying the hair on the stick with hair spray or coating it with wave set will give it more body.

Occasionally it is possible to use unstraightened hair if a very thin, fluffy kind of beard is needed. To prepare the hair, pull out the braid as far as it will go without cutting the string, grasp the braid with one hand and the loose end of the hair with the other, and pull in sharp jerks until a section of the hair is detached from the braid. The hair can then be spread out and fluffed up with the fingers. One method of fluffing is to pull the hair from both ends. Half of the hair will go with the left hand, half with the right. The two strands can then be put back together and the process repeated until there are no dark spots where the hair is thick and heavy. The curl is thus shuffled around so that it is no longer recognizable as a definite wave. If the hair is then too fluffy, it can be rolled briskly between the palms of the hands. This is nearly always done for mustaches when straightened hair is not used. The pulling and fluffing technique is particularly useful when skin should show through the beard in spots, as it sometimes does on the chin and on the cheek bones. It can also be used in an emergency if there is no straightened hair and no iron available for straightening.

Mixing colors.—Since combing wool crepe, even with a wide-toothed comb, tends to waste a good deal of hair, mixing can be accomplished more economically by first cutting the various shades of hair into whatever lengths you are going to need, always allowing extra length for the trimming. You can then proceed in one of two ways—either take strands of hair of each color and gradually put them together until the portions of the various colors you want mixed are assembled into one pile, or put together all of the hair you want mixed and keep pulling the strands apart and putting them back together until they are sufficiently mixed. The principle, though not the technique, is the same as for shuffling cards. You may be able to accomplish this with all the hair intended for use at one time, but more than likely you will have to do it in sections. If so, make sure that you use the same ratio of colors.

176

The first method will probably give you a more even mixture. For some beards you will want to choose colors that are not too strongly contrasting in hue or value; for others you will want stronger contrasts. You might even, for example, use such strongly contrasting colors as black, white, and red.

If you wanted to give more subtlety to the color variation in a beard, you might work with three colors (which can be referred to as A, B, and C), mixing A and B to produce one mixture, A and C to produce another, and B and C to produce a third. Added to your original three colors, that would give you six different shades, which might vary only value—variations of gray, for example—or both value and hue—perhaps some red or brown mixed with the gray.

Application of the beard.—There are several methods to apply beards and mustaches to the face. We will concentrate on the two most common. The hair is commonly applied with spirit gum over the surface to be covered. We suggest that you not apply foundation over the surface where the hair is to be attached, except for blending it into the actual hair line where some skin may be visible through the beard. If creme makeup or greasepaint is applied and well powdered, the spirit gum should stick. How well it sticks will depend largely on how much the actor perspires and on the quality of the spirit gum used.

You will already have determined the shape of beard you want. In applying the hair, always be aware of the natural line of hair growth, as shown in the diagram at the end of this section. The numbers indicate the most practical order of application.

The following procedure is recommended for one-time use or for beards that will be used a few times only. Again, proper care will determine the longevity of this kind of beard construction:

1. Paint a small area at a time with spirit gum, and allow the gum to become quite tacky. Lightly tapping the gum repeatedly with the tip of a finger will speed up the process. It's a good idea to have some powder handy to dust on the fingers or on the scissors whenever they get sticky. The scissors can occasionally be cleaned with alcohol and the fingers with alcohol or spirit-gum remover during the application.
2. Separate a small section of crepe from one of your darker blends and, holding them firmly between the forefinger and middle finger of one hand, cut the ends. The hair should be longer than required for the finished beard or mustache; they will be trimmed later. The darker hair usually should be used underneath, the lighter on top. In observing bearded men, however, notice that in gray or partially gray beards, certain

177

DIAGRAM FOR APPLYING CREPE-HAIR BEARD: Layers of hair are applied in the order indicated by the numbers.

sections are often lighter than others. Those areas normally match on both sides of the face.

3. When you have made sure that the gum is sufficiently tacky, apply the hair first to the underside of the chin. Usually the application should be in three layers. Push the ends of the first layer into the gum under the chin, about one-half or three-quarters of an inch back from the tip. Press with the scissors, a brush handle, an orangewood stick, a towel, or a damp chamois for a few seconds, then add a second and a third layer, the latter starting from the lowest point on the neck where the hair grows naturally. The hair along the edge of this line should be very thinly spread. If you are making a full beard, the hair should be carried up to the highest point at which the beard grows on the underside of the jaw.

4. Next, apply hair to the front of the chin. The hair can first be attached in a roughly

178

semicircular pattern following the line of the tip of the chin. Then add thinner layers of hair, following the line of the beard as outlined by the spirit gum. For full beards, the hair should be built up gradually, starting at the chin and proceeding to the sideburns. Since the hair is usually not so heavy on the sides of the face, a few applications will be sufficient. Each application of hair, cut at an angle to match the jaw line, should be pressed and allowed to dry slightly before another is added. Remember that ordinarily the thin layer of hair at the edge of the beard as grown from the follicle will be some-what lighter in color than the hair underneath.

5. When you have completed the application and have allowed the spirit gum time to dry, use a hair pick to gently comb the hair of the beard to remove any stray hairs that are not firmly anchored.

6. Holding your barber's shears horizontally, trim and shape the beard according to the style required. If the beard is to be straggly, little or no trimming may be required; but a neat beard requires careful shaping. Thinning the edge of the beard is done in holding the shears in a vertical or near-vertical fashion and snipping into the beard from this direction.

7. Usually you will want to spray the beard with lacquer so that it will hold its shape. This should be a clear acrylic spray carefully applied to the beard and mustache only. Even an unkempt beard will need spraying just to keep it intact and to keep it from pulling off during the performance; you will want to use the spray to maintain the disorder. To avoid over-spraying the acrylic onto portions of the face or nose, fold a paper towel to shield specific areas and spray in sections. When spraying the mustache, the actor may wish to have a tissue or paper towel to insert into his mouth, protruding enough to cover the lips. We suggest that you spray in a well-ventilated area (outdoors, away from the wind) and not in close quarters. As always, ask the actor to hold his breath and close his eyes before you spray. Keep the actor informed as to your progress and inten-tions while spraying, and gently lead him forward out of the area of spray as you finish each section, allowing him to breathe at comfortable intervals. Do not spray too heavily or it will bead up on the crepe and perhaps dry in that form. Again, you may wish to spray two or three coats over the entire hair appliance before you feel adequate cover-age has been applied.

Beard removal.—Before removing the crepe hair appliance (or any hair appliance), make sure the actor is draped with a waterproof material. The beard should be removed first if the wardrobe has a narrow collar and does not easily allow for it to be lifted over the beard without damaging it in any way. Especially delicate at the time of its first wear, the beard should be removed in the following steps :

1. With a brush or long-handled cotton swab, dip into rubbing alcohol and then press against the upper hairline beginning at the sideburn or outermost region. Let alcohol seep down into the beard where it adheres to the skin's surface with spirit gum. You may wish to hold a paper towel underneath the beard to catch the excess. In a matter of seconds the alcohol will have begun to breakdown the adhesive.

2. With a stiff brush or cotton swab, begin to lift the beard away from the face, gently pulling it off with one hand as you brush with the other.

3. Once the outer sideburn area is lifted, continue to apply alcohol at the top of the hairline regularly and brush upward from the neck towards the chin or jaw line as much as possible. Do not pull too hard on the beard, as you will stretch it more than you realize.

4. Once you reach the center of the chin from one side, you continue the same routine, this time from the opposite sideburn (or outermost corner), and work toward the center of the chin.

5. Usually, depending on the size of the beard and mustache, it is almost always easier to make an angular cut into the beard up toward the outside corner of the mouth on each side, separating the beard from the mustache still attached to the skin. The beard can then be lifted from the skin's surface and set adhesive-side-up on a cloth or paper towel.

6. Again, offer the actor a tissue to insert or hold tightly against the upper lip with guidance from the makeup artist so as not to inhibit the removal process. Then seep smaller amounts of alcohol onto the mustache area. One or two applications should be plenty; and the mustache can be removed from one side of the face, usually in one continuous, gentle, pulling motion from the outside corner towards the center. Do the same with the other side.

7. Set aside on the towel, adhesive-side-up as you did with the beard. Once the alcohol has evaporated, the clean-up process of the appliance will be done.

8. Meanwhile, now that all of the hair has been removed from the skin, clean the area where it was attached, first with the spirit-gum remover or continue with the alcohol. Alcohol usually is less expensive and will do the job at hand. If the actor has a heavy growth of his own beard stubble where the spirit gum was applied, then spirit gum remover or even acetone may be required. The more friction such as with a sponge, the easier and shorter the task will seem. *Hint: Do not let the sponge or alcohol-dipped cot-*

ton ball become too saturated with adhesive. It doesn't take long before you are working against yourself with the adhesive you have collected. With your usual makeup remover, you can then go over that same surface and continue to remove the other makeup from the actor's face, and so forth.

9. Once the entire skin surface is clean, a good astringent is advised. After that, a moisturizer should be applied to counter all the affects of the application and removal processes endured this performance.

10. Now that the actor has been released from makeup, the hair appliance needs some attention. In areas where the adhesive had been liberally applied, you may find the appliance has become tacky or gummy. It will need to be snipped off from the side where it attaches to the skin-surface, parallel to the underneath plane of the hairpiece. It should not affect the appearance from the front side.

11. From the front side, you may see areas where the upper line along the cheekbone may need to be trimmed for the same reason. Otherwise, the hairline should be left as is. Be careful to protect that delicate line of the appliance to keep the hair's appearance of growing from the follicle when applied the next time.

12. It is much easier to attach the second time when this next step is followed. Cut the beard into regions as in the diagram for easier storage and future application. Prior to storage, after all clean-up has been completed, spray the beard from the underneath surface with acrylic, two or three coats, letting them dry thoroughly in between coats. The mustache should be done in the same manner, also spraying with the acrylic. Once completely dry, it should be loosely wrapped in paper towels to separate each section from the others. Storage in a large zip-lock bag, labeled on the outside with a peel and stick label, is recommended. All hair appliances can be stored in plastic or cardboard containers. They should be packed in such a way that they will not be smashed nor crushed from within the container itself.

Future application.—The next time the hairpieces are applied, they should be applied beginning at the chin and working outward and upward. Do not be afraid to overlay the pieces where they were separated after removal the time before. The hair appliance should have no gaps or "seams" visible. From all appearances, it should be as if it were not an appliance at all.

Application of the spirit gum should be light: the acrylic is holding the appliance together; the spirit gum merely secures it to the skin surface. Do not apply spirit gum outside the area which the beard is to cover. Any excess should be removed with a cotton swab and alcohol before makeup or powder is applied. The beard should be carefully pressed; a plastic comb or blunt-edged hair pick is the best tool for the re-application of crepe appliances. The hair needs not to be crushed or matted at the surface that adheres to the skin. Again, a natural look is what you are striving for.

As you may have realized by now, one solvent for the adhesive is alcohol. Therefore, any ingestion of alcoholic beverages within twenty-four hours of the time the appliance is to be applied and worn only promotes its lifting from the skin surface regardless of how much spirit gum is used. It is an automatic result from perspiration. The body tries to rid itself of poisons through perspiration; alcohol is one of many found in the cleansing process of perspiration. This alcohol then causes the beard to loosen and even fall away from the skin surface.

Hint: The beard may need to be sprayed with acrylic each time it is worn, depending on its apparent strength, durability, thickness, and the abuse it undergoes with the directed action on stage. We have seen a beard created in this manner last only three performances and we have seen others hold up well enough to be believable in close-ups on film after eight applications. Occasionally, you may need to reapply spirit gum and crepe hair to repair the natural appearance of the thinner beard at the cheekbone line. Acrylic will preserve these touch-ups.

Latex Base.—If you need a beard to last through several performances, you can apply it with latex rather than attaching it directly to the skin with spirit gum. Before painting latex on the face, it's a good idea to protect the skin with a light coating of cleansing cream or oil. Then powder the oiled skin and brush off the excess powder. If you should feel a burning sensation on your skin when you apply the latex, try another brand. If no other brand is immediately available or if you find all brands irritating, use spirit gum.

1. Paint the entire beard area with liquid latex. If the character is to be aged, carry the latex application partially over the upper lip until the lip is as thin as you want it to become. When the first application is dry, add successive applications (usually two or three) until the latex seems thick enough to form a firm base.

2. When your crepe hair is ready to attach (i.e., straightened somewhat, cut and blended or shuffled), brush on in sections the final coat of latex and immediately push the ends of the hair into it. The ends will be firmly anchored when the latex dries. Since latex dries quickly, you should do only one small area at a time. Look at the diagram of crepe application for the sequence of latex application.

3. Gently pull or comb out loose hairs, and trim the beard.

4. A light coating of acrylic spray on a latex based beard is optional. If you choose to do it,

this is the time to apply it. The only other option would be to spray it once the beard has been removed from the actor's face.

The beard may now seem to be anchored solidly enough to leave it on for the first performance, but if there is much movement around the mouth or excessive perspiration, the latex may loosen and pull away from the skin. It is safer, therefore, to remove it as soon as the latex is dry and reattach it with spirit gum. This can be done simply by lifting one edge of the latex with a fingernail, tweezers, or an orangewood stick and pulling the beard off. The back of the latex should be powdered immediately to prevent it from sticking to itself. Rough edges should be trimmed before putting the beard back on. In trimming the latex, be sure to leave as thin a blending edge as possible.

In reattaching the beard, apply the spirit gum to the back of the latex, but only around the edges, unless there is to be so much movement that you would feel more secure with a greater surface of adhesion. Let the gum become slightly tacky before attaching the piece to the skin. After the piece is in place, press with a towel for a few moments, just as in laying the crepe hair onto the skin directly with spirit gum. To conceal the edge of the piece, add a row of hair to the skin along the top edge of the beard, this time with spirit gum. This added row of hair will usually be the lightest hair you have prepared for use in making the beard.

Latex beard removal.—In removing the beard, apply alcohol or spirit-gum remover around the edges of the latex to loosen it. Do not try to pull it off without first loosening the gum, since this may stretch or tear the latex. When the beard has been removed, clean all the gum from the back of the latex with remover. It is possible to reattach the beard with latex, but since there are inherent problems in doing so, this is not advised.

In making both a beard and a mustache with a latex base, make them separately or cut them apart after they are made to avoid restricting movement of the jaw.

Crepe beard stubble.—For an unshaven effect, crepe hair is cut into tiny pieces and attached to the beard area with beard-stubble adhesive. This is the simplest of several variations:

1. Wash the face with soap and water or clean it with alcohol or astringent to remove all grease. If the skin under the stubble is to be made up, apply makeup sparingly.
2. Choose the color of hair you want, then cut up tiny bits of it onto a piece of paper, your makeup table top, or any smooth, clean surface.
3. Cover the beard area with a beard-stubble adhesive. Uncolored mustache wax can also be used for the same purpose.
4. Push a dry rouge brush into the pile of hair bits (quite a few will stick to the brush),

and with the brush, transfer the bits to the face. The hair bits will spread out fairly evenly and will not pile up in clumps. (It would be best not to use your regular rouge brush for this but to have an alternate reserved for this purpose.) If you do not have a clean rouge brush available, you can transfer the hair bits to the face with a clean foam-rubber sponge. However, you may then need a clean brush (almost any kind of makeup brush will do) to remove clumps.

It is also possible to use a matte spirit gum product instead of the stubble adhesive, and it may be advisable to do so if there is likely to be any sort of activity that might dislodge the stubble from the wax adhesive. The spirit gum can be applied over whatever makeup you are using for the character. Regular spirit gum is not advisable because of the shine. When the gum is almost dry, the stubble can be attached by touching a fairly large clump of it to the gummed area repeatedly until the entire area is covered. Or you can spread the stubble over a cloth towel, then apply it by pressing the towel against the gummed area of the face. In either case, loose hairs can be brushed off and final touching up can be done with the fingers or with tweezers. The spirit gum can be used over any makeup, though grease or creme makeup must, of course, be thoroughly powdered. The stubble adhesive works better on clean skin.

Removal of crepe beard stubble.—Beard stubble applied with a wax adhesive can be removed with any makeup remover. When applied with spirit gum, it can be removed with spirit-gum remover or alcohol.

Cream beard stipple.—Beard stipple also can be done successfully with a cream beard stipple and a black stipple sponge. It should be tested on another area at first so as not to glob too much on any one area as it is applied. Watch for it along the top of the hair growth line where it should become thinner or more sparse, depending on the character's lifestyle and heritage. It must be carefully powdered, with a brush only, in stippling motions. Any smeared area will have to be removed and done again.

Cream beard stipple removal.—The beard can be removed with any makeup remover or alcohol. Follow with an astringent, and moisturizer.

The art of makeup is not one that just anyone can achieve. You must realize:
• the limitations of each medium, in combination with
• the physical characteristics of the actor to be made up, in conjunction with
• the actions and story to follow.

Not everyone can be taken from twenty-two years of age to eighty with just highlights and shadows, enhanced with pencils. If you want to pursue the difficult task of applying pieces that are purchased or custom made for the actor, then we encourage you to research various libraries and theaters, and practice what you learn until you have mastered the look you want. It can be done and you may just be the person who can do it!

Makeup Room

In the makeup room the following items should be found:

1. Tables and/or shelves with appropriate chairs, lights and mirrors
2. Clean water for makeup application and blending
3. White rubber sponges, red stipple sponges, orange stipple sponges, black stipple sponges, makeup brushes, etc.
4. Puffs, individually labeled for each performer, etc.
5. Paper towels, baby wipes, cotton swabs, cotton balls, tissues, makeup brushes, orangewood sticks, sculpting tools, etc.
6. Pencils, shadows, liners, mascaras, hair colors, character colors, bases (oil and pancake), body makeup, alcohol, makeup removers, moisturizers, spirit gum, powders, rouges, etc.
7. Miscellaneous adhesives, derma wax, putty, sealers, latex, etc.
8. Hair gels, sprays, colors, bobby pins, hair pins, wig tape, hair brushes, combs, picks, wig stands, wig pins, crepe-hair mustache wax, etc.

Acquiring Makeup Supplies

Research into local theatrical supply houses should be done to see:

1. what can be obtained at discount, and where
2. what the price ranges are
3. brands and items available at various houses
4. the purchase order policies, etc.

You will probably discover that the prices of theatrical makeup are quite higher than "street" makeup. You should also find that the quality is higher and often well worth the price difference. Good makeup saves time and therefore money.

AGING TECHNIQUES

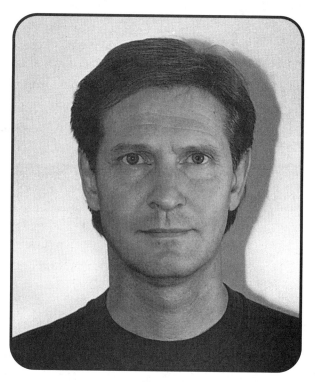

Before

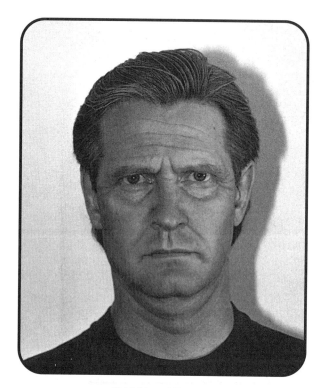

Highlights and Shadows

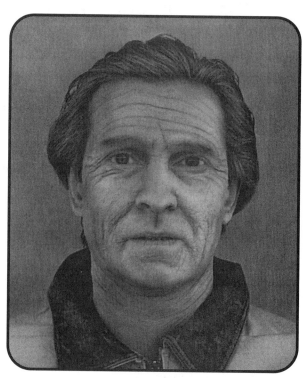

Latex and Tissue

CHAPTER 13

SPECIAL EFFECTS

One of the best ways to increase high production values is to create realistic and highly functional special effects (which are referred to as FX). These effects are usually aimed at the audience's eyes or ears. Handled well, they can sustain and heighten the illusion of reality you are creating with your production. Badly handled, they can shatter whatever illusion you have managed to establish to that point. For this reason, it is wise to spend whatever time and effort are required to make your effects as perfect as possible.

Where most special effects are employed, there is almost always a potential for danger. It is important that a qualified person be in charge of this department. Special effects require a higher standard of accountability to ensure that accidents are not the result of incompetence or inattention. If you use any type of fire or fireworks effects on stage, many states require licensing for pyrotechnics. Knowledge of rigging and safety equipment is a must for the effects man.

There is much a willing and capable person can accomplish using FX on stage, and you will probably be able to create your own. We give a few examples that we have used in some of our productions. For this purpose, we have them divided into two categories: Sound and Visual.

Sound

There was a time in theater history when visual and sound effects were the major concern of the prop department. Before the development of such sophisticated recording equipment, many sound effects were created mechanically by the prop department. Most of these machines are now obsolete since an adequate sound system can bring any effect to the audience with a truer quality and more sensitive control than the mechanical sound effect. However, we have included some of these machines at the end of this chapter. It might be effective to use these in combination with recorded sound effects.

A great variety of sound-effect recordings is available, but many of them may sound "canned" when used in live stage performances, unless high-quality sound equipment is used. Compact discs and digital effects on computers and synthesizers are also effective in creating extremely realistic sounds. These can be very effective, simple, and inexpensive. We suggest that you conduct thorough research into the wide range of possibilities with such equipment. Improvements in these areas are constant. Unless your church has the proper equipment, producing the sound effects manually may be more effective, more dependable, and easier to cue.

Recording may be necessary for certain distant sounds. Whistles and animal noises may be satisfactory when played at low volume, as well as some hard-to-imitate sounds (carrousels, bagpipes) and some very loud reverberating sounds (cathedral bells, thunder, etc.). If you use recordings, make sure that your sound man experiments with the available equipment to get the best possible result. Specific sound effects should always come from speakers properly located at the intended source, or from backstage, and not from public-address speakers out in the auditorium.

When recordings are used, transferring the sound to tape is advisable because tape is easy to mark for cuing, volume control (fade-ins and fade-outs) is easy to manipulate, and all the sound effects for the production may be taped in sequential order. Always remember to make a backup tape. Of course if computers and other high-tech equipment are available, they are preferable to tape.

It might be wise to start a sound effects file on tape. CDs and tapes can be rented or borrowed from local libraries or purchased at music stores. Don't limit yourself to sounds that you feel would apply only to religious or period plays. You might be surprised at the assortment of sound effects you may need in future productions.

In one of our plays we incorporated modern sounds into a period play. In one scene, while Christ was receiving 39 lashes, very quiet and subtle sound effects filled the audience: sirens, bombings, crying, news reports of crime and war, and such. These represented Christ taking on the world's sins, past, present, and future. This is one example of modern sound effects used in a period play.

Following is a list of most often required sounds in theater:

Rain.—Shake dried beans (for light rain) or "small shot" (for heavier rain) in a large round tin pan. Water poured from a sprinkling can onto various materials near a microphone is also feasible. For long continued showers or storms, a rain machine is easily built. Rain records also can be used, but be sure to test them out with your amplifying equipment.

Surf.—Use a large rectangular tray floored with plywood and topped with screening and containing shells and broken glass (about an inch deep). Tilt tray up and down. Or, rub two sandpaper blocks together. Or, shake shot in a large metal pan.

Thunder.—Use a thunder sheet, made of a three-foot by six-foot piece of 26-gauge sheet metal with battens sandwiching the top end. Hang it from this end and shake the lower end. Also, strike with a heavy drumstick or padded hammer for distant artillery effects.

Water effects.—Blow through a straw into water near a microphone. For splashes, pour water from one pail into another.

Wind.—Use a wind machine (a wooden drum with slatted sides that can be rotated). A sheet of canvas is fastened at one end of the mounting frame and battened at the other. The drum is turned toward the free end of canvas, which is held taut. Speed of rotation and tension of canvas vary the pitch and intensity of sound.

Hoof beats.—Use coconut half-shells struck together or struck against a flat surface covered with an appropriate material that will simulate the proper surface, such as a padded material for earth. Or, use rubber plungers if coconut shells are not easily obtainable.

Crash box.—This device is used for the offstage FX of a lamp or other glass objects being knocked down and broken. Make a wooden box approximately two feet square with two sides open. The open sides can be covered with wire mesh or screening, or something open yet strong enough to keep the contents in. Fill the box half-way with paint can lids, squashed cola cans, small chains, small pieces of wood, and such. Experiment with various small objects that might create the particular sound that fits your needs. Secure all edges of the box, attach handles to the sides, and you have a very inexpensive yet effective crash box.

Visual Effects

Although some visual effects have become electronic, most of them have remained mechanical. Smoke, fire, and flash explosions are usually electrically controlled; however, smoke can be made non-electrically if necessary.

Flashes of fire and smoke.—It is preferable to rent a flashpot from a theatrical supply house and follow directions. If you make your own pyro effects, always consult a professional first. *Warning: Never use pyrotechnics near actors or anything flammable.*

To make your own flashpot: A good flash pot consists of a metal pan or coffee can with a tight-fitting wire screen over it. The interior bottom is covered by a piece of asbestos board, to which two electric terminals are fastened (small brass screws will do), but they must be carefully insulated from the pan itself or a short circuit will develop. The two terminals may be about one inch apart. They are connected respectively to the two wires of a circuit that also contains a switch. For this you can cut the end of an extension cord and wire the two bare wires to the screws and splice in a switch near other end. Between the two terminals a single, very thin strand of copper wire is strung, wound firmly around each screw and lying flat on the asbestos board. A small quantity of flash powder is poured over this wire, covering all portions of it, and a piece of flash paper is added. When the switch is thrown, the thin wire will burn out, igniting the powder. After each use the wire and powder must be replaced. *Warning: Before replacing the wire, unplug the cord from the power source!*

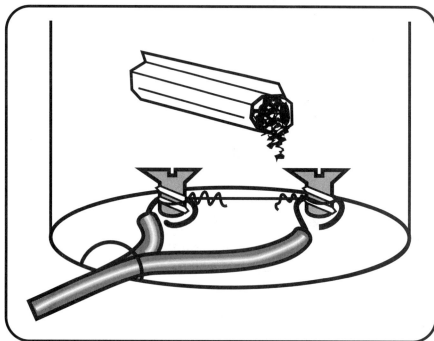

Homemade flashpot

A variation of the flash box is a fuse of very low amperage set in an appropriate fuse clip or socket. Gently break and pry out the glass window of the fuse, taking care not to damage the fuse link. The resulting cavity is then filled with the flash powder. As with the flash box, the opened fuse and the powder must be renewed after each use.

Flash powder, when set off in this way, gives a good burst of light, but little smoke. If smoke is desired, some sal ammoniac powder may be mixed with the flash powder. In any case, the flash device must be well protected with a screen and should never be fired close to flammable materials or to persons. For a more brilliant flash of light, place a piece of flash paper on top of the powder.

A most important warning: very little powder should be used at one time--and it should never be packed down, but poured loosely into place. As soon as a flashpot has fired, turn the switch to the off position and unplug the power source. As soon as possible,

190

remove the burnt fuse from the outlet. (*Caution: Add your combustibles before plugging into the electrical outlet, and make sure your switch is in the off position.*) Fire extinguishers should be present and functional at all times.

Disclaimer: The processes described above are dangerous and may require special permits or licenses in your area.

Smoke.—When describing certain effects, many people confuse fog and smoke. While many of the professional machines are called foggers and smokers, there are differences that may affect the look you want. Most of the professional machines produce a white, misty, gaseous visual of varying density and intensity. Depending upon the technique, you create either a "smoky" or a "foggy" look, though some of these devices are more readily applicable to one or the other effect. For most church applications it is important to know that fog hovers low to the ground, while smoke dissipates and floats high in the air. Both are effective depending on what is required for the scene, and in fact they can be used at the same time.

There are many types of smoke-producing devices on the market, and they have several characteristics in common. They all use either oil-based or water-based smoke fluid. This fluid is heated in a chamber by electric or gas flame above its boiling point and vaporizes into tiny liquid droplets, actually turning the liquid into a gas and creating what looks like smoke. *Caution: All vaporized smoke is toxic to some degree, so be careful to use it only in well-ventilated areas.*

These devices must be rented or purchased and are relatively expensive. There are many types and brands. We won't list them all. The best so far and most common to stage is the Rosco 1500 Fog and Smoke Machine. The Rosco is remote-controlled and produces an excellent volume of smoke or fog. One drawback to this machine is that once it has been disconnected from electrical power, it shuts down.

Smoke cookies.—These get their name from their round cookie-like shape. To use them, simply break a section off, ignite it, blow out the flame, and place it in a metal canister, can, or cup. Smoke cookies come in all standard colors. These work great for campfires on stage. They are relatively expensive, but a small piece of one goes a long way.

Smoke pellets.—Smoke pellets, or cigar smokers, are quite similar to incense and are excellent for live stages. In films they are used for smoking ashtrays and gun barrels, but they can also be used for campfires, barbecues, and atmospheric smoke. They vary from a quarter inch to two inches in diameter by four inches in length.

Spectrasmoke.—This is one of the best types of smoke products and can be purchased in powder or coarse granule form. Smoke powder is a fine substance that can be put into a pile and ignited. One inch of it burns in approximately 10 seconds. The powder comes in various colors: white, red, yellow, green, blue, gray, violet, off-white, orange, and pink. The solid granules give more volume of smoke per ounce and burn a bit longer. They are available in the same colors as the powder. Spectrasmoke can be ignited with a simple electric match or Nichrome wire. An electric match unit of 1 volt at 10 ml amps to 12 volts or 24 volts of DC can also be used. Never use an electrical power such as 110 or 220 volts. There are many firing devices and ignition systems available. Contact a Pyrotechnic specialist for advice as to the best system to meet your needs.

Smoke.—Theatrical supply houses also stock smoke pots (for dense smoke) or smoke powder (for mist, or light smoke). The latter is heated on a hot plate or used in a heating cone, which can be purchased for less than a dollar and plugs into a conventional electrical socket. (*Caution: With chemical smoke there must be adequate stage ventilation to prevent the smoke from spreading out into the audience.* A coughing audience finds it difficult to concentrate on the play.) Dry ice also can be used effectively to create smoke in some cases (see next entry).

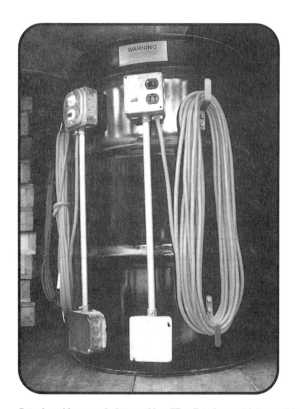 

Exterior of homemade fog machine: 55 gallon drum with internal heating coil. A basket of dry ice is lowered into the barrel of heated water.

Dry-ice fog machine.—The most common method of creating fog is the dry-ice fog machine. This is a dense, grayish-white ground fog that lingers and hovers just above the stage floor. This is excellent for tomb and garden scenes. The machine is about the size of a 55-gallon drum with built-in water heaters that raise the temperature to 160 degrees. Fill the barrel to the center with water. A wire basket is supported by a pipe inside the barrel and just above the water. After the water is heated to the correct temperature and just prior to cue for fog, dry ice chopped into sizes approximately three inches in diameter is dropped into the basket. Just prior to the cue, the basket is lowered into the water and fans are switched on. The fog is pumped out through vent hoses to the locations on the stage. The dry ice must not be dumped quickly because it will give off a tremendous volume of fog that will hover above the ground and will not dissipate unless it is blown off by a fan.

If it is to be seen through an opening in the set (doors, windows, etc.), hang a gauze drop between the set opening and the normal background. Light both the gauze and the background with strip lights on the floor, using separate dimmer controls on each unit. The gauze won't be seen when the strip light on the background is used alone. The fog will appear gradually when the light on the gauze is increased and the background light is dimmed. Reversing this process makes the fog disappear.

Fog can be created without a machine. Dry ice dropped into a basin of hot water and the resulting steam blown onto the set with an electric fan is effective.

Dry-ice fog machines can be purchased or rented. However they are extremely easy to make. Anyone with electrical knowledge about the fans and water heating coils can build one with common materials from the hardware store: a 55-gallon drum, a small fan, water heating coils, thermostat control, pipe, wire basket, dryer vent hose and electrical wiring.

The same machine can be constructed from a used or inexpensive water heater but will take much more time and work. You will need a blowtorch to cut the top off and create the basket system. The good side is that you won't need to install the heaters. With a little ingenuity it can be created.

Remember, you are using frozen carbon dioxide and no one should enter the fog or breathe it. It can be lethal. Never put this carbon dioxide fog over someone's head or engulf them in it because it displaces all oxygen. When breaking up dry ice, always wear protective gloves and goggles, as it is extremely cold (110 degrees below zero F). Flying splinters, chucks, or ice dust that naturally occur when you smash the blocks can be frightfully caustic, burning eyes and hands. Do not use ice dust in the basket or machine

An ice-skating pond is made of prefabricated teflon squares. These squares are joined together, then covered with a silicone spray. Actual ice skates are used. Notice the batting used for snow surrounding the ice pond.

because it will activate the machine ahead of time.

Snow.—For falling snow, plastic flakes can be purchased by the carton at any major theatrical supply company. When they fall they are light enough to float very realistically and they can be recycled. Instant potato flakes also can be used, but in quantity the plastic flakes are probably the least expensive.

For ground layers, synthetic cotton batting can be found at any upholstery shop. When this is spread around the set it has a very realistic look. White muslin should cover the entire set first; then spread the cotton batting around. For mounds and contours, place sacks of sawdust under the muslin. For flocking trees, the cotton batting is best.

Salt in the corners of windows and windowsills has a very effective look. To prevent it from falling off, wet down the surface before laying down the salt. Spray varnish over the salt. Never use salt if animals are on the set or if you are working near trees, grass, or shrubs.

Spray aerosol shaving cream on hard-to-stick-to surfaces like wire and chain-link fences. A few plastic flakes may also be dropped on the foam.

To make icicles without moldings dip Pycotex or Pycolastic, paraffin, or resin on a fine fiberglass cloth or on plastic wrap.

Frosting windows.—*Prismatic lacquer:* When frosting a window to appear frozen with ice, use a fine brush and apply prismatic lacquer in the direction you want. When it dries, it looks like frost on a window. *Epsom salts and stale beer:* Although an old method, using Epsom salts and stale beer has many applications and the advantage of simplicity. The formula is basic; one part of flat beer mixed with two parts Epsom salts. Let it stand for a few minutes and then apply evenly to a clean glass with a cotton ball.

Rain.—A long pipe with numerous perforations is hung just above and upstage of each outdoor opening in the set. Water fed into the pipe through a hose falls into a sloped trough underneath, and this drains into a receptacle. Throwing light on the falling water helps accentuate the effect.

Lightning.—Produced by flashing on and off light units located offstage in the direction from which you want the lightning to come. Use this effect sparingly, as it shortens the life of the lamp. Combine with thunder sheet or other storm noises. To heighten the effect, use one or more camera flashes in conjunction with the other light units. If it is necessary to have a forked lightning bolt appear, a lightning pattern (gobo) should be used on a designated unit and projected onto the cyc.

Water reflection.—This effect is simple yet extremely effective. A long, narrow, and shallow trough is place on rockers. Dozens of pieces of mirror of various sizes are placed on the bottom of the trough and several inches of water are added. By shining a light onto the trough, which is rocked slowly, the reflection spilling onto the set appears to be coming from water. Of course, the trough will need to be masked from the audience's view.

Fire effects.—Open fires are rarely convincing on the stage. And yet, all too often the demands of the script force the designer to put a fire in full view of the audience. Sometimes no flames are actually demanded, and then a mere glow, through crumpled gelatin (orange and red), broken glass splashed with translucent orange paint, or the like, will suffice. A glow on some form of rising smoke, streamers of chiffon or cellophane, blown upward by a small fan, is often used. Tin foil crumpled, stuffed in a hollowed log and lit from inside with red light, can simulate burning embers or coal. In every case, however, the designer is faced with this dilemma: whether to make the fire effects so realistic as to grab the attention of the audience—possibly to alarm them—or so phony as to arouse their ridicule. We strongly suggest that the less fire effect you can get away with, the more

Photo of gas fire effect.
"The Christmas Tree,"
First Baptist Church,
Van Nuys, CA.

fortunate you and your production will be.

Flames.—The realistic versus phony fire dilemma also applies to other open-flame devices such as torches, candles, and oil-burning lanterns. Torches are especially difficult. When faked (flashlight and silk), they almost always appear phony.

Oil-burning lanterns should never be used on the stage. They present a real hazard and their use is strictly against all fire and insurance regulations. In case of an accident the stage would become flooded with blazing oil. Fortunately, oil lanterns usually have glass chimneys which can be realistically smoke-stained to hide a small lamp bulb placed inside. If the lantern is to be carried about the stage, a battery must be hidden within it and a switch provided.

Unlike oil lanterns, candles which usually extinguish themselves when dropped, are permissible on most stages if properly handled. However, they are not advised if they can be avoided, as their bright flickering lights cause distraction to the audience. Very effective substitutes can be made with a small battery or pencil flashlight hidden in a white paper or plastic tube.

If it is absolutely necessary to use an open flame for purposes such as a campfire,

196

design it as much for safety as appearance. Following is one method we have used: Cut a piece of plywood in a round shape (the size of your campfire) and cover it with sheet metal. Bend copper tubing in a circular shape and close off one end; weld it tight. Drill several tiny holes approximately one inch apart, around the tubing. Connect the open end of the tubing to a camping propane bottle with the proper fittings. Check for leaks, then light it to test. Fasten this unit to the center of the sheet metal base. Surround the board with rocks and secure them with cement. Place artificial fireplace logs over the copper tubing. Turn the propane valve and light it with a match.

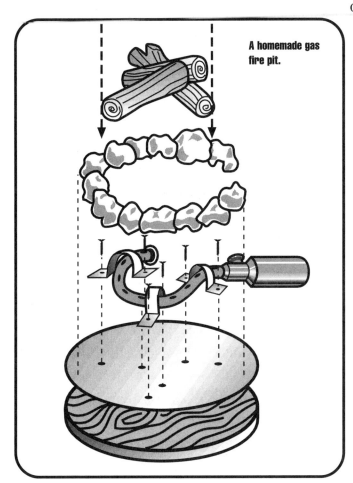

A homemade gas fire pit.

Any time you are using real and open fires on stage, contact the fire department and ask them to inspect the device and the set. If they disapprove, they may have suggestions as to alternatives. More than once a show has had surprise inspections by the fire department during dress week and has been forced to reconstruct weeks' worth of work to satisfy fire codes.

We once built a set in a church that required a "set" church to burn down. We used gas pipes from the church gas lines and ran them into the "set church." Gun powder and flash paper were placed on the floor and the beams and set to ignite at the same time the gas was turned on. The walls were built of strips of metal, suspended much like vertical blinds, and painted to look like the inside of a church. During the fire, the strips were slowly turned to reveal mirrors reflecting the fire, which gave the appearance of the walls aflame. When completely turned, the walls were painted black, giving the appearance of charring. It was extremely effective. We were required to have a licensed special effects man operate the gas ($300 per night), and two fire marshals ($200 per night) located backstage with fire extinguishers each night.

Moon and stars.—If the background is the form of a cloth drop or cyc, a realistic moon can be made by cutting the desired shape (fully round or crescent) into a large sheet of thin material such as cardboard or plywood; this is then placed behind the cyc and pressed flushed against the material. Then when a small spotlight is focused on the cutout, the moon becomes visible through the front of the cyc. If the background is not a cloth, then a projection from a designated unit with a moon gobo should be used.

Stars can be very effective, but are tricky to handle. The tiniest bulbs obtainable look like big blobs of light. It is advisable to tape over these allowing only a small pin-prick of light to pass through. When the cyc is made of plaster or wood, tiny holes can be drilled, and lights can be projected from behind. For soft or cloth cyc's, strings of low-voltage lamps with an appropriate transformer (bought at any hobby shop) can be used. Christmas tree strings can be also be used. Pressed against the cyc, these "stars" will only become visible when lit.

Stars can be projected from the front, but unless they are done by the gobo technique, they are seldom convincing.

Fluorescent glow.—Buy some glow-in-the-dark sticks that can be purchased almost anywhere now. Cut open the outer plastic (over a container to keep the fluid), but don't break the glass capsule inside. In another container break the capsule and keep the two fluids apart. Then on stage add one to the other and—*surprise*—the fluid starts to glow. This is fairly safe; just don't drink the stuff.

Jumping from bridge.—The suicide scene from *Les Miz* was extremely effective yet done with simplicity. The same technique could be used for any occasion of falling or jumping from heights on stage. The bridge that the actor was standing on was raised up when he leaped off, giving the effect of him falling. Once he hit the stage the bridge disappeared, and the lights formed a whirlpool effect as he spun around on the revolving stage. Highly effective and "low tech," depending on the actor with discrete assistance from the lighting designer.

Flying.—Last suggestions: (1) Make sure that all hardware used is load rated; (2) *never* use hardware that is labeled, "Do not use for overhead lifting"; (3) test the system without the actor until you *know* it is safe; and (4) *never* let anyone talk *you* into doing something that you do not know is completely safe. There are several types of flying harness in use today. The two most popular are the "Peter Pan" single-line harness and the "somersault" two-line harness, also called "flying shorts." The Peter Pan harness supports the actor from around the waist and the crotch. It hides very well under a costume, but should not be used when an actor has a lower back problem. Flying shorts support the actor from around the hips and the thighs. This is a comfortable harness and probably the best for your situation. There are also "fall harnesses" used by stunt people which might also work.

Hanging noose.—In a church, this effect would be used most often for the hanging of Judas. We reluctantly offer advice in this area, since it seems almost idiotic to put a rope around somebody's neck no matter how safe we try to make it. The effect could be created by silhouettes or shadowy projections on a cyc or building. However, if you must use a more realistic approach, you must think of safety first. Use the same type of body harnesses you would use for flying. The wire and clip should be attached to the rope from the end and run all the way up to the pulleys. The noose should be separate but attached to the end of the rope by Scotch tape applied loosely. If there were by some chance a "slip," the noose would break loose of the tape and the body supported by the harness and clip on the wire. Make sure that the noose is taped properly every night, and test the effect on dummies before trying it. There should never be any pressure around the neck. *A note of warning:* Don't attempt to manufacture a harness unless you have a good amount of detailed instructions from a reliable source (i.e., someone who does it for a living) and the necessary equipment and materials to finish the work successfully and safely. We all, by the very nature of our craft, find ways to solve our own problems. However, when it comes to putting someone in danger, spend the extra money. It really isn't that expensive.

Water to wine.—Many churches overlook this miracle when portraying the life of Christ. Imagine how dramatic it was when Jesus performed His first miracle. Anytime you are reenacting a miracle on stage, it is difficult to make it as dramatic as it actually was. Following are two methods.

Some theologians believe that Jesus turned the entire well into wine. This makes the illusion easier on stage. First build a well (waterfall) from plaster or plastic, or use an existing plaster waterfall base. This can be surrounded by papier-maché or plastic rocks. Use two reservoirs hidden below, that the water drains into. These can be as simple as five-gallon plastic buckets. The first is filled with clear water, the second with some type of bright liquid. Use a small waterfall pump in each and run the plastic pump tubing up to the top of the well, and fix them side by side. The clear water pump is turned on and circulates until Jesus performs the miracle, then it is switched off and the second "red" pump is turned on. You will need to experiment with the timing of the change over.

Another dramatic method for smaller churches is to use chemicals. This is effective when the audience is not far away from the stage. It is difficult to justify this method biblically,

"Jesus changes the water into wine." *Passion Play*, Bellevue Baptist Church, Memphis, Tennessee, 1997.

but it is nevertheless dramatic. What looks like clear water is poured from an opaque jug or pitcher into seven clear glasses. The colors change with each glass until the final which turns red. Chemicals needed are: 5 grams of tannic acid, a few milliliters each of saturated solutions of ferric chloride and oxalic acid, concentrated ammonia, concentrated sulfuric acid, and distilled water. Equipment needed: opaque jug and seven water glasses.

Put the tannic acid into the jug. Fill it with distilled water and stir well. Line up the empty seven glasses. Leave glasses one and three empty. Put 5 drops of saturated ferric chloride solution into glasses two and four. Put 15 drops of oxalic acid into glass five. Put 10 drops of ammonia into glass six. Put 5 drops of sulfuric acid into glass seven.

When you are ready to perform, pour water from the jug into the first glass. It will look exactly like water. When you pour water from your jug into your second glass, it looks like ink is being poured. When you pour from your jug into the third glass, it will appear as though water is being poured. When you pour into your fourth glass, it looks like ink is being poured. Now, pour the liquid from all four glasses back into the jug. Pour some of this liquid into glass one. It looks like ink is being poured out. When you pour this liquid into glass two, it still looks like ink is being poured. But when you pour this liquid into glass five, it looks like water! When you pour this liquid into glass six, it looks like *wine*! When you pour all the glasses back into the jug, it looks like you have a jugful of wine. When you pour this "wine" into glass seven, it looks like water again. *Caution: Do not drink this liquid!*

Fishes and loaves.—Under the set, stage, mountain, or whatever, construct and place a large sonotube or plastic conduit. Whatever you use should be at least one foot wide. Sonotube is best, and you can get it up to three feet wide.

Cut a circular plywood disc to fit just inside the sonotube and attach a handle to this. Push the disc up through the bottom of the tube. Fill the tube with the bread and fish (cut from foam rubber). When the basket (hole in bottom) is placed over the hole in the set, the "miracle" is created when the plunger pushes upward and the fish and loaves literally pour out of the basket.

Makeup Effects

Most makeup effects are covered in the makeup chapter. However there may be times when the makeup and FX departments will work together to create an effect. For instance, the retractable spear will need stage blood from the makeup department. To complete the effect, makeup can be applied to the tip of the spear, which when pressed against the actor's body would leave a "hole" mark. (See retractable spear description later in this chapter.)

As shown in the following section (Prop Effects), the FX hand nails are designed with a "blood packet" in the palm. This packet can be made by cutting a corner from a sandwich baggy and melting the open edges together, leaving a small opening for the stage blood. Fill the pouch with blood and complete the seal. These should be made fairly small and can be attached to the palm with spirit gum. When the hammer hits the nail over the palm, there should be just enough pressure to burst the pouch. A Roman soldier (masking his actions from the audience) could add to the effect by squirting a tiny squeeze bottle of stage blood onto his hand, nail and arm. This bottle, of course, should be hidden at all times and replaced in the soldiers accessory bag.

A larger version of this pouch could be made for wounds under clothing. Before adding the stage blood, poke a tiny hole in the center of the bag and cover the hole with a strip of Scotch tape. Tie a string to one end of the tape securely. Attach the entire pouch to a leather square or board that has belt straps. Strap this around the actor's waist (or source of intended wound) and run the string to an inconspicuous "pulling" location. When the string is pulled, the tape is removed and blood squirts from the baggy and soaks through the actor's clothing (the effect is best when the clothing is white). The actor can help the effect by clutching at the wound and forcing the blood out and onto his hands.

Malchus' cut off ear.—This scene, when done poorly, will break the illusion of reality and destroy the mood at one of the most important moments of a passion play. Usually, the actor has preset blood on his hand and ear. After Jesus "heals" the ear, the blood is still there, causing the audience to wonder just "what was the miracle." A solution: Place a latex surgical glove on the actor's upstage hand. Make sure to cut off the wrist portion and "tack" it to the skin with a small amount of spirit gum, then cover with skin-tone latex makeup. Place a bloody latex ear in the hand. After Peter swings the sword down past the upstage ear, the actor falls to his knees and holds up the bloody hand and ear. When Jesus kneels and places His hand over the upstage ear, Malchus unrolls the latex glove off of his hand so that it is inside out with the ear and blood inside. The latex is left on the floor unseen under the actors robe. When Malchus holds up his hand after the healing, it is clean of blood—a simple but effective illusion.

Stage blood.—Be very wary of using stage blood. Check with your costumers first, as stage blood stains horribly and is very hard to get out. Mixing a little liquid soap into it helps the cleanup process tremendously. An alternative is well-strained ruby orange juice, which looks just as good from more than a few feet and washes out easily. You also can buy commercial stage blood products. If you use commercial stage blood, it should be nonflammable and nontoxic. Read the labels of commercial products. Test any stage blood you are unsure of for flammability.

Below are formulas to create your own stage blood.

Corn Syrup Base

4 parts - Karo clear corn syrup or equivalent

2 parts - Chocolate syrup (Hershey's or equivalent)

1 part - Red food coloring.

1 part - Water

1 drop - Blue food coloring per 59 cc (¼ cup).

For a one cup batch use a 1 oz. bottle of red coloring, 2 tablespoons of water, 4 tablespoons of chocolate syrup, 4 drops of blue coloring, and fill the balance of the cup with corn syrup. Mix well. This formula looks good on skin and fabric. You may wish to experiment with the ratios a bit.

Flour-Base Blood Formula

7.5 cc to 10 cc plain all purpose flour per cup (250 cc) of water (7.5 cc = ½ level tablespoon, 10 cc = 2 level teaspoons). Mix flour into water completely (no lumps) before heating. Bring to boil, then simmer for ½ hour. Stir frequently. Stir in any surface scum. Let cool before adding food color. Makes a good base for stage blood. Slightly slimy. Fairly low surface tension. Soaks and spreads well.

One-cup batch: 1 oz (29 cc) red food coloring; 1/8 teaspoon (6 cc) green food coloring. Add flour base described above to a total of one cup. Some makeup artists feel that this is more realistic and simpler than corn-syrup, chocolate-syrup, and food-coloring based formulae. There is no sugar and very little food in this formula so it's probably less attractive to insects. Shelf life is fairly short (days) at room temp. Does not go rank, but ferments a bit and loses viscosity.

A + B Blood

Two clear liquids when joined together turn red. This effect was created several years ago for a movie scene requiring a knife cut. You can purchase the A + B Blood at most theatrical supply and makeup shops. However, you might find it less expensive and more interesting to make it yourself.

Chemicals needed: 25 grams potassium thiocyanate; 5 grams ferric chloride; salt. Equipment needed: two glass beakers. Add a few milliliters of water to each beaker. Add the potassium thiocyanate (solution A) to one beaker and 5 grams of the ferric chloride (solution B) to the other beaker. Add a small pinch of salt to each beaker to make a saturated solution. Both A and B solutions are fairly clear and cannot be seen when placed on various objects.

Example: Dip a knife blade into one of the solutions. Take a cotton swab and dip it into the other solution. Take the cotton swab solution and rub it into your hand or arm or any part of your body. Stay away from your eyes or mouth. Take the knife that has been dipped into the other solution and draw it across the part of the body you put the other solution on. It will turn bright red and look just like blood.

Other uses for A + B Blood: Saturate a white wall with the A solution. Dip your finger into the B solution and you can write on the wall in blood.

Experiment with this effect as it pertains to your scene. One or more of the solutions may need to remain wet. The timing in which you apply these solutions during the show is critical.

Safety Factors: As with all chemical effects, take precautions. Keep chemicals away from eyes and mouth.

Bloody lip.—Edible stage blood in gelatin capsules held in the mouth and bitten open on cue can make a good bloody lip effect for fist fights. Empty gelatin capsules in various sizes are sold by many pharmacies in the U.S.

Prop Effects

The FX and prop departments will be working closely together to develop most special effects. FX will take their designs to Props who will solve the problems of constructing them.

One of our sets was constructed in the shape of forty-foot cross that extended from the baptistry and sloped down over the first six pews. The entire cross was built of one-inch thick plexiglass (painted stained glass and lit underneath) that the actors walked on. We wanted an actor to stand at the bottom of the cross and appear to rise to the top. The FX department designed a system and turned it over to the prop department. One of the men worked at an aircraft company and had access to the tools necessary to construct such an effect. He cut a square of plexiglass large enough only for the actor to stand on. Four tiny wheels were added that raised the square only a fraction above the surface of the cross. A super-thin wire, attached to the back of the square, ran up the length of the cross and under the stage to a large drum and crank handle. The actor stood on the square with his arms out and was pulled the length of the cross. The square and the wire were nearly invisible on the cross and the effect was astonishing.

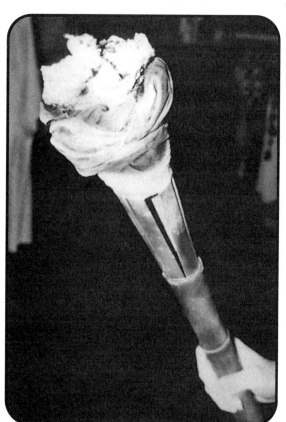

A tiki torch wrapped with flame-proofed cloth and crumpled tin foil around the inside candle.

Torches.—The use of real flame on stage is always more effective but always more risky. A relatively safe torch can be made which uses real flame. Specific actors should be chosen and given lengthy safety instructions. These actors should be the same for every performance and should not pass the torches off to an untrained performer.

Take a cheap bamboo "tiki torch" that can be purchased in most stores. These generally use an oil and wick in a small metal container. Soak a strip of dyed muslin in flame proofing liquid and allow it to dry. Wrap this material around the top of the store-bought torch, partially over the sides of the bamboo handle. This is a very effective look and the single wick flame is relatively safe. Again, actors who carry these torches should be choreographed or blocked with the awareness of the other actors, trees, and potentially flammable props, costumes, and such in his vicinity. Proper containers for dousing or extinguishing the flames should not be far off stage or incorporated into the set design.

Cat-o'-nine-tails whips can be made to give a realistic effect for whippings. The leather (naugahyde) strips can be covered underneath with red makeup which will leave welt marks on the actor's back. Long strips of blood packets may also be applied to the actor's back which will break open upon striking with this whip. All these should be believable to the audience, or they should be revised. Low light levels during these special scenes will not only help hide the effect, but could be used to intensify the mood.

One extremely dramatic effect we have used in the past involves the nails for the crucifixion. Cut the head from a large nail or spike. A railroad spike is best for this. In a machine shop, bend a narrow band of steel (approximately 5 inches) in a U-shape to allow the width of a hand to be inserted. Weld the nail head at one end and the nail at the other. This is like the old arrow-through-the-head trick. Paint the metal strip blood-red. Drill a hole in the cross-arms just large enough for the nails to squeeze through (tight). Cover the holes with masking tape and paint to match the cross. A soldier will pull one of these nails from his accessory bag and place it on the actor's hand, covering the metal band with his left hand. Guiding the nail into the taped hole, he pounds it with a hammer, driving it into the cross. The blood pouch bursts (a soldier squirts blood on the hand), and it appears to the audience that the nails are being driven through the actor's hand. When the crosses are up and the actor is hanging, his hands are resting on the metal bands, now covered with blood.

Retractable spear.—If you want to add an extra touch of realism to the crucifixion scene, the retractable spear may be worth the effort. We caution you: this effect is so realistic that it usually elicits a strong reaction from the squeamish.

In our opinion, a play about the crucifixion should illicit a strong reaction. Realism should be the goal when a message of this importance is being dramatized.

Following is a guideline for making the retractable spear. You may discover an easier and more effective method of creating the same effect as you go. Much of it may be trial and error until you have it working properly.

- Screw on cap from 3½' plastic bottle. Cut shape of slit for the blade to pass through.
- Cut from wood—sealed with water sealer—coated with several coats of varnish painted silver and varnished again.
- Cut plastic circles slightly less than 1½."

FX SPEAR (BLOOD)

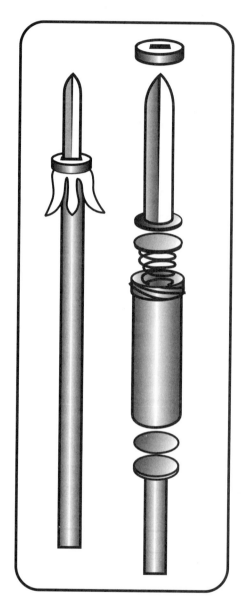

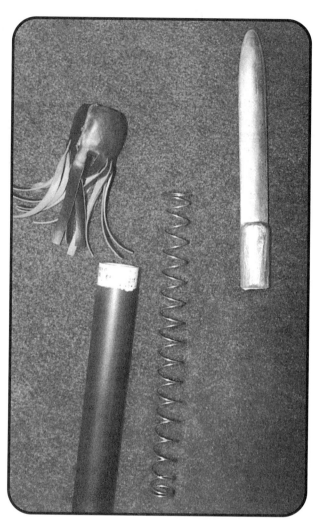

Photo of retractable spear during a performance.

- Spring—glue on and coat silicone.
- 1½" thread cut from plastic bottle and glued to conduit.
- 1½" plastic conduit
- Cut plastic ornamental pieces to glue around the base of threads.
- Plastic circle is glued inside and sealed heavily with silicone.
- Plastic circle is screwed to top of wood pole, then glued to the bottom of the conduit.
- Wrap the entire pole with papier-maché and paint it to resemble wood.
- Fill the conduit with stage blood and assemble.

Earthquake

One of our most elaborate FX undertakings we have experienced in a church play was the earthquake scene at the crucifixion. It required the collaboration of almost all departments.

As the earthquake began, flashes of lightning (strobes) were set off behind the cyc. A large lightning bolt was projected onto the cyc from a light pattern. The base of the bolt was adjusted to end at a large rock next to the center cross.

207

The rock had been constructed of papier-maché, cut apart in "puzzle" pieces and reassembled (all sides were painted). Under the rock was a spring-loaded catapult arm. When the lightning bolt "hit" the rock, the spring was released, exploding the rock all over the set.

The set platforms on one side of the stage were built on mini "roller coasters." These were covered with upside-down carpet and painted to look like ground and mountains. The platforms were connected to a cable running offstage. When the wire was pulled, the set rolled in a wave and split in two, opening a crevice. To heighten the effect of the crevice, a Roman soldier guarding the cross screamed and fell in. The set closed back up with only the soldier's hand sticking up from the crack.

Large speakers were hidden on each side of the set on the house floor. Only the lowest base settings were used as tape recordings of rumbling were played. The base vibrations were so intense that the floor of the auditorium shook.

Actors on stage helped the effect by screaming and falling. Taped music played which helped to create the "frenzy" and panic on stage. The lights dimmed and fluctuated throughout the earthquake, which lasted approximately two minutes.

This effect was so realistic that we printed a statement in the program warning the audience that the upcoming earthquake scene would only be an illusion.

Baptism of Jesus with lighting and water-mist effect.

CHAPTER 14

PUBLICITY

The most important part of every production is the audience. They must be considered before anything else is done. You want as many people as possible to see your production, and so publicity must be handled the right way. Even if the production is not meant to be an outreach tool, you should not simply assume that the members of the church will fill the seats for more than one or two performances. Publicity should be carefully planned and executed to gain the maximum benefit.

Advertising for the show should be thought of in two separate actions: publicity and promotion. They differ in that publicity is usually free of charge, and promotion is paid for. Both should be used to the utmost of your resources. By careful planning, you may be able to cut your costs sharply while successfully increasing the public's awareness of the show.

There is much to be considered when planning a publicity strategy. A campaign that is "preachy" may turn away non-churchgoers in the community, while a more secular approach might anger some church members. Answers to certain questions will determine how your fliers and posters are designed and distributed: What is your target audience or audiences? Will it be a secular or non-secular play? Is it a premiere or an old favorite? (among other questions).

From our experience, we have learned that the publicity should be about the play itself. Emphasis should be placed on the actors, the effects, the set, its production values, its uniqueness. Try to avoid phrases such as "Come fellowship with us" and "Join us in our joyful celebration." This is language used only in church crowds and will turn-off the general public. Separate fliers and posters containing these or similar phrases can be distributed to other churches and religious organizations.

Like everything else in the production, imagination and creativity are your greatest resources when developing the publicity strategy. However, let us make it really clear that the producer or director (or both) will need to be included in the strategy and schedule of the publicity department at all times. This division of your production staff will need to be sharing their ideas and vice-versa with the creative executive staff of the production team. Posters, fliers, announcements,and such are the first things that most of the attending audience will see. You are establishing the quality and professionalism of the production in their minds at that time. Your publicity must be of the highest quality. Keeping with the style of presentation that the director is going with will be as important in the design process here as on the stage. The theme of the play and its style of presentation must be enhanced or supported in the art and all graphic presentations. Verification of information and the content itself that is to be included in the various published articles, fliers, posters, and so forth is also a factor. (Misrepresentation here is unforgivable.) Is it stylized, realistic, contemporary, exaggerated, or bigger-than-life in any one realm? Coordinating their goals with the completion or ready-dates of certain costumes, props, set or scenery pieces which may be required for photos that will be incorporated in this campaign is imperative.

Who prepares all the bulletins, fliers, and similar items that you presently release within your church and to your community? You will most likely know someone, either among your church membership or an outside acquaintance, who is either artistic or has graphic art experience. Enlist them to provide sketches and then the final graphics. It is often tempting to allow the first volunteer to design the posters and fliers; unfortunately many times the quality is well below an acceptable level. Resist this. It is very important that the work be done by a professional or someone who is qualified with experience, talent, and creativity.

Fliers

The flier can be a miniaturized version of the poster or a completely separate design. Again, the person in charge of publicity should use imagination. Strategies should be tailored to your town and neighborhood. You may want to make up several different fliers that target different populations. For instance, you may be sending one to each church of each denomination in town and a different one to non-religious organizations. Fliers released periodically may carry a continuing theme or point of interest that keeps the community interested and can be used much like billboards in that way. If you decide on this approach, it is important to track the distribution process and maintain the mail-outs for each release.

If your church does not have an on-site printing facility, you may be able to get a discount with a print shop, especially if the order includes posters. Your church may have a mailing list and/or a bulk-mail permit. You should have at least enough to accommodate that list plus enough to distribute door-to-door to your surrounding neighborhoods, and on cars in near-by shopping centers. Because the posters have been highly visible for several weeks, the best time to distribute fliers is one or two days before the opening of the show, or the weekend prior to its opening. You will want to estimate also the fliers that cast, crew, and church members will want to have to give to family, friends, and co-workers as a way to encourage community attendance and to create opportunities to build relationships that will lead to sharing their personal faith.

Posters

Posters should be larger than fliers and made of heavier stock. They can vary in size: 16 x 20, 11 x 14, 24 x 36, and so forth. They should be at least two colors that complement each other and draw the eye to the image, such as red on black, black on red, black on white, yellow on black, and black on pink. They can have pictures, graphics, sketches, or just words arranged artistically. They can be glossy or matte finish.

However, to keep the professional look, we suggest that the posters be glossy. They are worth the additional expense. In quantity you should be able to get a fairly good rate per poster. Generally, you will not need as many posters as you will fliers.

Again, use your imagination as to where to place them. Look through the yellow pages and find addresses of all schools, churches, civic groups, and the like in your county. Get permission to put them in your local movie theater(s), the windows of grocery stores, beauty salons, barber shops, and such. Anyplace you can think of where large volumes of people would pass on a daily basis would be a good location. Restaurants with waiting areas, fast food restaurants, or places where people stand in line such as banks, post offices, or the DMV, should be approached. Place the posters where people will see them.

Bulletins and Pulpit Announcements

Of course, you expect your biggest support from your own church membership. However, this may require as much publicity as you would generate outside your church. Start weekly "blurbs" in the Sunday bulletin or weekly church newspaper, at the same time you start pre-production. This could be months prior to opening.

One way to generate publicity is to place an insert in the bulletin. The insert could be a questionnaire requesting information about volunteers, talents, or a list of items needed for things such as donations, props, and sets. These forms should be collected during the service or as people exit at the close of the service.

Each Sunday that these appear in the bulletins, an announcement should be made from the pulpit. The speaker could mention the needs and give the name of a person to contact (probably the production manager), or some of the actors could do something different each week to spark interest. For instance, an actor or actors in full costume and makeup could make the announcement.

Tickets

One creative and inexpensive way to advertise is to print business-card-size tickets with the name of the show, the location and address, phone number, and the words "Admit one free" at the bottom. Another alternative is to have the word "Complimentary" appear on the ticket itself. If there is to be a donation at the door, then it is advisable to indicate that a ticket donation of your asking price is requested. Keep in mind that a donation is exactly that. If someone should choose not to donate towards the ticket price, the laws of most states require that those people are still provided a seat.

Whichever way you go, a heavier paper such as card-stock is suggested. A dozen tickets (business card size) can usually be printed on an 8 ½" by 11" sheet, then cut. Another way to do this is to actually have business cards printed with the same information. These can be printed at minimal cost.

Choir, cast, crew, and church members can pass these out to their friends and co-workers. Having these in hand makes the approach much easier when inviting someone to your church production.

The Set

Once the set is under construction, the church congregation will begin to watch its progress each Sunday, prior to the performance. This will generate more curiosity and publicity among the church members than anything else.

Of course, when the final set is complete and it is of the highest quality, they will be impressed enough to invite others to see what's going on in their church. Many church members are embarrassed to invite their non-churchgoing friends to see a poorly produced production in their church. Others are even afraid to invite their friends to church for any occasion. But we have discovered that when there is something at their church that is unique and of which they are proud, their inhibitions, fears, and embarrassments fade. They gain a new boldness to seek out friends, co-workers and even strangers to invite to their church.

When the set begins to develop with a quality that they are not used to and are themselves impressed with, this boldness begins even before they see the production. After they see the production on the first night, word-of-mouth becomes one of the greatest forms of publicity. Some of our productions were intended to be done for one weekend and, because of crowds, had to be extended to include a second and third weekend.

Publications

Newspapers and magazines can be your greatest form of advertising since these publications usually reach hundreds of thousands of people. Even so, the advertising must be handled just right or it won't do any good.

Newspapers.—Most newspapers sell advertising space either by the square inch or in page divisions at one eighth, one quarter, one half, or full-size with prices graduating upward accordingly. The prices are adjusted to accommodate the number of times you want the ad to run. For instance, if you run it every day for one month, you will receive a big price break on the daily rate.

You may want to run it in your paper's special weekend sections, such as *Calendar, Living,* and *Metro*. In this case, you may want to run it for four to six weekends at a special rate.

Usually, the paper requires that your ad be submitted "camera ready." That means that all print, graphics, and pasteup should be complete and ready for print in the paper. The paper will take a picture of your completed ad, reduce or enlarge it, then run it in the paper as you submitted it. With the right use of graphics and catchy wording, your ad will catch the eye of the reader.

It is acceptable to advertise in the religious section of your paper; but you should also advertise in other sections, such as entertainment (theater) and the others mentioned above. The religious section will probably cost you the same and reach a lesser amount of readers. Usually at Easter or Christmas season, the religious sections are packed with ads of other churches and their programs. Your ad may get lost amongst them.

The best thing you could do would be to get a feature article written about your production. If you can sell a reporter on its uniqueness and high production values, he may feel that it is a human interest story. Try to get him out to the set during a dress rehearsal. He could take pictures and interview several key figures involved in the production. Pitch it as being a major event in your city.

You may also want to place an ad or get a feature article in the newspapers of all local schools and colleges.

Magazines.—Your local area may have county, valley, or city magazines. If you submit early enough, usually several months prior to the opening, these magazines may list your show in their "Things to Do This Month" sections. Like newspapers, you should also pitch for a feature article.

Your denomination or church association may have their own monthly magazine or newspaper circulation which would be accessible to you. These publications may be more open to writing feature articles on your production.

Some denominations even have state magazines or newspapers. These may not necessarily bring more audiences to your performances, but it helps increase the reputation of your church for future performances. It also may reach surrounding communities that are within driving distances.

Radio and Television

Don't be afraid of these mediums; they are much more approachable than most people think. Many radio and television stations have policies that provide public service announcements. You may be able to get interviews and feature stories on local radio and television stations just as you can in newspapers and magazines.

One Easter, a local news station came to our church on opening night (Good Friday) to interview us "live." The set was magnificent, we were in full costume and make-up, and we did the interview on the set just before the House was opened. The next two nights the audience was packed out.

Find out what paid advertisements will cost for your local radio and television stations. Television is usually more expensive than radio, but you may be surprised at how low some of the quotes can be. You've got nothing to lose by inquiring.

This kind of advertising and promotion takes boldness. The person in charge of publicity should have a bold and aggressive enthusiasm for the production. He must be excited and believe in the quality of what he is presenting to the public. The producer should enlist someone with these qualities and then continually encourage him in his boldness, enthusiasm and creativity.

Invitations

Invitations can be extremely useful if sent with cover letters and fliers to various clubs and organizations who may support the production with a pre-arranged group attendance. This can be implemented by the producer, director or administrative staff, but utilized by any church member who has influence or acquaintance with any such group. Cover letters can be modified to address each group and presented in person or via any mail or courier service. Follow-ups should definitely be made whenever an invitation is released. You can also use them to give to groups or any persons who have purchased significant advertisement space or made contributions of materials or funds that have enabled your to reach your production goals on time and within budget.

Programs

The main purpose of programs (sometimes referred to as playbills), passed out by the ushers as they seat the audience, is to supply the audience with information to follow the production easily and intelligently. This information includes the names of the play, the author, the director, the designer, the musical director, and anyone else who has made a contribution to the production. It also includes all the key information about the play itself: the period, place, and time where the action occurs; the sequence of scenes; and any other information that may help avoid confusion. It includes the names of the cast and the parts they play, as well as the various staff members and the nature of their contributions.

In addition to this vital information, the program also may include additional information about the play, cast, or staff. These program notes will ordinarily consist of brief biographies of the leading actors, actresses, production staff, and crews. Additional notes on the play, the author, and occasionally notes from the director or producer are included.

Finally, the program should include acknowledgments for those people, businesses, or organizations that have contributed materials or services to the production. And if any organizations were significant donors, there should be some description of each of those organizations and the work it performs.

The program can be simple or elaborate. We suggest that as much care and effort be made on the playbill as on all other aspects of the production to uphold your standards of "quality."

Preparation.—Program material should be assembled as early as possible during the rehearsal period. Usually it will be collected or written by the publicity people or by someone especially designated for this task. Before the program is actually duplicated, the production manager should check the proof sheets for its general content to make sure that no one has been omitted, that everyone is properly credited for the work he has done, that no one's name has been misspelled, and so forth. Only after this final check should the printer be instructed to run off the programs.

The program should be arranged in a logical order with the most important items of information given the most prominent positions. The cover, or inside page, should include the name of the play; the name of the author; the name of the group or church presenting the play; and the theater, auditorium or church where the performances are being given. The name of the play is usually the most important item. These pages might also include the names of the director, the designer, the musical director, and the dates of performances. In addition, the cover might be decorated with a design appropriate to the play. The inside pages of the program should be arranged with the same care as the cover. The program layout is at the discretion of the program designer.

The cast and scene information (important to the audience) should be given the most prominent positions. If advertising has been sold, the program would have to be expanded, and the arrangement of material may be somewhat different.

Biographies.—Most biographies (bios) are simple paragraphs detailing past credits, awards, and training of the key production staff members and principal performers. Some may use the space allotted to them to make political appeals or expound on their personal philosophies or beliefs. Some try to be amusing. Most actors in church productions do not have a long list of acting credits, but there should still be some type of interesting information about the actor in his biography.

When Richard Dryfeus performed in *The Hands of Its Enemy* at the Doolittle Theater in Los Angeles, his biography said something to the effect of, "I love my wife and daughter."

Advertising.—Program advertising, if someone is willing to undertake the task of selling it, can be a source of substantial income. A group should not underestimate the value of advertising in its program. If, for instance, you sell ads at a minimum of $100 a full page, $50 a half page and $25 a quarter page, two or three pages of advertisements could pay the entire cost of printing the programs. More could supplement the cost of the set or lights, and still more could pay for the entire production.

The question is, what businesses do you target to sell ad space? While some types of businesses might be expected to benefit from such advertising, others might have nothing to gain. Any attempt to browbeat the latter into taking ads will damage community relations. It is much better to concentrate on those businesses that stand to profit from program advertising—shops, local stores, restaurants, service organizations—than to waste time on big businesses such as chain stores. However, these larger organizations may wish to make a donation, in which case they would be acknowledged in the program.

Let's look at what you can do to make the acquisition of advertising support as easy and straightforward as possible. It is essential that the production be represented in a most professional manner. Your attempt to gain the support of other businesses through their purchasing space will depend on your professional and personal integrity and credibility. Therefore, it is recommended that you prepare a publicity package to present to those from whom you hope to gain this support. Items to include in this package are:

a cover letter from the producer,

a flier of the production itself,

two forms specifying type of space to be purchased (the PM will retain one copy upon completion), and

a sample page of advertisements, or of the type of program you intend to provide.

The purpose of the cover letter is to introduce the production and perhaps the person soliciting advertising space to the business owner or manager. It must be on letterhead of the church or of the production itself, depending upon the preference or current policies of your church and your budget. Often you can create your own letterhead for the production or a logo to be cleverly incorporated onto the existing church letterhead. This then can be used for all production correspondence.

The flier and the letter will serve to establish the professional integrity with which all advertising space will be presented to the public. If the quality of the graphics and presentation is poor, then those you approach can only assume that their image to the public will be presented in the same manner. However, if it is of the highest quality, printed on quality stock, with an attractive or eye-catching layout, then each business owner is more likely to be impressed with the degree of professionalism which will carry over to his business.

The form(s) you use to identify the space purchased must clearly state:

- the name of the production and the dates it is expected to run
- the name of the site where the production will be held and its street address
- the name of the person selling the space, the name of the producer, and a contact number for same
- the size(s) and cost of available space
- the state of the "copy," and instructions as to its presentation
- the deadline for camera-ready and non-camera-ready copy
- the date, signature, and contact number of the person purchasing the space
- the date and signature of the person selling the space
- if the ad is purchased through the exchange or trade-out of services, space should be left to clearly identify this transaction
- the amount of money received
- the form of payment (cash, check [and check number], money order) to whom checks and money orders should be made payable.

The sample of the program should be included only if you have ones that contain such advertising, and only if they match the standards with which you intend to produce this current program. As we presume this is your first attempt to secure advertising in a program, we suggest that you paste-up a mock advertisement page which would show the format, or presentation of the various spaces you are providing in actual size.

In preparing this paste-up, you can use business cards which are camera-ready (i.e., are already typeset with appropriate graphics, logos, etc.) and easily reduced or enlarged to accommodate the spaces available. If you include one sample of a personal advertisement, it may generate interest from a business or individual to pursue that angle. Any businesses represented in your paste-up should be with their permission. Certainly there are people in your church who would appreciate extending that to you; it serves to help their business, the production, and the church.

The sample publicity package pages should include a cover letter, advertising agreement, and sample advertisements, as well as a flier, production staff and cast sheet, and biographies of key staff and principal performers. Any well-known name—even if just within your community—that is associated with the production can help boost publicity.

As these advertising packages are assembled, we recommend that they be inserted into the type of folders which have pockets on the inside. These pockets can hold envelopes which should protect the copy, and additional fliers, should the purchaser wish to have some to distribute from his store.

Advertising space can be secured by any church member. All members should be encouraged to participate, even if they are assisting in any other capacity of the production. The package needs to be reviewed with all persons attempting to secure advertising space for the program. Though it is relatively straightforward in its contents and presentation, there will be some questions that they should be prepared to answer. Some of these questions may be:

- Is there an extra charge if an ad is submitted that is *not* camera-ready? You should not expect that any "personal advertisements" (i.e., well wishes towards the cast or even a certain member of the cast from family, co-workers, or friends) will be submitted camera-ready. We recommend that you price the ads so that the number of ads which will need to be made camera-ready can easily be absorbed by the overall income generated by the advertising campaign.
- Does the deadline for submission change if the copy is *not* camera-ready?
- Do I get to proof the ad before it goes to print?
- Are there incentives to encourage the purchase of full-page ad spaces (i.e., a certain number of complimentary tickets, etc.)?
- Can you reduce or enlarge the camera-ready submission at no extra charge to me?

However, no person should attempt to do answer such questions without the package in hand. If a church member finds himself in the position of talking to someone about the opportunity to purchase space and does not have a package in hand, then he should not make any definitive statements about the terms. He should talk in general terms and then set up a time to return with a package, or arrange for a production representative to return with the information package. Misquoting terms often leads business owners to make commitments they may not want to uphold once the actual terms are known. This only puts them in an awkward position of paying more than anticipated or even retracting their intentions. Whichever way you end up compensating for inaccurate information, it usually leaves them with a negative feeling towards the production and the church.

Inquire as to the printer's deadline and the time required to complete the task once delivered to him so you can adjust your time-line accordingly. You will need to have this information in hand before your deadlines can be established for the return of biographies, notes, advertisements, and such with enough time to assemble and prepare the layout. If your printer is preparing the camera-ready version, then your preparation time will be proportionately diminished. As with every aspect of production, planning will eliminate numerous problems that present themselves. Needless to say, you will want to be certain to provide programs to all persons and organizations that have contributed in any way to your production, whether in the donation of materials or the purchase of advertising space.

We have presented some samples throughout this chapter of the various tools you have available to you. We are doing so merely to assist you in preparing your publicity strategy. Note also that there are forms in the production forms chapter that will assist you in your approach to acquiring and assembling the information that you need. It may serve merely as a springboard to propel you into areas that are not included here. We hope that is the case!

CHAPTER FIFTEEN

BUDGET

Preparing a budget is not simply a matter of creating a list of itemized expenses under appropriate headings. The budget must reflect, as accurately as possible, the final form the production will take. The challenge in creating an accurate budget for a church production is that there is usually a "fixed amount" established first and the production must be mounted within that figure.

Let's say, for instance, that the church has allotted $10,000 for your entire production. The total amount you then allot to all departments must not exceed the production budget of $10,000. If you are able to cut costs from one department, the funds released from that department can be funneled into another.

However, if you are given a budget that is unrealistically low, it is still possible to mount your production with the same quality, if you capitalize on your available resources. A $10,000 budget could be equivalent to a $30,000 budget if you add donations of money, materials, manpower, and so forth.

It is always better for the church to invest as much as it can into its first productions. Keep in mind that most of the materials, sets, and costumes will be stored and reused in future productions. Most of the budget on your initial productions will be a "one-time cost" of building an inventory of set, costume, and prop pieces that will dramatically reduce future expenses in those areas, allowing funds to be channeled into other areas.

Preparing the budget.—The budget breakdown of any production can not be established without your first having selected the play. However, depending on your church policy, the history of previous productions (if any), and the department responsible for the production, the amount of money set aside (from which the budget will be derived) already may have been determined and may not be negotiable.

Once the play has been selected and the producer and director have agreed upon the concept of presentation, then a preliminary budget breakdown can be prepared. Usually prepared by the producer, this breakdown will have taken into consideration the following:

1. The expenses to obtain the property to be produced (i.e., the fees for the rights, the score, the scripts, etc.)

2. The type of presentation to be produced in relationship to:

   - The mandatory expenses incurred with work for hire which cannot be avoided (i.e., union performers and crews in a union house, fire marshall or pyro-technician for on-site special effects, etc.)
   - The resources in storage
   - The potential resources that can be borrowed
   - The availability and cost of services to be acquired and items to be rented
   - The time from the onset of pre-production to opening night and the qualified manpower to create, construct, and assemble these necessary items within that time
   - The cost of materials from which these items will be constructed
   - The possibility to offset production costs with donations of money and/or materials, ticket donations, sale of program advertisements, or even acquiring an outside associate producer to share expenses and sometimes, responsibilities (The publisher of a new musical may ask your facility to present the premiere performance of it, and therefore agree to provide funding towards its production; or perhaps a local service club would be willing to donate money or services for the youth in your church to mount a production during the summer, or as a benefit or fund raiser for a local charity, etc.).

The budget breakdown should be completed by the time of your first pre-production meeting with your key production staff. It will be the responsibility of the production coordinator to make sure that the breakdown within departments is accurate and manageable. You cannot allow the set designer, for example, to spend all money allocated to his department on the set acquisition and construction, thereby leaving no monies for necessary set props and dressing. It is suggested that the PC work with each department head in breaking down the needs of his department. The PC will carefully monitor the release of purchase orders and petty cash to departments on a daily basis. Remember, the PC will also have all information regarding the potential donation/acquisition of materials or services related to all areas throughout production. The receipt of these materials or services may affect or alter the budget breakdown. How monies are reapportioned upon receipt of same will be the responsibility of the production coordinator in conjunction with the director and producer.

Charging Admission

This is one of the biggest controversies in church theater. There are those who feel that charging admission is wrong for the church. And since the church is a non-profit organization, the word *donation* would have to come after the admission price in order to "sell" a ticket legally.

Others feel that it is perfectly acceptable to charge for the quality of production the audience will be seeing. We are not going to make a judgement either way here, but we will present all options and their advantages and disadvantages.

If the production budget is relatively small and would not be a financial burden upon the church, then you may not want to charge admission. Freewill offerings and donations could close the gap enough to reduce substantially the total cost of the production.

If the decision has been made to mount a production with a high budget, it may be necessary to charge a nominal fee (with "donation" on the ticket). Those unable to afford the ticket price should still be allowed in since laws vary regarding a nonprofit organization's right actually to charge admission.

If the production is produced on a larger scale, the budget could go into the hundreds of thousands of dollars. A union orchestra could run as high as $30,000–50,000, depending on its size and the number of performances you have scheduled.

With this kind of overhead, a high media advertising campaign to elicit and sustain a moderate ticket admission should be conducted to cover expenses.

The psychology behind this is:

"Most people believe that when they pay for something, it must be worth the price. For example, a friend of ours had decided to sell an oil painting for a price of $30 and months went by without it selling. The price was changed to $300 and the painting sold immediately. The painting was then deemed valuable.

It is possible that by asking a ticket donation as low as $4.00, you may find more people attending than if it were a "free" event. A good publicity person can create an atmosphere that would have the phones ringing off the hook with people making advance reservations.

Some churches send mail-outs with order forms to those on their mailing lists. These forms are to be filled out and returned to the church office, along with the admission price, to receive the tickets for a particular night.

Some churches have seat and aisle numbers on the seats with corresponding numbers on tickets. Audience members have an opportunity to choose seats in advance (from reviewing a house diagram) according to availability. This also encourages them to buy early, which secures advance money to offset the budget.

The church pastor, deacons, and other administrators will probably be in long discussion and prayer when making the decision regarding admission. As stated above, we will not make a judgement either way. The decision should be left to the leaders of the church. The cast and crew should happily, and respectfully, abide by that decision.

The following page contains a sample of a detailed production budget. Each line item should take into consideration the expenses required by each need listed in the following pages. Following the sample "Production Budget Top Sheet" is a listing of various areas and items within those areas which the different departments should take into consideration in preparing a budget using the same format as the sample. After each department has submitted its "needs list," the budget can be totaled and put in the top sheet. The person in charge of your finances (producer/ executive producer, etc.) may need to use several different versions as "cutting" and "juggling" becomes necessary.

The forms are mostly self explanatory. ACCOUNT—This number is to simplify bookkeeping. It makes it easier to keep track of expenditures. CLASSIFICATION—This is the name of each department. There are other sub-divisions within those, such as the MISCELLANEOUS section. We suggest that you read the entire budget through several times to become familiar with each item.

PRODUCTION BUDGET TOP SHEET

TITLE: _____

Production No.		
Date:	Version:	

Account	CLASSIFICATION	Page			
001	STAFF	1			
002	GENERAL & ADMIN.	2			
003	TALENT	3			
004	MUSIC	5			
005	SET	7			
006	LIGHTING	11			
007	SOUND	15			
008	COSTUME	17			
009	MAKEUP & HAIR	18			
010	SPECIAL EFFECTS	24			
011	AUDIO VISUAL	25			
012	PUBLICITY	26			
013	SAFETY & SECURITY	27			
014	LOCATION	28			
015	MISCELLANEOUS	29			
016	CONTINGENCY	30			
	TOTAL COST				
Prepared by:			Date:		

Staff

Executive Producer
Producer
Director
Writers
Music Director
Production Manager
Other

General & Administrative

Telephone
Taxes & Permits
Accounting
Insurance
Office Equipment & Supplies
Local Travel and Mileage
Copying & Printing
Secretarial
Other

Talent

Leads
Special Guests and Cameos
Cast
Chorus/Dancers
Bit Parts

Music

Conductor
Composer & Lyricist
Arranging & Copying
Studio Rental
Sync Licences
Rights / Royalties / Buyouts
Cartage & Instrument Rentals
Rehearsal Piano & Drums
Other

Orchestra

Conductor
Concert Master
Violins
Violas
Cellos
Trumpet
Trombones
Saxophones
French Horn
Baritone
Clarinet
Oboe
Flute
Bass
Harp
Piano
Synthesizer
Guitar

228

Percussion

Other

Production

Set Designer

Construction Foreman

Scenic Artist

Wood

Two by Four

One by Three

Two by Two

Firring Strips

Plywood

Luan (doorskin)

Other

Paint

1 Gallon Cans

5 Gallon Cans

Spray Cans

Tempra/Poster

Artist Oils and Acrilic

Brushes (Hand)

Brushes and Rollers

Dropcloths

Spray Equipment

Masking Tape

Fire Proof

Other

Hardware

Nails

Screws

Nuts & Bolts

Razor Blades

Saw Blades

Brackets

Hinges

Casters / Wheels

Other

Miscellaneous

Glue

Sandpaper

Duct Tape

Muslin

Canvas

Naugahide

Scrim

Cyc

Backdrops

Duvetyne

Plexiglass

Wire / Cable / String / Chain

Other

Lighting

Lighting Director

Assistants

Units

Ellipsoidals

Fresnels

Pars
Scoops
Peppers
Blacklights
Striplights / Cyclights
Spotlights
Accessories
C-clamps
Barn Doors
Gel Frames
Edison Connectors
Pin Connectors
Twofers
Threefers
Cable
Cable Clips
Trees
Stands
Bars
Sandbags
Fixture Wrenches
Safety Chains
Gels
Lamps / Bulbs
Gobos
Other
Control
Console (Control Board)
Dimmer Packs
Other

Sound

Sound Director
Assistants
Microphones
Handheld
Lapel
Stand
Choir (overhead)
Wireless
Other
Cable
Speaker
Microphone
Speakers
Speakers
Monitors
Other
Systems
Amplifiers
Mixers
Equalizers
Tape Decks
Compact Disc Players
Other
Accessories
Stands
Power Supplies
Batteries
Connectors
Intercom Systems
Other

Costume

Designer
Wardrobe Person
Tailor
Seamstress
Fabric & Thread
Wardrobe Racks
Irons & Steamers
Sewing Machines
Cleaning
Other

Makeup & Hair

Designer
Assistants
General
Foundations
Contouring Colors
Liners
Mascaras
Lipsticks
Powders
Pencils
Body Makeup
Moisterizers
Make-up Remover
Alcohol
Other

Specials
Stage Blood
Teeth
Spirit Gum
Spirit Gum Remover
Latex
Bald Caps
Crepe Hair
Wax, Putty
Hair Colors
Hair Pieces
Other Appliances
Other
Brushes
Eye Liners
Mascaras
Lip Brushes
Blush Brushes
Body Brushes
Shading/Contouring
Brushes
Eyebrow Brushes
Other
Tools
Sculpting Tools
Scissors
Bobby Pins
Double Stick Tape
Hair Brushes
Combs & Picks
Dryers

Rollers & Clips
Elastic Bands
Hair Sprays
Mousse
Ribbons & Decorations
Spray Bottles (Water)
Other

Perishables
White Rubber Sponges
Q-tips
White Tissue
Paper Towels
Baby/Wet Wipes
Powder Puffs
Stipple Sponges
Orangewood Sticks
Cotton Balls / Pads
Other

Accessories
Tables
Chairs
Mirrors
Mirror Stands
Mirror Lights
Bowls
Containers
Other

Special Effects

Licensed FX Person
Firemen

Equipment
Smoke Machines
Fog Machines
Strobe Lights
Mirror Balls
Chase Lights
Rope Lights
Sound FX Tapes & CD's
Bubble Machines
Color Wheel
Laser FX
Breakaways
Other

Audio Visual

Projector Operators
Camera Operators

Equipment
Slide Projectors
VCR's
Video Cameras
Movie/TV Cameras
Screens (Front)
Screens (Rear)
Tripods
Cables
Batteries
Lenses
Mounting Racks
Film/Tape
Other

Publicity

Posters
Flyers
Newspaper Ads
Magazine Ads
Radio
Television
Playbills / Programs
Tickets
Other

Safety and Security

Head Secrurity
Qualified Safety Person

Security
  Walkie Talkies
  Beepers
  Cellular Phones
  Flashlights
  Batteries
  Other

Safety
  First Aid Kit
  Fire Extinguishers
  Glow Tape
  Night Light
  Hard Hats

Location

Rental
Utilities
Resident Personel
Custodian
Janitorial Supplies
Insurance
Other

Miscellaneous

Transportation
Childcare
House
Strike
Gifts
Food
Other

Contingency

CHAPTER SIXTEEN

SAFETY & SECURITY

In professional theater the subject of safety and security is one of the most important areas of concern. On first thought, it would seem unnecessary to be concerned with safety and security in a church environment. However, we have discovered over the years that this subject is as important in the church, if not more so, as in the theater world.

To some extent, loss of property due to theft or vandalism has occurred on almost every church production. Over time, we have "lost" thousands of dollars' worth of tools that were somehow removed from the properties of various churches by opportunists. More than once, sets have been destroyed by vandals in the middle of the night. Though much of this may be due to negligence associated with misplaced trust, it proves the need for some type of security measures in addition to any system or policies the church may be using already.

Most churches' insurance policies cover such losses and injuries to persons on the property. However, the high-risk circumstances of the production could possibly bring an injury lawsuit due to negligence. You need to take every precaution to create a safe working environment for your cast and crew. One way to do so is to form a safety and security department to work alongside all other departments. The safety and security department should make sure that everyone involved is aware of safety and security rules. After all, it only takes one person to cause a serious accident or security breech.

Security

Keys should be assigned to a limited number of persons involved with the production. The producer, director, production coordinator, and stage manager would normally have keys to the buildings designated for use during the production. The appropriate key holder should arrive at least fifteen minutes prior to a scheduled work or rehearsal time. Usually the stage manager or production coordinator is at all scheduled meetings and will possess any alarm codes and their procedures. Likewise, the stage manager or production coordinator should be the last one to leave after securing all doors, locks, and alarms, or make arrangements for it to be done.

Each time you meet on the church property, steps should be taken to insure the security of those involved in the production. Security in the early stages of pre-production may be as simple as walking team members to their cars at night and making sure that all exterior lights are in proper working order. When pre-production begins, you may want to inform the local police of your schedule and ask them to give extra patrols to the parking lot and streets surrounding your church.

Once rehearsals begin, it is always a good idea to have only one door to the facilities being used unlocked, with someone monitoring those who enter. There should be a "sign in" system in place for accurate records of those coming and going and their whereabouts on the property.

Any minor, whether accompanied by a parent or authorized adult leader, should "check in and out" with the stage manager or person dedicated to this task upon arrival and before leaving the building, whether for that particular day or just momentarily. The kids may be escorted simply across the street to the donut shop or to another building for separate practice sessions or to be fitted for costumes or just to play while waiting, but a designated person on your production staff should always be aware of that. Parents rightfully will become upset if they arrive to pick up their children and no one knows where they are. More about this subject is covered in chapter 6 (discussing responsibilities of the production coordinator and stage manager.)

Tools belonging to individuals should be marked with their names. The production coordinator should keep a record of all tools which are stored on site, and of their owners. Tools should be centrally located during use and properly locked in storage during the off-hours.

Depending on the neighborhood and history of crime in the area, special security may be necessary during off hours (usually at night). Once the set has been loaded in, it may be necessary to request extra police patrols for the parking lot and bordering streets. If the risk is high and the budget allows, a security guard could be hired to patrol the grounds at night. One or two cast or crew members may volunteer to sleep at the set if circumstances require this additional precaution. We have had to do this more than once, especially when renting a hall or auditorium to house a production that the church building could not easily accommodate. (In such instances, perhaps the hall was providing the security as a part of the rental fee and it was not sufficient to meet our requirements, etc. In one production, it was the provided security personnel and cleaning crews that were in fact stealing costumes and prop pieces during the week of dress rehearsal!)

Performances yield greater security risks due to the volume of people: hundreds or thousands on site for each performance. Usually, ushers are capable of handling indoor security during the performances. The three weak areas of security are the stage area, the backstage area, and the parking lot.

As the audience enters, it will immediately become curious at the sight of the set, especially if it extends into the aisles and seating area. Undoubtedly some children and a even a few adults will want to wander onto the stage or touch some props. Ushers or security personnel should be stationed to prevent this, and if necessary, signs should be posted. You don't want your many months of work to be destroyed in a few seconds. Props or special effects may be set to work at critical times during the performance and if disturbed may bring the show to a halt. The stage should remain off limits even after the show, and "guards" should remain posted until the building is clear. There is also a liability issue to be concerned with—you don't want an audience member to fall off the stage or trip over a light cable.

During performances, security should be provided to the backstage area including the dressing rooms. The entire cast and crew may be occupied at the same time, leaving all valuables in the dressing rooms vulnerable to theft. (We once had all purses and wallets stolen from a locked dressing room during a performance.) Because during each show certain actors need to make entrances and exits that are not perhaps from an ordinary location, certain doors are left unlocked in order to accommodate such moments in time. Your security staff will need to be alerted to those places and once the moment arrives can verify the action having been completed by that performer prior to securing the door for the remainder of the performance. If a door is to be accessed by more than one performer, it should be monitored by cameras or a designated person for the duration of each show.

After the production has closed, security should be applied to the storage of the sets and props. They should be secure and safe from vandalism and weather. They are a valuable investment that you will want to continue to use in future productions.

Safety

Concentration on safety should be in the foreground of every production for a variety of reasons. Consideration for the health and safety of others, the loss of time, and the loss of a key performer due to injury are just a few of the concerns.

Most accidents and injuries occur during the construction of the sets and props. Only qualified carpenters and electricians should be allowed to handle equipment appropriate to their trade. It is not advisable to allow teenagers or inexperienced persons to operate power tools or electrical wiring. A qualified expert may supervise or even train one of these persons to do so; however, care must be taken in the selection of such persons. There are plenty of other "set" jobs to which volunteers can be assigned.

You should have a very thorough first-aid kit available and accessible during all rehearsal, construction, and meeting times. Following is a list of some basics. You may have means of collecting a more complete kit, and if so, you should.

- *Cuts and abrasions:* assorted Band-Aids, assorted gauze, surgical tape, adhesive tape, tourniquets, antiseptic cream/spray, peroxide, iodine, pressure bandages
- *Sprains and breaks:* ice packs, heat packs, splints, slings. Icy Hot (Ben Gay)
- *Internal:* aspirin, Tylenol, antacid tablets, ipecac syrup (induce vomiting)
- *Burns:* burn cream, cold pack, saline solution, large gauze, distilled water
- *Other topicals:* alcohol, betadine solution, sunscreen, antiseptic sprays/creams
- *Equipment:* scissors, tweezers, splinter removal kit (needle, tweezers, magnifying glass), Q-tips, thermometer and sleeves, airway, sharp knife, razor blades, medicine (eye) dropper, measuring cup, matches, flashlight
- *Eyes:* eye wash solution, gauze squares, surgical tape, eye patch.

You should also have a first-aid manual in the kit. Most of these items are recommended by the American Red Cross's "Standard First Aid & CPR" course. Among other things, you may wish to include:

- a trauma blanket (useful not only for shock, but also for the American Red Cross approved method of splinting legs, ankles, and possibly other body parts),
- plastic airways, and
- latex gloves.

A vital part of any first aid kit is a large supply of disposable latex gloves. The individual performing first aid should, as a matter of regular practice, slip on a pair of gloves when dealing with *any* sort of open wound. The protection goes both ways, and beyond the actual protection offered, there is a psychological protection offered as well, especially if gloves are used in *every* case. While this may seem extreme, just look at any emergency room. It's good medicine even beyond the concerns of blood safety. There are diseases other than HIV (contrary to what many people would believe) that you should worry about when dealing with blood and other bodily fluids. Hepatitis B, for example, is more contagious, and can be transmitted through respiratory droplets (coughing), blood, feces, and other methods.

The procedure when entering a trauma scene as we have been taught is to consider the following questions:

1. Is the scene safe? (Put gloves on.) Can I enter without being hurt? If not, make it safe or call the experts.

2. What is the mechanism of injury or nature of illness? How did the person get hurt? (Pipe dropping on head, hand caught in saw, etc.) What is the major problem that they are complaining about? (Abdominal pain, chest pain, etc.) Some injuries can hide from you, especially serious ones.

3. How many patients are there?

4. Do I need help? Should I call 911? If the person is apparently badly hurt, has an altered mental status (are they dizzy or disoriented?), is unconscious, or has trouble breathing, then call 911 before you do *anything* else. If you know CPR, then you will know what to do to assess the patient for Basic Life Support. Also look for any apparent life threats, such as huge amounts of blood on the floor, major open wounds, punctures of the head, chest, or abdomen, and so forth. Calling the paramedics out of their base is not a crime, especially if you are uncertain as to how badly someone might be hurt.

Your budget should include all appropriate safety items such as gloves, safety glasses, dust masks, and hard hats. Safety glasses should always be worn when using power tools. Gloves can prevent minor cuts, burns, and splinters. Dust masks help prevent sickness from inhaling fumes and dust, and hard hats are used when working under high sets or overhead lighting equipment.

Check all tools and equipment for "shorts" and malfunctions. Never use faulty equipment for convenience or budget reasons. It is worth the cost to repair or replace these tools. The old adage, "the right tool for the right job," is one to remember, as it may save time, produce quality, and prevent injuries.

Special safety precautions should be taken when using ladders and scaffolding. Use whatever precautions are necessary, making certain you include harnesses and safety belts and use good judgement according to the task. There should always be several others below to guide, advise, supply, and if necessary "spot" the persons above. When working on lights from a grid, the lights should be hoisted up by rope or cable from the grid and not carried up the ladder.

On one production, one artist we know resisted our warnings and stood on a board stretched across the top of two six foot-ladders. This was obviously a safety risk. While he was painting scenery, the board slipped off the end of a ladder and he fell to the floor, landing on his back. He was not seriously hurt, but the bucket of paint dumped on the organ and the carpet and splattered the front pews. Easily avoidable are these kinds of very expensive and near-fatal safety violations.

The design and construction crews should be concerned with the safety of the performers, as well as themselves. You may or may not receive a surprise visit from the local fire department. You should work under the assumption that you will. It is a good idea to take all original designs and plans to the fire department in advance of construction and ask their advice and help. Fireproofing certain materials prior to construction and assembly may be required to meet certain fire codes. You might be surprised at their support from that point on. Make sure that you meet all safety and fire codes throughout the production process. All fire extinguishers and fire alarms should be serviced to date and extra fire extinguishers placed around the set.

The performers will trust that the sets and props they use were made with complete safety in mind. Platforms should be built with the proper material strength and size, properly braced, and free of sharp and hazardous edges. Any overhead sets, lights, cables, and such should be secured with safety cable and tested for strength.

Each day after construction and with ample time before rehearsal, all tools and hazardous objects must be removed and secured from all audience, stage, backstage, and dressing areas. Floors should be cleaned and checked for nails, wood shavings, and the like.

We once had an unfortunate accident result from such a safety violation. Our construction crew was laying carpet on the stage and securing it with industrial staples. All tools and equipment were secured prior to rehearsal, but the stage was not thoroughly checked or swept. At rehearsal, dancers were performing "mule kicks" (jumping to a handstand and pushing back onto their feet). One young man landed his hand on a row of industrial staples, slicing a deep cut through the muscle. That required hand surgery. The man had to be replaced and his part learned by someone else. The crew, the producers, and the church had to take full responsibility for the accident.

During rehearsals and performances, there will be cables and cords running in aisles, on the stage, and even dangling from above. All these should be properly secured and taped. Wide duct tape is excellent for taping down cords. If, after taping a number of cords together, the bump is too high, they should be covered or marked to prevent tripping.

The safety and security department should be aware of the location of all emergency telephones numbers for nearby medical and fire facilities, and the whereabouts of the nearest hospitals and medical centers, and have access to a phone. They should pass this information on to the entire crew and staff at the beginning of the production. In your original questionnaires to the cast and crew, ask for anyone who has any qualified medical training and CPR training. You might be surprised to find nurses, paramedics and even doctors right in your own group. This gives a little extra comfort to the safety and security department. They should also know whom to contact (the production coordinator and/or stage manager) who has the emergency and medical information release forms for cast and crew. They too should be aware of persons with medical problems such as allergies, heart conditions, asthma, and epilepsy, and should pay close attention to those people during production time.

During one production, we were aware that a carpenter had severe heart problems and was wearing a pace-maker. Had we not been aware of this, and exactly what to look for, we might not have recognized the early symptoms of a heart attack that he was experiencing even as yet unknown to him while he was working alongside another building a stage platform. We were able to get him to the hospital in plenty of time, and we have been fortunate to work with him numerous times since this incident.

The cast and crew will endure many weeks of full schedules and long hours. Fatigue and stress will undoubtedly increase susceptibility to colds, viruses, and other communicable diseases. Stress the importance of rest, vitamins, and good hygiene to the entire cast and crew. Ask the hospitality crew to provide hot tea and honey, and plenty of other liquids. Throat lozenges and cough drops may also be placed at the same location. Only non-prescription, over-the-counter medicines should ever be provided by the church. Once we had a pharmacist donate samples of a well-known cold medicine. A cast member took one for a cold without realizing he was allergic to it. Within hours his skin turned red, all his extremities swelled, and it was necessary to take him to the emergency room. Again, this was properly handled and he recovered fully after treatment was rendered—no loss, no lawsuit, no problem.

Accidents may happen during performances. There should be someone, not actually involved in the performance, waiting backstage and prepared for such a case. One common event during church productions is fainting from heat, stress, or excitement. Along with a complete first-aid kit, ammonia inhalants should be accessible.

CHAPTER SEVENTEEN

DRESS REHEARSAL WEEK

Months of preparation, hundreds and sometimes thousands of collective man-hours, have all led up to this week. This week leading into the opening performance is also known as "Dress Week." We believe that from this point forward, we would best be serving your needs by outlining the sequence of events that should now take place and the persons responsible for those events. Let it be understood that by this time, everything that will be used during the performance will have been acquired. Whether it was borrowed, leased, purchased, or made, it is now ready for use during dress week. This applies to *all items*—items used by the crew, the cast, and even the audience. Needless to say, everyone involved in a non-performance capacity has been well-informed and confirmed for their commitment from this week through the close, and where appropriate, the strike.

Let's work backwards from the first performance to now and lay out a suggested Dress Week plan. For example, let's decide that for this run of performances, the shows opening weekend performances will take place on Friday, Saturday, and Sunday evenings. This allows four week-nights in Dress Week for working and running the show.

The weekend prior to Dress Week can then be utilized by the technical staff and crews to conduct the "Dry-Tech" meeting (which is detailed later in this chapter). In preparation for the actual instruction and practice of equipment operation, the tech director will supervise the final equipment set-up, running cables to power sources and the control boards (usually located within the tech booth), and run a general test of all equipment. Back-up microphones, batteries, light bulbs, and such are ready to be placed in the wings and booth for easy access and replacement as necessary during the performance run.

Let's review what should be in place and ready to go before Monday's rehearsal. The set, constructed and utilized during previous rehearsals as much as possible, has been finalized, painted, and dressed and is "show-ready." All set and character props are ready as well. Lighting and sound crews have hung their equipment, or placed (in previously established locations) all items that will be used during the performance. All cords are taped, secured, and masked wherever possible, and safety chains are securing the lights. The sound department will have placed all stationary microphones (and determined assignments for all radio microphones) and sound monitors. Glow tape has been attached to all the set pieces, set props, and areas in the wings as pre-determined by the stage manager, lighting and/or set designers. Makeup and special effects items that need to be applied have been prepared, costumes and accessories are ready, musicians are rehearsed, and ushers and child-care workers are lined up. Everyone is excited and anticipation is high. Dress week is finally here.

Dry Tech

It is often during the weekend prior to Dress Week that the director (often along with the technical director) will meet with the tech crews to give them their scripts and cues. The tech scripts (laid out to allow room for appropriate cues to be identified alongside the corresponding music or dialogue) should have been prepared and ready for distribution at this meeting. *Note: all crew members already should have read a regular script and attended one or more run-through rehearsals.* At this meeting, everyone sits where they can comfortably write *in pencil* their cues as previously determined by the director onto their respective scripts in the section dedicated for this purpose while viewing the actual set or the set model. (During this tech rehearsal or meeting they do not yet have to be at the positions they will occupy during the dress rehearsals and performances.) The director will assign the sequence and explain his general, predetermined cues to the crew members (knowing these cues may change in sequence or intensity, once they're seen in the context of an actual dress rehearsal). These cues will be identified by a coded system (alphabetical or numerical) by whoever will be "calling the show," most often the production manager or the technical director.

Our suggestion would be to have the production manager call the show, thereby leaving the technical director free to respond to any critical needs that may arise during an actual performance. If this is true in your case, then the PM and the director already will have reviewed the cues that are now being relayed to all crew members, and the PC's script will reflect those cues, already coded. Let us strongly suggest that the director recognize and capitalize upon this time to reinforce the authority of the PC at this juncture approaching dress week in the presence of all the crew. He can do this most effectively by acknowledging the responsibility of the PC and step aside, allowing him to give the cues as coded to the crew at this meeting. (The director will still be there to explain the intent or purpose of certain sequences as necessary and so forth.) Although the stage manager will be positioned backstage to coordinate the flow of cast members and props, wardrobe, makeup, and stage hands during the run of the show for each performance, it is important for the stage manager to be present if possible at this dry tech session, too. The stage manager will be in direct, constant communication with the PC (who will be stationed in the tech booth) via headset during the remaining rehearsals and performances, and will be aware of all occurrences happening in the tech booth, in the audience, and on the stage, that might necessitate some kind of change. Likewise the PM will be made aware of events and occurrences on stage and in the wings by the stage manager, so as to "call the show" appropriately. Therefore, directions from the PC may be relayed to the SM, that do not correspond to any rehearsed cues, but will need to be adhered to without question or explanation. This must be made clear to all cast and crew alike at the first combined rehearsal, your cue-to-cue rehearsal.

Headsets will not be used during the dry-tech meeting, but will be required for the cue-to-cue and all rehearsals and performances thereafter. As the manner in which cues will be given to the various crews is determined at this meeting, it is important to have prepared for this prior to the dry-tech with your tech-director and perhaps the head of the sound department. Headsets may be limited due to their availability or to restricted communication channels. Therefore, determining who will be using them (other than the PC and SM) will depend upon the following:

- the location of the tech booth and its proximity to the audience
- whether the booth partitioned off, via glass, a wall, or by whatever means, so the crew is not heard in the audience
- the ability of certain crew members to receive/give audible and/or visual cues to those within an enclosed or well-secluded booth, station, or backstage area
- the placement and number of combined spotlight operators, backstage crew, and special-effects crew members who may be able to share or take direction from someone with a headset.

Let us suggest, depending on the size of your crew, that headsets should be allocated at the very least for the following positions: PC, SM, light board operator, sound engineer, conductor or assistant to the conductor (your conductor may already have another headset for the music click track), and house manager. From that core group, it is advisable to dedicate headsets to various crew members (spotlight operators, property master, runners for mics, special effects, costumes, security, head usher, etc.). The technical director may have one, but usually will be stationed in the tech booth, and if emergencies arise, he will attend to them and then have contact with the booth via those persons with headsets for whom he is resolving problems. Also a consideration will be the number of cordless headsets, headsets hard-wired to a specific point, and intercoms that may be accessible from the booth, and/or other dedicated backstage points accessible by the SM that will not disrupt the performance on-stage.

Following this dry-tech meeting, those persons responsible for the actual running of the equipment should be instructed on the proper operation and care of the equipment: spotlights, radio microphones, special effects devices, moving set pieces, or props, and so forth. If you can arrange to follow this meeting and instruction period with a cue-to-cue rehearsal, that would be ideal. Otherwise the cue-to-cue should take place the Monday evening of this particular dress week.

One more aspect that we have not yet addressed would be the dress requirements of your crew members. Stage hands, runners, spotlight operators, and anyone who may be seen by the audience at any time are almost always dressed in slacks, long-sleeved shirts, socks, and shoes that are solid black in color. This keeps them as inconspicuous as possible and less likely to distract from the events on-stage, especially in those scenes when your "stage" is expanded to include the audience area or when a stagehand, whether backstage or offstage, is unexpectedly within sight-lines of any audience member during the performance. This should begin with your tech dress rehearsal (at least in a limited format of perhaps all black shirts) and then be fully instituted with your final dress rehearsal. Let all cast and crew be in full costume for this last rehearsal on Thursday night!

Cue-to-Cue Rehearsal

The cue-to-cue rehearsal involves the principle actors (and supporting cast whenever possible) on the set, with "actual" props if available or "working props" at the least. The cues should be given from the pre-set levels of what has been established in the house and on the set prior to the admission of the audience into the auditorium. These cues would be for pre-show music, house and stage lights. If you are to have a live orchestra, the rehearsal pianist and/or organist are all that is needed for this rehearsal. Taped music should be included, however, if it is used in any part of the show. Naturally, the lights and all technical elements of the show should be operational and safely secured in place. At this rehearsal, do *not* run through the show with full dialogue and music. Run instead from the first cue-line or direction that will bring a change in any cue for music, lighting, sound, sets, costumes, props, or special effects. Note also that the entrance or exit of any cast member must also be included as a cued-moment if it affects either lighting or sound departments. The director will instruct the actors as to how much dialogue should be spoken prior to his moving them to the next cue-line. The purpose of this rehearsal is to allow the tech crew to comply with the instructions given at the previous dry-tech meeting. This allows them to see, firsthand, the person(s) they may be responsible for following with the spotlight (e.g., noting their exact position[s] on stage). Therefore, it will be necessary for all headsets to be in place and functional before this rehearsal is begins. Going from cue to cue should require approximately half the time of an actual performance. Preliminary changes can be penciled-in.

Tech-Dress Rehearsal

The tech-dress rehearsal will require full running and tech crews with the cast members getting into full costume and makeup. If following the cue-to-cue rehearsal, then this call-time will need to be adjusted to allow all cast and crew members time to become show-ready! This will be the time to verify the pre-determined call-times of the cast and crew. Therefore, the child-care and nursery workers need to be ready to receive the children of those with the earliest call-times. Providing time for those who were called for the cue-to-cue to grab a bite to eat is important. (You may want to provide them with food, at either their expense or that of the production.)

By this tech-dress rehearsal, presumably on Tuesday night of your dress week, all crew stations are set up with the necessary equipment to be operated, along with tables, chairs or stools, as appropriate and available. Small, directional lights (gelled if necessary) for the stands or tables, which hold the cued scripts during the show, should be in place. Though only the pianist (and organist) shall be present at this tech-dress rehearsal, the orchestra seating is arranged with music stands, lights, cables, monitors, and the like in their respective places. Prop tables are marked and may also be dimly lit, as will the back stage areas where spillage or bleeding onto the set is not a possibility. Prop lists and sequences of all the acts and scenes are posted in the wings. Sign-in sheets are posted for all cast and crew members. Bathrooms to be used exclusively by the production company and not available to the general public have had signs posted on them (indicating their restricted use and directions to other facilities that have been reserved for the general public). Costume and makeup crews have prepared their strategy for each of their respective responsibilities, developing assignments for alternating call times for actors to report to costumes and makeup. Assorted clutter has been removed from the wings and the dressing areas. The dressing rooms have racks for the wardrobe and racks or boxes for accessories as well as the personal belongings of the cast and chorus. It is a good idea to have a character list posted, with the items of each person's wardrobe identified, and to have their names taped into those garments or items whenever possible. The crews' emergency items are packed and accessible: that is, tape (masking, duct, Scotch, double-sided), black and white thread, needles, scissors, seam-rippers, safety pins, string, hair spray, bobby pins, tissues, Vaseline, smelling salts, Band-Aids, cough drops, bottles of water, cups, aspirin, and such. Set crews have their kits of cordless drills, screws, and duct tape, and sound crews will have the same in the way of batteries, double stick tape, and so forth. The room in which all cast and crew will assemble prior to the call "Places!" needs to have ample space for all, even if it is a tight squeeze. Chairs may be provided for as many as possible.

Tech-dress is the first rehearsal in which the director will be focusing on the proper integration of all performers with the music, the sound, the lights, the makeup, the special effects, the props, and with one another. The director will use this rehearsal to preview the quality and levels of sound, the intensity and colors of lighting, the lead time of music to action or movement of some kind, etcetera. From this, he can determine if the pre-established cues suit the purposes intended. If not, they can be changed easily without wearing out the energy levels of the cast in a full-on performance rehearsal.

Once it starts, it will be conducted as a run-through. The tech crews and running-crews will be at their appointed places, performing their respective jobs. Allowances for stopping should be restricted to such problems as the taped music equipment malfunctioning, feedback from the microphones to be handled, and circuit overloads resulting in power-loss. Otherwise, it will go from start to finish with actual intermission time allotted only if one is scheduled during the performance. All performers should be well beyond the need for line interpretation, or cue-lines to be fed, for that matter. However, it often happens that, for one reason or another, an actor will enter before the sound cue has been given or that the lighting operator, despite the prompting call given by the Pc, will be slow in responding to his cue sheet. These are what this rehearsal is for. The actors need to be prepared for their inevitability, and not frustrated that the performance as a whole is not as perfect as they perceived it would be by this time. After all, this is the first time it has all been put together. It is a rehearsal, *not* a performance.

Following this run-through, all cast and crew members will sit together. Lead by the director, production coordinator, and technical director, they will review the rehearsal, ask questions, and point out potential problems. Some cast or crew members may think it is unnecessary for them to stay for this portion of the rehearsal. It must be stressed that this discussion is a very critical part of the rehearsal process. If conducted following the cue-to-cue rehearsal, cast and crew alike are bound to be exhausted, even irritable or on-edge. It is important that the sharing of problems be done in a light, matter-of-fact style.

Allowing for humorous interjections will keep any one person or department from perceiving it as a personal affront or a criticism of his ability.

Problems that will be noted should be those pertaining to the integration of the tech crews with the performers, such as:

- microphone cords which need to be lengthened or shortened
- minor refocusing of lights, gels, barn-door
- batteries to be replaced
- glow tape to be added
- monitors to be relocated
- relocation of set and character props (both on and offstage)
- adjustment to the moving of set or prop pieces (pertaining to sequence or possibly the person who was first assigned and how it affects his ability to meet his next cue)
- costume/makeup changes and the time allotted for same
- distribution of radio mics to various cast members and hand-off to assigned crew as planned during or after the performance
- possible changes in the timing or sequencing of cues pending the capabilities of the cast and the crew to meet their next cue to be evaluated at this review.

Opening/closing barn-door to control the coverage of light on a specific area or group may need to be done during this meeting, while you have the full cast/chorus there to take their places on stage while this adjustment is made. The director also may ask to see certain cues (with the appropriate actors in place on stage), to see if he wants to decrease or change light levels, colors, sequencing, and so forth. Also, the adjustment of certain props, costumes, and the like may need to be done with some individuals. Those people may be asked to stay after the general discussion, to clarify their needs with the department responsible for their particular problem.

However, keep in mind: not all problems need to be resolved before the dismissal of the cast as a whole. Some problems will be more technically based and may require more experimentation to develop the most effective solution.

Giving notes, encouraging all persons in cast and crew alike, and thanking them for their personal sacrifices (in the context of the production) prior to dismissal, are some of the most important tasks of the evening. Once these are accomplished, the production coordinator may ask the stage manager to be available immediately to assist the cast, wardrobe, and prop crews as the cast prepares to go home. Once the cast have been released and their needs taken care of by the running crew members within the wardrobe and makeup departments (leaving the department heads to continue meeting with other crews), those crew members should rejoin the crew meeting for their additional input. Proper cleanup, care, and storage of props, costumes, and such can be dealt with at the close of this crew meeting. Once the formal crew discussion is closed, the various crews will need to attend to those tasks deemed necessary from this tech rehearsal, either now, or prior to the call-time of the next rehearsal. The next rehearsal will be a complete dress rehearsal which must run from start to finish without a hitch of any kind. After all, there are only two rehearsals left to "get it right."

The director, production coordinator, stage manager, and technical director now have a keen awareness of all the small things yet to be done, to pull this production together. This first dress rehearsal (and subsequent meeting) was probably very enlightening, letting you see just how far you really are, and how much more remains to be done! Both are exciting and overwhelming prospects.

The PC is responsible for assisting each crew member and/or department in identifying the tasks left to be done, and determining the priority in which they must be accomplished. Lists of things yet to do probably include such items as:

- applying finishing touches and/or repairs to various set pieces, props, costumes, special effects
- picking up those perishable props that need to be replaced with every show
- arranging for proper cleaning of the entire grounds, which will require your having all items in their proper place (making sure all props are put away and not lying on the prop tables for someone to break or misplace, or in the costume room, or on the set, or in someone's car!)
- returning most trash receptacles to their original locations (by now you have probably borrowed just about every one the church owns, with the exception of the one in the nursery, of course)
- printing the program and getting people to fold, assemble, and package them in bundles appropriate to your maximum seating capacity per performance
- arranging the opening night presentations for appropriate cast and crew members
- confirming the nursery workers, ushers and security personnel, etc., one more time.

As usual, following every rehearsal and performance, the SM and PM will need to secure the buildings, noting and compensating for things which may have escaped the attention of other members of the cast and crew. This post-performance walk-through is a mandatory procedure regardless of the size, the experience, or the professionalism of the cast and crew. It should be thorough, and it is recommended that two people share this job, both to double-check each other and for safety reasons. Notes for yourself would include the review of each crew's station to see what can be done to make it a more efficient, clean, quiet, or comfortable place to work. Never assume that the crew is incapable of overlooking that which may seem very obvious to you:

- Are all lights and power units off or disconnected at the main switch?
- Are the sound and radio microphones turned off and the batteries removed from designated units?
- Have all appropriate items been stored in a locked cabinet?
- Are the headsets collected or stored in the assigned stations?
- Is litter strewn about any of the work areas or in the auditorium?
- Has anyone gone home without "checking-in" their props or wardrobe?
- Has anyone left behind any personal items of great personal or monetary value (i.e., their wallet, jewelry, eye glasses, etc.) which they may need to retrieve prior to the next scheduled meeting?

As tired as you may be, making immediate notes of things you observed during your walk-through, as opposed to "in the morning," really does save a lot of time. It allows you to come back the next morning with goals already established. You will not lose time trying to recall the various things that you thought sure you would remember from the night before. Having a list to refer to, and to prioritize once you have "slept on it," helps you to establish a clear direction for the day.

As stated in a previous chapter, it has been our practice never to allow any one person to leave the grounds or the buildings without the knowledge and the companionship of another. It is a precaution that sometimes seems silly or unfounded, but should be adhered to in the strictest sense. This custom should begin with the first pre-production meeting and continue until the last item is stored away at the close of the strike.

Dress Rehearsal & Piano Dress Rehearsal

Usually, the key staff/crew people have arranged to spend the full day working on the necessary tasks to be done before tonight's rehearsal. This actually will be the first time to run through the production as if it were a true performance. The tech crews will have had their first taste of the play, as a show, the previous night, and the actors will have experienced the reality that this is really coming together. The *piano dress rehearsal* will include the full orchestra for the first time with the cast and crew.

Because this is a dress rehearsal in every sense of its meaning, we are also rehearsing the getting-dressed part of the pre-performance schedule. Therefore, let's look at what is expected of the cast during performance nights so we can put it into practice now. They should arrive earlier than their call-times, to sign in their children with the child-care providers; and to confirm or verify the placement of certain props in the house, on or back stage, prior to either their call-time in the dressing areas or prior to the time the House is scheduled to open. Prior to arrival they need to have eaten and made whatever phone calls had to be made. Their call-time should have allowed them time to "warm-up" physically and/or vocally, and run any scene or special effects device that was not properly working the previous night, if requested by the PC on behalf of any crew. For this they may need to confer with the PC first, who will either inform the actor of the revisions made, or refer them to the appropriate crew member for instruction before the House is "open."

The actors should not be allowed to roam the property once in costume or make-up. This includes taking something to their car, their mate, or their parents. The illusion of reality you establish from the moment the audience arrives on the grounds and enters the House will be next to impossible to achieve if any member of the audience should encounter a member of the cast already in costume and/or makeup. All actors should remain in the dressing room area or in the general meeting room once they are ready. Ideally, they will not be allowed to eat or drink anything that will stain or alter the look of their character in any way. Therefore, it is suggested that even cherry-flavored cough drops be substituted by the honey and lemon varieties, as they do not discolor the tongue in any significant manner. Once in the general meeting area, the cast can continue to run lines and to warm up vocally or physically until the general assembly meeting or group warm-ups are started.

All actors and specified crew members must participate in the general assembly of cast/crew which will take place before the start of every show. It should even be considered as the start of the show itself. This time is critical for the dispensation of information, to share and resolve minor problems, to bring unity of purpose, and to uplift both cast and crew so that everyone is performance-ready physically, psychologically, and spiritually.

It must also be noted that once the show begins, it begins for everyone, regardless of the time that may pass before an entrance by a particular character (or group of charac-ters) takes place. They should wait quietly in the assigned areas and not interact with each other or fellow crew members so as to distract them from their cues.

On occasions where you have stationed certain performers to wait a few moments in the lobby or other "non-restricted audience areas," from which an entrance must be made, they may be approached by audience members with questions concerning water fountains and rest-room facilities, and so forth. The performer should instruct them to see an usher, if one is located nearby, or give clear direction themselves in a quiet manner, only if it does not prevent them, or anyone else, from keeping their next cue. Ideally, they should not interact with members of the audience at all, and at the very least any interaction should not be initiated by them. It goes without saying, but indulge us anyway. The actors who will be stationed in such areas will have specific call times which should be cued into the script as to when they are to arrive at that particular position from which to make an entrance, hand off a mic, or whatever. They should wait quietly and not bring attention to themselves by their movement or even quiet talking among themselves, with nearby crew, ushers or those persons in that area, so as to distract from the performance in progress.

It follows then, that the play is not over until it is over. Therefore, when a performer or crew member is done with his respective performance/duty, he is not free to mingle with anyone outside of the production team, nor to leave until...

- the entire play is performed,
- all costumes, props, etc. have been signed-in by the appropriate crew member,
- notes are received regarding the next call-time, and/or
- they are officially released.

One reason for this mandate is to maintain the illusion-of-reality for each member of the audience. Another reason is to preserve the unity of the team and to keep them well informed as to possible changes that may occur from one performance to the next. Perhaps most important is the task of being certain that all things and all persons are accounted for at the opening and close of each performance.

Though these points are essential for the production to run smoothly and with integrity, it is important that they be conveyed at the right time, with the right attitude. By the time you reach Dress Week, the cast and crew have invested an enormous amount of time, energy, and money, and made personal sacrifices of which certain members of the production team may be unaware. Therefore, it is suggested they be informed of these rules at the close of a rehearsal prior to Dress Week. However it is done, it should not require a long period of time to review. Many of the requests are already incorporated or practiced by most members of the cast/crew, and they just need to be identified or reinforced one time with all persons present. Having them in writing is helpful, perhaps on the call-sheets which will be distributed for this rehearsal week. They should be reviewed from the standpoint of preserving all the work done thus far—and out of respect for the production itself and its purpose.

The crew members will also have call-times to observe and duties to fulfill before the house is open. Crew members in the makeup and wardrobe departments usually have an earlier call due to the hours of preparation required. Those crew members will need to have all items unlocked and set out on shelves or tables for ease in access and use. Ironing or "distressing" will be under way, if necessary, by those in the wardrobe department. The property master will need to have access to all items for which he is responsible in order to distribute them to the appropriate characters and places. Persons running lights will need to verify the proper functioning of all boards and light units. All cables and cords will be checked to be certain they are still properly connected, taped, secured, and masked. The same should apply to the sound, special effects, and stage crews, with ample time for cast members to be on-stage for vocal warm-up and quick rehearsals of problem areas if needed and planned by certain department crews or performers beforehand.

The house manager will be responsible for the seating areas, the foyer or lobby area, the rest rooms, and even the general grounds. These areas need to be clean, orderly, and appropriately supplied with towels, soap, programs, and such. The placement of all on-stage props, and the verification of all lights, sound, and special effect items must be done *before* opening the house.

Let's define now this phrase, "opening the house." This refers to the moment when the audience members are allowed to enter the auditorium or area where they will be seated to watch the show. This means they will be seeing the set for the first time and interacting with members of the ushering team. This is why the pre-set lighting cues have been cued up already, all on-stage props have been placed earlier, and any on-stage rehearsals of cast members, singers, and others have already been done. Pre-show music cues may have been determined for the entire period from the opening of the house to "curtain," or may be called at a mid-way portion after the house has been opened and prior to curtain. It is important to distinguish the difference between opening the house and allowing audience members into the foyer or lobby areas where they may wait for the house to open. Since the cast and crew may be working on-stage during the time that this occurs and may be overheard by those waiting audience members, you may want to plan for your audience to wait in an alternate building, such as a fellowship room or hall where they have access to rest-room facilities, water fountains, and even perhaps refreshments service (either complimentary or for set prices or donations only). You may want to provide this opportunity to your audience depending on the season and corresponding weather conditions, and the time of the performance itself (i.e., whether it is a night performance, or a performance following a matinee where the cross flow of audience exiting one performance and those waiting for the next may be intermingled, etc.).

Finally, the pre-set lighting and sound levels will need to be adjusted and cued up before the PC will cue the house manager to open. Once the house is open, the performance is under way in many respects. No last minute activity should have to be done at this time that will be noticed by audience members visually or audibly. The finishing up of prop placement backstage may continue if it can be done quietly, though it should be completed by the time of the general assembly. (Usually, the general assembly takes place thirty minutes prior to curtain and coincides with the opening of the house.)

General assembly.—To allow for as many crew members to participate in the general assembly as possible, ushers may be stationed to ensure that no one tampers with any of the equipment or props, nor enters into the areas restricted for cast/crew only. The production coordinator and stage manager will lead the entire assembly time. Group notes are given, vocal warm-ups and stretching exercises can be conducted, highlights of audience responses from previous performances may be shared, and prayer will take place during this time. The director, music director, choreographer, tech director, and others will each have an opportunity to address the group, but should do so mostly to inspire, encourage or reinforce the notes already relayed by the PC and/or SM. *Note:* Most of the notes each of those persons may want to give will be communicated to the group by PC/SM in the most appropriate manner. (The PC may choose to relay the initial notes to individual departments or crew members before the general assembly of cast and crew, and then reinforce them to the group as a whole. This way, respect to that department or individual is given with the advance notice and even a suggestion from that person or department that can be communicated at the general assembly may be received that is extremely helpful.) The production coordinator or stage manager may need occasionally to duck out of the meeting to observe the activity of the audience, and to make sure that the security staff, the ushers, and the skeleton crews are experiencing no difficulties with their pre-show responsibilities.

Places.—The PC, who will be calling the show, must consider the status of several items before ever calling "places" to crew/cast members. The number of audience members waiting to be seated, including those in the rest rooms, is of course the primary factor. Essentially, opening the house to the audience means the cast and crews are all ready, so the audience becomes the focus at this time. Often, depending on your facility's capabilities, you may wish to flash the lights in the lobby and rest rooms as well as in the house to alert all audience members that the program is about to begin. Ushers may need calmly to notify people in the lobby or even in the immediate exterior of the building that it is time to be seated. A live or pre-recorded announcement indicating the same may be your choice, or any combination of the three.

Also to be considered is the time which the program is scheduled to begin. It should never be started before the scheduled curtain, regardless of the circumstances. Your house may be full, the cast and crews may be ready—so be it. You still must wait to begin the show at the advertised time. The professionalism of this one aspect will gain you much respect and appreciation from your audience and your production team as well. Starting within two minutes is acceptable; starting any later than five minutes should be avoided. When this is necessary, a concise announcement should be made to inform your audience of the delay and that the show will begin momentarily (if that is the case). If you anticipate an extended delay due to technical difficulties which must be overcome, that must be communicated also.

Additional pre-show music, live or taped, should be standing by for such an occurrence as this, and periodic announcements may be made. ("We anticipate starting in five minutes. We thank you for your patience and understanding during this time.") Persons who require use of the rest-room facilities will be able to make judgments accordingly and anyone who may decide the delay is too long can choose to depart, hopefully encouraged by the house manager to return for another performance.

The crew is usually "called to places" approximately five minutes prior to the beginning of the show. The running crew (i.e., those persons responsible for specific tasks during the performance itself) should all be at their places within thirty seconds after receiving their call to places. This thirty-second response time applies to all persons—cast and crew—when their call to places has been given. Verification that no changes occurred during their absence and that all headsets are functioning properly must be done immediately. It should be clear that crew members are at their positions with scripts/cue sheets in hand and headsets "on" so as to respond to a cue within seconds of its being directed. This way, last minute instructions can still be given before the show begins. The skeleton crew, which missed the general assembly, can be notified of changes affecting them such as solo reassignments and spotlight changes.

At this time, all orchestra members should be in their positions, tuned up and ready. The orchestra sign-in sheet has already been reviewed, and any member still absent has been noted by the SM and conductor. Modifications to accommodate any absence should have been handled already by the conductor/music director and SM with the production manager. Should the absent member arrive after the performance begins, appropriate stage personnel will be alerted to assist that person upon arrival, per directions given by the PC.

Holding the show for any person—cast or crew—should never occur. Having understudies for all lead roles and backup crew is always a good idea. The tech director can always take over a crew position himself or have another crew member assume a more demanding task (which he is capable of handling) and pull in a novice to occupy a more minor position, or he may choose to double up responsibilities whenever possible. The PC will work with the tech director and all departments in determining the adjustments to be made in the absence of a critical position or role. Regardless, the crew and orchestra should be ready when actors are called to places. The PC has a moment to confer with the ushers, and to communicate with various crews and the SM that all members of the production are ready for the show to begin.

The cast will be called to places two minutes prior to the show's start-up. Once the "ready" confirmation is made by all crews, and it is curtain time, the PC will call the beginning of the show. In cases where there may be a prolonged overture or musical prelude at the onset of the show, then actors may be called to places after the downbeat of the music has occurred. In either case, the show is now up and running! Break a leg (and all that stuff)!

During this rehearsal, as with any performance, the director, tech director, music director, choreographer, stage manager, and production manager may inconspicuously keep notes which will be discussed at a later time. It is never permissible for any one of these persons to override the performance with their input during the performance itself. If there is a major flaw, which is not already obvious to the general audience and can be inconspicuously corrected, then there is a course of action which may be taken. Either one of those persons, or the security staff, or the head usher must feel that in an emergency they may approach a technician with a headset to ask them to relay a specific point to the PC and SM. It may be something as simple as a monitor being out on one side of the house which has not been detected by the sound engineer, or something as serious as an injury sustained by a member of the cast, crew, or even audience which requires immediate action. Oftentimes, instances such as this may be related to the director who can then calmly, yet swiftly take them to the PM or tech director. The Director may be more accessible to the security staff or ushers than will the PC who is running the show. During a performance, any emergency requires swift action and should be brought to the immediate attention of the PC, via any possible means.

End of dress rehearsal.—Though this is "just a dress rehearsal," it is a performance nevertheless, and there is an audience just the same. When the performance rehearsal is completed, it is best not to have the audience stay for the notes that will be shared upon its conclusion. Let them have a moment with their friends and family members in the cast or crew, while the department heads briefly discuss the plan of action for the remainder of the evening. Then, announcements can be made by the SM or PC as to what action the crews, actors, and chorus should take (such as, do they stay in costume for notes or change to street clothes and return for notes in ten minutes?).

When notes are given, there may be reactions of the rehearsal audience shared by various persons of the cast or crew. These reactions may both support and counter what has been done thus far, and must be handled very carefully. Emotions are on the surface. Whether they are ones of exhilaration or discouragement, people are tired, and often their perspectives are not objective.

In either case, the director must consider the following. He may be far from where he wanted to be at this time. To encourage the crew and cast, that a flawless evening was not expected by him, nor should it have been from themselves, is critical. However, attitude, compliance, and effort on the part of all cast and crew must be undergirded. Therefore, the director must choose whether or not to play upon this fact, to "lay it on the line" and push for another run-through *tonight*, regardless of the time. He may even decide to go the other way, quietly thanking them for their endless hours of hard work, acknowledge that they are overtired and need to go home and rest as much as possible between now and tomorrow night's final dress rehearsal. Tomorrow is, after all, his last shot to make it right, to make it what he has envisioned it would be all along. It may be a long evening and certainly there is no letup between then and the weekend's performance run. It is a tough call, perhaps one that he should not make alone; seeking input from the PC beforehand is advisable.

He may also be right on track and have this time to praise them, yet warn them too of the dangers of being over-confident. Let them have tonight, but make them aware of the implications of letting down too soon, and the carelessness that often accompanies this attitude of complacency.

Do not neglect to pray for families that have patiently supported you, both here and at home; for your responsibilities outside of this play—giving thanks for all that has been learned and accomplished. Pray for increased trust, faith, and fellowship of individuals and of the church body through the discipline of hard work; for the upcoming run and the health of all involved. Remember, too, the audience members who will come, that they will feel not only welcome, but that they will be drawn to a deeper understanding of what it means to be a child of God, whether from the play's message itself or from the "message" they see in the lives of the membership.

It is imperative, however, that a small audience be invited at least once, perhaps on this final dress rehearsal Thursday night. This generates a sense of purpose that may not have been realized until this time, and it also brings a reality to the cast and crew of the impending opening. This audience should be selected carefully, perhaps to include the following: mates of those in the show (who are not participating as a member of the cast or running crews), ushers, security persons, and perhaps child-care workers (many of whom will be unable to see a show, as they have responsibilities elsewhere on the church grounds during the actual performances). Since this is not a polished performance meant for critical review, it should be composed of supportive persons. They should be asked to arrive as you would have the audience arrive on opening night, between curtain and thirty minutes prior to curtain; no earlier than that. They should not be allowed to go into the actors' dressing rooms, makeup rooms, backstage, on-stage, and so forth. Keep it, as much as possible, like you would have it for the performance run. During intermission, they may not interact with the cast nor crew. They are here "playing the part" of the audience and should "act" accordingly.

Likewise, Thursday would be the perfect evening to incorporate the ushers as a team and to give them instructions about their responsibilities before, during, and after each performance. Once they have seen the performance, they will have a better understanding of the sequence of events on and off-stage and respond from a more informed sense when given their respective assignments.

It cannot be over-emphasized that this particular team has an enormous responsibility for the safety of audience members (and from a creative aspect—for maintaining the illusion of reality established by all other departments) by keeping audience members out of restricted areas. The importance of doing so in a manner that is not easily mistaken for that of a drill-sergeant is also necessary. Their contact and interaction with individuals of the audience may be the first impression those audience members will have of the church. Perspective and balance are not to be lost now!

Making them aware of the following points or how to handle the following situations is imperative:
- reserved seating for special guests, handicapped seating for those with wheel chairs, the hearing impaired, visually impaired or other special needs
- late arrivals and late seating
- those with small children who may need direction to child-care facilities if such is to be provided to the audience in general or only to those who find themselves in exceptional situations
- how to deal with youth who are not accompanied by parents and are not behaving in an appropriate manner

- staff positions and areas of authority for each within the framework of the production and how those positions may be different from their church staff positions (In other words, if one of the pastors should make a request of an usher that would require him to leave his post or to override instructions given his assignment, it must be handled delicately but appropriately. The usher can always seek the assistance of the head usher or another person as appropriate to assist the pastor in his place, or to cover his position while assisting the pastor, or to gain permission for the pastor to perform whatever function he is attempting to do at a time that would be better.)
- when and which cast members are ever seen off-stage in an area accessible to the general audience is one factor (Keeping the audience, and even unfortunately members of the cast and crew from intruding into areas where they should not be before, after, and especially during the performance is one of their main functions. Though instructed otherwise, cast and crew members want to show their friends "how it all works." Though this may be appropriate for certain individuals, exceptions that are made must be communicated to those ushers by the SM or PC only).

Though there are many issues that you cannot foresee which may arise, you must take steps to prepare all members of your team to meet the challenges that they will face and to know when and from whom to seek assistance.

Also as members of the crew, they will have assigned call times and sign-in sheets or persons with whom to check-in, a dress code to follow, and so forth.

Final Dress Rehearsal

If your final dress is in fact your piano dress rehearsal, then rehearsal prior to your opening is now done. The next gathering will be for the "real thing." However, if this is not your situation and you have one more go at it, then let's make it count. Your tech crew has had time to work out all the bugs and polish the fading into and out of scenes, from every aspect. Just think how much you have improved from Monday night! Pray, as always, that your motives continue to be right, and that lives of both church members and guests will be affected by the performance and its inner message, and by the growth and love evident in the lives of those who have worked so diligently and so hard to bring together your church and your community.

CHAPTER EIGHTEEN

OPENING, CLOSING, & STRIKE

Opening Night

There is nothing that can compare with the range of emotions your cast and crew will experience throughout this day and night. Predominant will be feelings of anticipation intermingled with anxiety on the part of most participants. Last minute items, no doubt, have required attention on the part of the production coordinator, who in turn may have requested the assistance of various other crew members to be truly "show-ready" before opening tonight. Checking and rechecking the agenda, the notes, the set, and backstage areas to be certain nothing has been overlooked is inevitable.

General Assembly.—Another tradition within the theater world must also be included in tonight's general assembly prior to curtain. It is that of presenting acknowledgments to such persons as the leading lady (or ladies), the music director, technical director, and the director of the production itself. If appropriate, the rehearsal pianist and/or organist may be acknowledged as well. Originally a tradition honoring the key female figures involved, it has now expanded to include persons in positions without whom this evening would not be possible. The initial acknowledgment may be in the form of a card, a small gift, or a flower or flowers.

Keep in mind that, following the closing performance, there is often a "wrap-party" or gathering wherein gratuities of various sorts are also awarded. Sometimes these are limited to the director, the production and stage managers and those people behind the scenes who have dedicated themselves to bringing the most professional production possible to their church and their community. Usually a card that has been secretly passed among cast and crew will be presented to one or more of those to be recognized. Also, a bouquet of flowers or some small gift is presented then, especially if there were only verbal acknowledgments on the opening night. These gifts may be supported from collections taken among the group or partially accounted for within the production budget, or they may have been included in trade-outs for tickets, advertising in the playbill, or any combination thereof.

In this particular general assembly, it is important that no one person make any speech that is too long, or in any way demoralizes the energy and purpose of the pending performance. That includes the PC and SM as well. Of course, there will be critical reminders which must be relayed, but the attitude, tone, and sequence in which these are shared are also elements which cannot be devalued. As the PC intermittently will be checking the status of the house and the skeleton crews still in the auditorium, the positive reports brought back will help sustain the energy and adrenaline for this opening performance.

Let us take this time to share our thoughts about the performances themselves. Each is strictly that—a performance. The "show" is a composite of each individual performance of every member of the production team, cast, and running crews. Therefore, the show is not over at intermission, nor at the final curtain. The means of bringing closure to a show will vary from church to church and from production to production within each church. Closure, from the audience's perspective, is critical. Therefore, even after the applause has died away, it is important that the actors and crew recognize that the illusion of reality so carefully established earlier still remains. Though it is imperative to uphold that throughout the entire performance, it is also critical not to bring it to a shattering end once the performance is over. The behavior and interaction of the cast and crew, both with one another and with audience members, is still under the observation and scrutiny of those same audience members. Let's not extinguish too soon the "magic" of the theater. Let's not downplay nor brag about what everyone has worked so hard to make look effortless. Likewise: cynicism, sarcasm, bad-mouthing, or pointing out mistakes of that night's performance should not be done where any audience member may overhear—not inside, not in the parking lot, not the next day. You can destroy in a moment what you have sacrificed so much to gain, and never be the wiser. Be careful! (This point may be one of the topics you will want shared during the general assembly.)

It is the responsibility of the PC to watch the clock and not let this assembly time overextend into actual performance time! Often, the pastor may want to address the group for comment or for prayer before this first performance. It would be important to invite him to do so and to arrange the timing of this moment to get the group further into a show-ready state of mind.

And now, let's hope they are show-ready, because it is show time whether they are ready or not. *"Places,* everyone!"

Starting the show.—The exact moment the show is started is the sole responsibility of the production coordinator, if as established in the previous chapter, the PC will be calling the show. He alone will know when the cast, crew, and audience are ready. He will give the first cue that starts everything in motion. If anyone other than the PC should decide to intervene in this procedure, it could be disastrous.

Once, we were working with a church who had asked us for assistance in mounting a rather large-scale production for them. There were well over one hundred people in the cast and chorus, a large set with moving set pieces, and special effects devices throughout the play. During one particular performance, the music director (who was also the choir director) became concerned that the batteries in the radio microphones might not be sufficient to last the performance. He instructed one of the stage hands to go out and get some. This stage hand knew the level of authority this director had with respect to his position within the church and therefore did not question the request. Regretfully, he also did not inform anyone else that he would be leaving his post, his assigned responsibility, and the building altogether. Had he done so, he would have been instructed to stay put. There was a supply of batteries purchased just for that purpose prior to the onset of the performance of which the music director was unaware.

Secondly, had the concern been legitimate, the PC could have assigned this task to someone not specifically trained to run this special effect. As it turned out, the stagehand had to go to more than one store to get what was requested and was strolling into the front of the building, batteries in hand, when he heard the music cue for his action coming up. He literally threw the batteries at the confused head usher and dashed backstage to get to the lever to perform his one responsibility a fraction of a second later than called for. Thankfully, this delay did not break the illusion of reality nor did it cause anyone to get hurt. However, the SM (who had only just realized the absence of this crew member) was trying to cover two simultaneous actions himself when the misguided stage hand ran in at the final moment.

Intermission.—Again, let us share an incident from a different occasion, at a different church; we had a problem of a different kind. The director was one who had worked as a stage manager for a professional theater company for over eight years, and subsequently went on to direct at the college level. This was his first production in California and he requested us to assist by producing, handling the design of the production, assisting with publicity and other areas, to name a few. The play was a Neil Simon comedy which was quite involved and required the male lead to conduct extensive changes in his appearance during the intermission. On one particular night, the actor had encountered some difficulty effecting these makeup changes and asked for an additional time of two minutes. The PC took into account that it was a full house and knew it would take at least two minutes for the audience to be seated once the end of intermission was called. So, intermission was extended by two minutes, and then they were called to take their seats. The PC then went backstage to confirm the readiness of this actor and was en route to the tech booth to call the second act when it became apparent that the house lights had already gone dark and the music segue had begun. The PC literally ran back upstairs to cue the actor and then back to the tech booth (via the alternate door so as not to disrupt the show already in progress). However, because the show was mis-called by a director (who panicked in his ignorance of the situation, and who should have known better from all his years of "experience"), the two actors on stage were left to ad-lib and "carry" the scene until the actor could make his entrance. (This character would normally have had an entrance only ten seconds into the second act.) It was an unbearable minute and a half for them, for their fellow actors backstage, for the audience, and for the actor who had to "go on" without having time to finalize his character's appearance. It became evident that something was amiss, especially when the corresponding music segue came to its natural end (on the tape). As it was, because the director rushed into the second act in this manner, there were two couples who had to be seated in the dark and another after the act was up and running. This only compounded the awkwardness of this scene for cast and audience alike. The audience could only conclude that the lead actor was late for his entrance, when in fact, he was not. The director apologized to the PC and the actor, but the damage was already done. The main point here is that it was an unfortunate circumstance that could have been avoided had everyone been allowed to do their respective jobs. The PC is responsible for the entire show. As stated in the previous chapter, certain events may arise —known to only certain members of the crew—that will necessitate a change or modification in rehearsed cues and events which may not be communicated to other staff members outside of the running crews and cast involved.

During intermission, the PC will need to monitor the passing of time and the tasks to be accomplished within that time. The SM should be making sure that the stage, sets, and props are being reset or prepared for the next act. The PC will want to verify this with the SM as well as keep tabs on the audience with the ushers. Make sure that enough time has been allocated for use of the rest-room facilities for all who require it, that the hospitality department is having no problem, that the ushers or crews are watching to prevent unauthorized persons from going backstage, on stage, or any other place where they should not be. The PC will have to keep the cast and crew focused on the second act, rather than discussing the pros and cons of the preceding one. Uplifting, positive, humorous, and/or straight-forward remarks will keep them on this forward course, regardless of what faux pas may have occurred already. Do everything possible to get it started on time. After all, it's not over until it's over, and intermission is as carefully blocked and conducted as any other aspect of the performance.

End of performance.—Generally, notes shared with a cast at the close of this first performance will be limited to the cleanup and fulfilling requirements for the next call-times. The crews which interact with the cast will have made a list of items that need attention or simply checking before the next performance. All tech crews will need to meet briefly (hopefully) with the SM, PC, and other key leaders to get notes on what went well and not-so-well during this first presentation. Cast members already will have relayed their concerns to the SM and/or PC so that attention to those matters can be given. Reasons for inaccuracy can be identified so that the department heads and SM and PC will be able to determine what modifications they need to make to prevent similar problems during the subsequent show(s).

It is quite possible that at the conclusion of this tech meeting, call-times for the next performance may be altered to incorporate these modifications. In the event that the people affected by these changes have already left the premises, they will need to be telephoned or contacted immediately with the updated information by the PC and or SM.

It is never a wise plan to accomplish these modifications just before the next performance. Always plan for the unexpected (e.g., the supply house does not have the attachment you need to modify the overloaded circuit, blown the previous night; or the cable pulley for the hoist is visible from the audience when the weight is on it and needs to be raised or masked in a different manner. When fixing it, you encounter another sight-line problem and require input from the Tech Director before resolving that issue). Arrange to make necessary changes in the morning so that there is some leeway between its completion and the next call-time for cast.

Performance Run

Your performance run refers to the "run" or term of scheduled performances, whether it be for one weekend or several weeks or months. It would include any show, whether it be a matinee presentation or an evening performance. Generally the run is also broken down by the number of performances weekly. If you are running three weeks, Friday and Saturday evenings, with a Sunday matinee, then: you are presenting a three-week run, three shows weekly. If you have performances on Wednesday through Sunday nights plus two matinee performances, one on each Saturday and Sunday, then: you are still present-ing a three-week run, seven performances weekly. The days/nights for which no perfor-mances are scheduled are referred to as "dark." In other words, the theater and stage will remain dark for non-performance days, and you will be "running" on the performance days. "Up and running" refers to the status of each performance, indicating that the first cue has been dispatched and executed and that "for better or for worse" the current show is underway.

There may have been, in the back of most minds, that slight element of doubt dur-ing the premiere performance. The anxiety of missing a cue, dropping a line, or hitting that certain note was doubtlessly felt by all. Though few, if any, may have expressed such thoughts aloud, it was converted to become the personal energy source which sustained cast and crew alike. Consequently, the exhilaration and/or relief that swept over cast and crew upon its conclusion most likely carried over for some time, requiring a let-down peri-od before sleep.

During the run, it is important that this energy level be sustained, that familiarity does not lend itself to complacency and carelessness. Usually, the nervous anxiety and adrenaline rush that get every production through its first performance are sorely lacking for the second one. The fear gripping the performers is somewhat less since they now know they "can do it." Their confidence is intact. The process of getting into makeup and wardrobe may be shortened for some; the need to "run lines" may not be so pressing for others. However, it seems, regardless of the number of shows we have done and the emphasis that we have put towards the presentation of the second performance, it still has yet to match the vitality of the first, even though it may run without a flaw. Watch for this second-show syndrome. Do not be surprised if you experience the same. Acknowledge it, forget it, prime your cast and crew for the third, and go forward.

If your run will be for more than a single weekend, you may need to have a line rehearsal or "pick-up" rehearsal before the first performance following the "dark" days. You do not have to conduct this rehearsal in character, by any means. Though not all cast members may require it, or perhaps only a particular scene or scenes may need to be reviewed in this manner, all cast members within that range of scenes to be rehearsed must be present and on time. The pick-up can be conducted in a very low-key way. The running of lines can be held before each performance or just before the first performance following your dark days. It can be the night prior to your first performance following the period in which you have been dark. It can be done in a room while makeup is being applied, or in the green room after they are dressed and ready, or even before costume and makeup crews arrive. If it is to be done after they are in costume and makeup, the call-times should allow for this to be completed before the pick-up begins. Caution: It is to be taken seriously, but let's keep perspective throughout this whole process. *This is not brain surgery.* Let's have some fun, too!

Understudies.—Working in understudies, whether it is a pre-planned event or one that takes place out of necessity, is not just a courtesy, but is also very important. Though all players may know their lines and cues, the time to rehearse on stage should be arranged for understudies of principle characters if at all possible. The need to replace old habits or expectations of line delivery, subtle blocking differences, and so forth is important for the other actors who will be playing off that person, as well as for the crew. They should not assume that an understudy will give the same audible or visual cues the regular actor gave. You could sabotage your production if you do not attempt to teach him any new or subtle cues that have been incorporated since his initial role rehearsal.

Makeup and wardrobe will need to make adjustments for an understudy. Let them be as prepared as they possibly can. Sound may choose to alter the microphone selected for that actor. Lighting may have to establish different boundaries for certain "specials," props will make sure the understudy knows exactly when and where to pick up his props, and so forth.

The same care should be given to substitute crew and musicians. For instance, if you bring in a new pianist for any given performance, both that musician and the principles who have to work so intimately with each other must have the option to rehearse before the house is open. You are a team; do not underestimate the importance of this concept.

During the run, the cast and crew should always keep in mind the importance of the audience. You may have done the show eighteen times, but most of the audience will be seeing it for the first time. When we were running *You're a Good Man, Charlie, Brown,* we had a special performance for a school of emotionally handicapped students. We, as a team, felt that we could not do this without first presenting this opportunity to the entire cast and crew. After a short discussion, it was agreed that we would not only conduct the performance, but invite them to stay afterwards for a question and answer period. The invitation to the class was presented and quickly accepted. The cast was advised that this performance would be unlike any other, and it was. Some of the jokes went without response, and other, not-so-funny lines were met with uproarious delight. The audience laughed without inhibition, talked to each other on occasion, and even to the characters in the play during the play. At the end of the performance, some had questions for the characters and some for the actors. It was truly a delightful experience for everyone. As you think about who your audience is, ask yourself:

- How many persons are viewing this production for the first time?
- How many are repeat guests who have certain expectations of this particular performance?
- How can we make each performance better than the one before?

Closing

The closing of any show is almost always accompanied by mixed emotions. Whether the run has been one week or several, the standard rehearsal period preceding it has no doubt been long. People are tired in a way they may not have experienced before. Their lives have not been routine; sacrifices on the part of individuals and their families have been numerous.

And yet, the benefits cannot be denied. They have challenged themselves to do this show, have put a lot on the line to make it happen, and the personal gratification at having achieved it can never be taken away. More often than not, the relationship between individuals and departments within the church has deepened and so may their commitment to undertake further challenges. It may or may not be evident as yet whether your nonchurch audience members have responded in a positive way towards God and Jesus, or in seeking a greater understanding of what it is all about and what your membership has that they do not. You must build on the present opportunity to bring these people into your circle again and soon.

General assembly.—It should come as no surprise that this last show is bound to be emotional: both exhilaration and sadness at its finality will be in the range of feelings you will be experiencing and dealing with in others. Make this work for you as you meet in the general assembly of this closing night performance. Notes about the show itself, about the events which will be forthcoming upon its conclusion tonight, and expectations of the upcoming week's activities will need to be shared. Everyone has been made aware of the schedule for strike earlier in the run of this final week. They know whether or not they are striking any or all of the set and crew stations tonight and whether or not it will occur prior to the wrap party, or immediately following.

As mentioned earlier in this chapter, perhaps closing night acknowledgments will be planned for this general assembly or even are being held over for the wrap party that will follow.

One important note that must be shared concerns the unique humor exclusive to closing night performances that surfaces, yet one more "tradition of theater."

It is common to have the cast and crew alike plan "surprises" for this last performance. They are usually small alterations which may be visible only to certain members of the cast, or things that will be visible to the entire audience, but may not have the same meaning as they do to those within the production. A running joke may be "played-up" on this night. It is imperative that these "tricks" *do not* distract the audience or interfere with the presentation of the show. If there is the slightest chance that the show will be jeopardized or that someone could be hurt (emotionally or physically), then the trick should be saved for another time (perhaps the wrap party) or omitted altogether.

By now your mind is likely to be reeling with the possibilities, so let me share a few such tricks that we have observed, just to give you an idea. One time we were doing a show where one of the props was a family photo album. While looking through the album, two "brothers" were sitting on a couch and reminiscing about the past. (To help them in developing a history, we actually had the actors don camping garments and we took pictures of them "camping." We also had them bring individual pictures of themselves in other activities to help them establish and sustain their illusion of reality). On the last show, the prop person had removed certain shots and replaced them with photos of the crew, including some with captions! It was a small gesture that was known only to those cast members, and the prop master was certain that those two individuals could carry the scene and not "break." *Note:* The prop master did not follow through with his idea until he had sought the input of the director and let the PC and SM in on his intentions. That way, he was able to confirm his perception of the actors' ability to maintain their characters and did not risk "throwing the scene" with what he considered to be an innocent joke. The ad-libs that were shared by those two actors during the scene were caught only by those who were aware of the joke. No one in the audience was misled or confused by their comments. They made it work for them, and yet managed to convey to the crew that they "got the joke."

On another show, a musical, we had one of the soloists who was a member of a comic trio pull a stunt all on his own. His character was a hillbilly in the most stereotyped way, and on this last night, he decided to come out with a live chicken under his arm for this one number. Well, the chicken provided some additional laughs for cast and audience, not to mention some additional clean up when the show was over!

These jokes or tricks should never be conceived as an opportunity to trip-up someone or to undermine the performance of anyone, either in your cast or crew. Another reminder now during your general assembly though it is just before curtain, doesn't hurt! Let's not forget as our thoughts are carrying us beyond this performance into the events that will follow, that there will be people in the audience who need to be given our best efforts on all levels. There are people who have traveled or sacrificed on some personal level to be in attendance, and we need to recognize our initial goal to meet their needs by allowing them to see Christ in us individually and collectively. Let us pray for everyone who has participated on any level once again and perhaps plan a gathering in two weeks' time to get a report on the impact that this production has created in our own families and lives, and in those who have attended. It is almost time for "Places!" Are you ready?

Wrap party.—The whole production team will need to have a general idea of what to expect at the wrap party. Is it to be cake, coffee, and punch, or will food be provided? Is it to be a potluck on site, or will everyone be going to someone's home? Perhaps it will be held in a banquet room of a local restaurant. Will all be expected to pay their own way or will the production be taking care of all expenses? Are the children in the nursery to be invited, as well as those volunteers, or will they be asked to provide extended care?

Another item for consideration would be whether or not it is appropriate to invite some or all of those in your community who have assisted you with the production in a significant way. You may wish to extend an invitation for them to join you in this last performance, regardless of how many other times they may have seen it, and to share in the party to follow.

At the close of one show, we had a person (who had come to see the show several times) invite the entire cast and crew to a local restaurant which he had reserved for our production exclusively. He had even hired a photographer to shoot pictures of the party. The entire evening was his way of expressing his gratitude for what the production had meant to him.

At the close of another show, all persons who were involved and their families were invited to go to an ice cream parlor following the close of the show. They were treated to free ice cream sundaes. It was a great time, and great to have all the kids with us where we didn't have to be "shushing" them all the time. One expects squeals of delight from young ones at an ice cream parlor! It happened that the owner of the shop had donated both money and props for our use during the run of the show and had placed a coupon as advertising in the program. When invited to share in the closing night performance with us, he proceeded to extend this invitation. This was not the intent of our invitation, yet we felt it would not be right to deny him this opportunity. We did, however, persuade him to allow us to pick up a portion of the tab before we agreed to accept his generous offer.

On another occasion, we made arrangements with a local restaurant to grant them free advertising in the program in exchange for trade-out of monies to be applied towards the cast party. We had given them the back cover page (the most ideal location in the program) in exchange for $350 to be applied toward the cost of the cast party. We then were able to invite the cast and crew to this location and let them have whatever they wanted. We had budgeted a certain amount of money for the wrap party with which we could then supplement this trade-out. As a matter of principle, we made it clear from the onset that we would *not* pick up the tab for anyone who chose to have any beverages containing alcohol. We had a great evening, wonderful food, did not have to arrange for anyone to cook or cater for us, and no party mess to clean up before the strike. What a deal!

As you can see, the possibilities are many. The production team will have to make the best possible choice for your production after weighing all factors.

Strike

Preparing for the closing of any show requires as much effort and forethought as did the mounting of it, because the closing of every show is accompanied by the strike of that show. You can't have one without the other. How the strike is to be organized, the time of its occurrence, and those who will participate must be determined before you plan the wrap party.

During the strike, it is important that you maintain the same standards of safety and security as you did throughout the production. You may have a number of volunteers assisting with the strike. It may be that some are not members of your church, or that some are not familiar with your policy for the wearing of gloves and hard-hats as the set comes down. As with other workdays, you will need to consider the provision of child care and refreshments as well.

Let's identify the tasks involved in the strike and the ideal sequence in which they should be done:

1. All tech-department items must be removed from the set first. Such items would include microphones, cords, cables, wires, and special effects items that must not be damaged or destroyed with the striking of the set itself. All tree stands and certain spot lights may have to be removed depending on their location and susceptibility to sustain damage. The exceptions might be the overhead lights and speakers that will not be affected by the set strike.

2. Following this, or simultaneously if it can be arranged, should be the striking of the orchestra pit area (music scores, stands, lights, gels, cables, cords, headsets, etc. if applicable).

3. All set and character props should be removed and prepared for storage (or for

return to their original owners) before any set structures can be struck.

4. The set can be tackled next. Extreme care should be taken so as to preserve most items for reuse in a future production.

As you contemplate these tasks to be done, the decision of whether or not to strike immediately following the closing performance will be dependent upon many factors. Some of these factors are:

- the size and complexity of the set to be struck
- the number of technicians and volunteers lined up to assist with the strike immediately upon the conclusion of the last performance and those available the following day (Your entire cast and crew are standing by at the close of this last performance—what you can do in one hour with all of them is amazing!)
- the deadline by which all areas used by the production must be returned to their original appearance, and the necessary cleaning time after the strike is completed for this to be realized (Are you renting a hall or auditorium that must be vacated and returned to its state as it was prior to your occupancy by a specific date and time? Do you have the transportation vehicles to load all the equipment onto with the appropriate man-power standing by?)
- the date of return of all leased and/or borrowed items (lights, cables, boards, microphones, monitors, costumes, props, flats, music scores, stands, etc.) Where is the corresponding lease form and or contracts to accompany the return of these items and how is payment and or deposit reimbursements to be handled?
- the available transportation required to accomplish the return of all necessary items such as those referenced above.

As you consider these factors, keep in mind that you have the availability of the entire cast and crew upon closing the last performance, with child care already provided. You may want to strike all the tech equipment, or at least remove them from the set and stage areas to a pre-assigned location within the building from which they can be properly wrapped and prepared for storage. This may be true of all departments: props, wardrobe, sets, make-up, etcetera.

As you complete the process of packing away what may seem to be "all the elements of the last few months of your life," realize that this too is part of the growth from having served in this capacity. It is not to be taken lightly nor carelessly. The strike is also not done until a walk-through has been conducted in every space occupied by any part of the production at any time since the beginning of the performance run. Once the church is satisfied that the production team has restored the church to pre-production status and all keys have been returned—then the strike is over; the production has come to an end.

It has become a custom with us that when the final tasks of clean-up have been done, we treat those few die-hards (and by now you can be sure it will be no more than a handful) to breakfast, lunch, or dinner, whichever is appropriate to the occasion. It helps to bring closure to a show that has consumed all of your energies and most of your time in the past months.

It also helps to alleviate the onset of "post-production blues." This syndrome is unavoidable and will be felt by everyone. It may take different forms or appear at different times, but it will occur without fail. Some will be feeling it before the final performance is actually over. Others will be experiencing it during the wrap party or during that evening's strike. You may find some people with tears and still others who have indicated their intentions to go home, yet may stay long after they have quit working to stand by, idly watching the continuing strike. In their subconscious mind they know that when they walk out the door, it is over. They are unconsciously prolonging the reality of its ending. (Or perhaps they are consciously avoiding the work at home that has been neglected the past few weeks!) It is all part of the same syndrome. Some may not feel it until the following day or days, when they find themselves missing the people they had grown accustomed to seeing on a daily basis, or even just missing the busy routine of the show. For this reason, it is important that you have some event planned soon after the show closes to give people a direction in which to go. It may be a church picnic, or a time to visit a convalescent home or nearby children's hospital. You'll know as you approach the close of the show what would best suit your situation.

Storage

The initial organization of all items from their respective areas into a central location makes for an easier cleanup process. All items can be separated into groups by departments and then broken down into one of two categories: items we own and items to be returned. Both categories can be divided further into sections, depending upon the type of cleaning to be done and the location of their ultimate storage. Some items may need to be wrapped or sealed to keep out dust and moisture. Others may just require a box or container for storage in a safe, dry location. All boxes or containers should be clearly dated and labeled, stating their contents. Notes regarding all inventory should be kept and held by the production coordinator upon completion. You may decide to code the containers and have detailed descriptions in the notes regarding the contents of all containers.

For example: C-1-6 may appear on the box. The corresponding notes would indicate that the "C" is indicative of the costume department, the "1-6" would indicate it is one of six containers. Your corresponding inventory list would indicate that "C-1" contains 8 Men's Robes/Over-garments: Small–4, Medium–4; 8 Men's Shifts/Undergarments: Small–4, Medium–4.

However it is done, the production coordinator should have worked with all crew heads to:

- pre-determine the means for packaging and storing all items
- provide the coding system to be used if applicable
- provide the sheets for labeling all containers and the corresponding inventory list to each department
- provide permanent markers and tape or plastic to seal the label once completed
- determine if a value is to be attached to the entire contents of each container or to each item stored therein (in lieu of possible damage or loss for insurance purposes or perhaps to determine possible deposits required for use by other authorized parties).

It also must be made clear as to who has responsibility for all production property once the show is over. The thought given to the storage of all items is critical. Whether you are storing them on church grounds or in someone's garage or leasing space from another facility, they must be well cared for. Who is authorized to release any one or all of the items (obtained for this production) for use by a church member or class or outside group? What if an outside group should ask to borrow or request to lease items from your church production? Who is responsible to make sure that they are properly maintained, so that the flats are neither punctured nor warped? Who keeps track of the production inventory?

We suggest that the production coordinator keep a copy of the production inventory list generated or modified so as to be current upon the close of this production in the file that has been maintained since pre-production. It is also advised that the PC return the original files to be kept on file within the church and keep an additional complete copy for safety reasons. It may be in the form of three-ring notebook(s) or in marked files in a file storage container. If all the data has been input into a computer system, then disks can be maintained within the church and minimal hard copy data will be in actual file folders. The church's set may be located in the department that presented the production (such as Youth, Music, or Drama Ministries), but that department may not be authorized to release it to outside groups. You also may choose to keep it in the main office of the church.

When the need arises to retrieve something from the production's inventory, whether it be for use by a church member or member of your church association or community, then the inventory list should be all you need to locate a particular item or items. As you increase your own in-house resources with well-constructed set pieces, props, costumes, and such you will find yourself becoming a resource for other community groups or churches. They may be coming to you for assistance in achieving state-of-the-art performance capabilities. Thus, your inventory sheet should contain spaces or columns therein to note for every item:

- the date of its removal
- the person authorizing its removal
- the responsible party and contact number of the person taking that item
- its condition upon release, and the intended date of return
- the terms of its release (Is a deposit required? Is it going out the door as a rental item? a loaned item? Is a deposit required to cover its loss only if it is lost, damaged, or never returned?)

Whether in stages or in one session, you are establishing a precedent that will be continued for years and productions to come. Let's make it easier for the next time around. After all, isn't the next pre-production meeting on the calendar for next month?

CHAPTER NINETEEN

DRAMA IN WORSHIP

When drama and theater are combined with the gospel, they become a powerfully effective ministry tool. Though most of the information in this book addresses the issues of a full production, the concepts applied to the three-minute sketch or the puppet show or the clown segment are the same as the ones we have discussed for the two-hour play. The commitment to quality by pre-production, careful planning, and an adequate number of rehearsals are imperative, regardless of the size of the script. In this chapter, we will briefly explore some other uses of drama and theater as exciting and effective ministry tools.

The most common use of ministry drama is "drama in worship." To properly define the concept of drama in worship, we must first independently define the words *drama* and *worship*.

Drama.—The word *drama* comes from a Greek word meaning "to do," which is usually associated with the idea of action. Drama is traditionally defined as a form of literature, either prose or verse, usually in dialogue form, which is intended for performance. Most often, drama is thought of as a story about events in the lives of characters. The adjective *dramatic* describes the ideas of conflict, tension, contrast, and emotion which are usually associated with drama.

When you think about it, any performance has only two basic elements: a performer and an audience. Drama is a moment that dramatically illustrates a message or a moral, eventually leading the audience to a conclusion or at least to a consideration. This illustration can be effected in countless ways. It can be scripted, improvised, or mimed, or it may even be so spontaneous that no one on earth expected it. You can use props, the audience, existing stage furniture, or nothing at all. There may be several actors in a sketch, one actor performing a monologue, or just the pastor acting out a pulpit drama. Drama can be created in any number of formats, each of which elicits some kind of emotional response from the audience. Drama shoots darts into the hearts of the audience and pulls them out with the emotions attached.

Worship also can be described with a countless number of adjectives such as praise, fellowship, evangelism. From the dictionary: "1: to honor or reverence as a divine being or supernatural power 2: to regard with great or extravagant respect, honor, or devotion...to perform or take part in worship or an act of worship."[1]

Let us focus in on the word *praise* from the above definition. From a thesaurus we find many other descriptions of praise: accent, acclaim, acclamation, accolade, accredit, adulation, aggrandize, applaud, applause, approbation, benediction, blarney, bless, champion, cheer, citation, commemorate, commend, commendation, compliment, congratulate, congratulations, consecrate, credit, crown, dedicate, dedication, deify, distinguish, elevate, elevation, endorse, enshrine, eulogize, eulogy, exalt, exaltation, extol, felicitate, flatter, flattery, further, glorify, hail, homage, kudos, laud, laurels, magnify, ovation, praise, puff, reference, salute, thank, thanks, tout, tribute, worship. Many of these words could be used to define drama.

Let us now explore the dictionary definition of *praise:* "1 : to express a favorable judgment of : COMMEND 2 : to glorify (a god or saint) esp. by the attribution of perfections ...to express praise."[2] To express praise!

Let's take a look at some definitions of *express.* "1 a : DELINEATE, DEPICT b : to represent in words : STATE c : to give or convey a true impression of : SHOW, REFLECT d : to make known the opinions or feelings of (oneself) e : to give expression to the artistic or creative impulses or abilities of (oneself)....*syn* EXPRESS, VENT, UTTER, VOICE, BROACH, AIR mean to make known what one thinks or feels. Express suggests an impulse to reveal in words, gestures, actions, or what one creates or produces (*expressed* her feelings in music)."[3]

Following this line of thinking, *worship* is *praise* which is *expression* of the artistic or *creative impulses* or abilities of oneself . . . which is drama. Therefore by definition, worship is drama.

History.—We have heard many church leaders describe drama as the "new thing." Drama or creative arts ministry appears to be a relatively new concept in churches today. But in reality, the omission of creative arts in the church is a modern tradition. Drama in the church has had a slow resurgence of popularity since the mid-sixties but, in fact, drama in worship is nowhere near what it was during the time of David. The following passage (2 Chron. 15:25–16:8) describes a full production of worship and praise. Notice the different methods used to worship and the many talents it took to accomplish it: costumers, poets, writers, singers, instrumentalists, dancers, set builders, and performers, as well as many behind the scenes.

So David, and the elders of Israel, and the captains over thousands, went to bring up the ark of the covenant of the LORD out of the house of Obed-edom with joy. And it came to pass, when God helped the Levites that bare the ark of the covenant of the LORD, that they offered seven bullocks and seven rams. And David was clothed with a robe of fine linen, and all the Levites that bare the ark, and the singers, and Chenaniah the master of the song with the singers: David also had upon him an ephod of linen. Thus all Israel brought up the ark of the covenant of the LORD with shouting, and with sound of the cornet, and with trumpets, and with cymbals, making a noise with psalteries and harps. And it came to pass, as the ark of the covenant of the LORD came to the city of David, that Michal the daughter of Saul looking out at a window saw king David dancing and playing: and she despised him in her heart. So they brought the ark of God, and set it in the midst of the tent that David had pitched for it: and they offered burnt sacrifices and peace offerings before God. And when David had made an end of offering the burnt offerings and the peace offerings, he blessed the people in the name of the LORD. And he dealt to every one of Israel, both man and woman, to every one a loaf of bread, and a good piece of flesh, and a flagon of wine. And he appointed certain of the Levites to minister before the ark of the LORD, and to record, and to thank and praise the LORD God of Israel: Asaph the chief, and next to him Zecharaiah, Jeiel, and Shemiramoth, and Jehiel, and Mattithiah, and Eliab, and Benaiah, and Obed-edom: and Jeiel with psalteries and with harps; but Asaph made a sound with cymbals; Benaiah also and Jahaziel the priests with trumpets continually before the ark of the covenant of God. Then on that day David delivered first this psalm to thank the LORD into the hand of Asaph and his brethren. Give thanks unto the LORD, call upon his name, make known his deeds among the people.

Modern history.—Ironically, theater in the form of liturgical drama was reborn in Europe in the Roman Catholic church. If you've ever witnessed a Mass, you probably witnessed something dramatic. The responsive songs of the Mass suggested a type of dialogue. In the 9th century, certain holidays were celebrated with theatrical qualities, such as the procession to the church on Palm Sunday. An anonymous three-line Easter play written and performed about 925 is considered the origin of liturgical drama. It consisted of a dialogue between the three Marys and the angels at the tomb of Christ. By 970 a record of directions for this playlet had appeared, complete with costume elements and physical gestures.

Over the next 200 years liturgical drama slowly evolved, with various stories from the Bible enacted by the clergy or by choirboys. At first these were simple, using only the actors to tell the story, but soon they evolved into elaborate productions with costumes and scenery. Soon these scenes developed into full plays where Bible stories were presented sequentially, usually depicting scenes from the creation through the crucifixion. These plays are often called Passion, mystery, or miracle plays. Appropriate sets were erected around the nave of the church, with heaven usually at the altar end and a Hellmouth (an elaborate monster's head with a gaping mouth representing the entrance to hell) at the opposite end of the nave. All the scenes of the play were represented simultaneously, with the performers and spectators moving from one area of the church to another as the scenes demanded. The plays usually spanned thousands of years, and included many separate sets and scenes. These plays did not always display conflict and tension. Their purpose was to dramatize the salvation of humankind.

Although the church encouraged early liturgical drama because of its moralistic qualities, entertainment and spectacle became increasingly prevalent, and the church once again voiced distrust about drama. Unwilling to relinquish the beneficial effects of theater, the church compromised by removing presentation of drama from the church building itself. The same physical stagings were re-created in town market squares. While the drama retained its religious content and intent, it became increasingly secular in its presentation.

By the 14th century the production of plays was associated with the Feast of Corpus Christi and had evolved into cycles of up to 40 plays. They were produced by the community as a whole every four or five years. The productions might take from one or two days to a month to present. The production of each play was assigned to a trade guild, with an attempt to correlate the guild with the subject of the play. For instance, the boatwrights might stage the play of Noah.

Because the performers were often illiterate amateurs, the plays tended to be written in an easily memorized type of verse. Selective realism was employed in staging. Costumes and props were all contemporary. Whatever could be depicted realistically was, and in fact many instances were reported of actors nearly dying from too realistic crucifixions or hangings and of actors who portrayed devils being severely burned. On the other hand, the parting of the Red Sea might be indicated by the separation of a red cloth that would then be draped over the pursuing Egyptians to suggest the sea swallowing them. The mixing of the real and the symbolic did not seem to bother the lesser sophisticated people of that day. Spectacle forms were used wherever possible. The Hellmouth was usually a show of mechanical wizardry and pyrotechnics. Despite the religious content of the cycles, they seemed to be viewed mostly as entertainment.

The staging became portable and the plays went out among the people. Pageant wagons were small rolling stages similar to a modern-day parade float, that would move from place to place in the city. Spectators would assemble at each location and watch the actors performing on the wagons and on a scene created on the street or with an adjoining platform.

During this same period, folk plays, secular farces, and pastoral dramas developed. All these influenced the evolution of the morality play in the 15th century. Although drawing on Christian theology for theme and characters, the moralities were secular, allegorical, self-contained dramas, usually performed by professionals such as the minstrels. The plays, such as *Everyman,* generally dealt with the individual's journey and conduct through life. The allegorical characters include such figures as Death, Gluttony, Good Deeds, and other vices and virtues.

20th century.—Somewhere between the 17th and 20th centuries, the church turned control of all creative arts, including theater, over to the secular world. In the 20th century, the styles and attributes of these plays progressed with increasing levels of quality.

In the 1920s musicals were transformed from a loosely connected series of songs, dances, and comic sketches to a story, sometimes serious, told through dialogue, song, and dance. The form was perfected in the 1940s by the team of Richard Rodgers and Oscar Hammerstein II. By the 1960s, much of the spectacle had gone out of musicals and they became more serious, even somber. In the late 1970s, however, possibly as a result of increasing economic and political problems (from which audiences want to escape), lavish musicals returned (many of them revivals) with the emphasis on song, dance, and light comedy. The trend toward spectacle continued into the 1980s with the musicals of Andrew Lloyd Webber, including the Broadway productions of *Cats* (1982), and *Phantom of the Opera* (1988). A counter-trend was also evident, as musicals such as *Dreamgirls* (1981) and Stephen Sondheim's *Sunday in the Park with George* (1984) brought a new, more thought-provoking dimension to the form.

In the late 1960s, the church began to write and produce musical plays. However, these were never written with the same level of quality as the secular world had already perfected when it came to the elements of style, technique, and production values. Christian publishers today continue to write these so-called musicals as a "loosely connected series of songs" unconnected to any kind of storyline. Too often the excuse for these is a lack of resources such as talent and money as compared to the secular theater.

Not only is this excuse untrue, but it should never stop the church body from striving for quality when delivering the message of Christ in whatever medium.

Modern worship tradition has utilized only a small portion of the creative talents available in the church body. In most churches the gifts used in worship are music and preaching. Those who do not possess these talents must sit back, observe others, and worship from the congregation. Fine arts, poetry, dance, acting, writing, sewing, designing, and woodworking (to name a few) are God-given creative abilities that are often overlooked as means of worship. Those with such creative energies are often forced to exercise their talents outside the church.

But the Bible is clear about using one's special abilities in service to God.

> But that isn't the way God has made us. He has made many parts for our bodies and has put each part just where he wants it. What a strange thing a body would be if it had only one part! So he has made many parts, but still there is only one body.
>
> The eye can never say to the hand, "I don't need you." The head can't say to the feet, "I don't need you."
>
> And some of the parts that seem weakest and least important are really the most necessary. Yes, we are especially glad to have some parts that seem rather odd! And we carefully protect from the eyes of others those parts that should not be seen, while of course the parts that may be seen do not require this special care. So God has put the body together in such a way that extra honor and care are given to those parts that might otherwise seem less important. This makes for happiness among the parts, so that the parts have the same care for each other that they do for themselves. If one part suffers, all parts suffer with it, and if one part is honored, all the parts are glad.
>
> Now here is what I am trying to say: All of you together are the one body of Christ, and each one of you is a separate and necessary part of it.
>
> (1 Cor. 12:18–27, TLB)[4]

If a body part is not used it will atrophy, wither, and in some cases it must be severed. We are allowing many parts of our body to wither from lack of use. Too often these "parts" deliberately sever themselves from the body to prevent their own withering or death.

From thirty years old and upward until fifty years old shalt thou number them; all that enter in to perform the service, to do the work in the tabernacle of the congregation. (Num. 4:23–28)

He also exalteth the horn of his people, the praise of all his saints; even of the children of Israel, a people near unto him. Praise ye the LORD.

Praise ye the LORD. Sing unto the LORD a new song, and his praise in the congregation of saints.

Let Israel rejoice in him that made him: let the children of Zion be joyful in their King.

Let them praise his name in the dance: let them sing praises unto him with the timbrel and harp.

For the LORD taketh pleasure in his people: he will beautify the meek with salvation.

Let the saints be joyful in glory: let them sing aloud upon their beds.

Let the high praises of God be in their mouth, and a two-edged sword in their hand;

To execute vengeance upon the heathen, and punishments upon the people;

To bind their kings with chains, and their nobles with fetters of iron;

To execute upon them the judgment written: this honour have all his saints. Praise ye the LORD.

Praise ye the LORD. Praise God in his sanctuary: praise him in the firmament of his power.

Praise him for his mighty acts: praise him according to his excellent greatness.

Praise him with the sound of the trumpet: praise him with the psaltery and harp.

Praise him with the timbrel and dance: praise him with stringed instruments and organs.

Praise him upon the loud cymbals: praise him upon the high sounding cymbals.

Let every thing that hath breath praise the LORD. Praise ye the LORD. (Pss. 148:14–150:6)

And David and all Israel played before God with all their might, and with singing, and with harps, and with psalteries, and with timbrels, and with cymbals, and with trumpets. (1 Chron. 13:8)

And David and all the house of Israel played before the LORD on all manner of instruments made of fir wood, even on harps, and on psalteries, and on timbrels, and on cornets, and on cymbals. (2 Sam 6:5)

Sing unto him, sing psalms unto him, talk ye of all his wondrous works. (1 Chron. 16:9)

It came even to pass, as the trumpeters and singers were as one, to make one sound to be heard in praising and thanking the LORD; and when they lifted up their voice with the trumpets and cymbals and instruments of music, and praised the LORD, saying, For he is good; for his mercy endureth for ever: that then the house was filled with a cloud, even the house of the LORD;

So that the priests could not stand to minister by reason of the cloud: for the glory of the LORD had filled the house of God.

Then said Solomon, The LORD hath said that he would dwell in the thick darkness.

But I have built an house of habitation for thee, and a place for thy dwelling for ever.

And the king turned his face, and blessed the whole congregation of Israel: and all the congregation of Israel stood. (2 Chron. 5:13–6:3)

The first description of God is found in Genesis 1:1, "In the beginning God created..." The first thing we learn about God is that He is a creator. He has the power to create anything and everything out of nothing. He picked up a handful of dirt and created us in his image. If God is the Creator and we are created in His image, then it stands to reason that we are creative beings.

Since the first creation day, we have made an incredible journey of progress, fueled by humanity's creative energies. Billions of human beings have combined their individual, unique, and God-given talents to create the wonders of the 20th century. Although degrees of creativity may vary from person to person, we all possess the basic ability to create.

In the time of David, the entire congregation was used in worship. Each one was a valuable part of the one body. Drama in worship is one way of using all of the parts of the body. The ways of using drama in worship are as vast as the creative mind God gave you.

Just as music is often selected to set tone and theme for worship, other art forms can be used. Poetry or performance poetry, dance, art, and instruments, for example, or combinations of these, also can be used to enhance or even illustrate the message.

Sketches.—A sketch is a short scene or vignette. Sketches can be any length but are usually around three to five minutes long. A sketch, by definition, is an illustration. It's best use in the worship service is to illustrate the topic of the sermon or service.

The pastor should meet with the leader of the drama ministry at the beginning of the week and make suggestions for the illustration based on his sermon topic. The drama department would then write the script, select the cast, and rehearse the illustration during the week. Once perfected, they would perform the scene for the pastor for his approval. When the scene is performed during the worship service, the pastor should immediately tie it into his sermon. The worship leader or music director should plan the music to complement the scene and the sermon. This could be done each week in a variety of ways.

Following is an example of a short script with sermon notes, from the book *Scripts and Sermons* by the authors of this book, John Lewis, Flip Kobler, and Laura Andrews.

OTHER WORLDS TO SING IN

SCENE 1: 8 years old

Fade in.

We hear the sobs of a little girl in the darkness. The lights come up to reveal an old crank-handle wall phone mounted on a stand or a wall. Little 8-year-old Kathy walks to the phone, still crying. She stands on a stool, picks up the receiver, and cranks the handle.

OPERATOR 1: Operator.

KATHY 1: Information, please.

OPERATOR 1: Yes, can I help you?

KATHY 1: My mommy said that if I ever needed anything when she wasn't home to call "Information Please."

OPERATOR 1: What's your name?

KATHY 1: Kathy.

OPERATOR 1: How old are you, Kathy?

KATHY 1: Eight.

OPERATOR 1: Why are you crying, Kathy?

KATHY 1: My pet canary died.

OPERATOR 1: Oh, I'm sorry. I bet you're going to miss him.

KATHY 1: Uh-huh.

OPERATOR 1: Did he sing pretty?

KATHY 1: Yeah, but now he can't sing no more.

OPERATOR 1: But you know what, Kathy?... You don't have to cry for your canary. He's OK. I want you to always remember... there are other worlds to sing in. Do you know what that means?

KATHY 1: He went to heaven?

OPERATOR 1: That's right. And you don't have to be sad for him. Just close your eyes and imagine you hear him singing.

Kathy closes her eyes, then begins to smile.

OPERATOR 1: Do you hear him?

KATHY 1: Yeah. I can hear him singing.

Fade out.

SCENE TWO: 14 years old.

Fade in.

286

Kathy, now 14, runs happily to the same telephone and rings it.

OPERATOR 1: Operator.

KATHY 2: Information, please.

OPERATOR 1: Hi, Kathy! How was school today?

KATHY 2: Oh, wait till I tell you! You know that boy I was telling you about?

OPERATOR 1: The one you're sweet on?

KATHY 2: Yeah. He gave me a flower today.

OPERATOR 1: Oh, Kathy, that's wonderful.

KATHY 2: I finally have a boyfriend.

OPERATOR 1: You see? I told you, didn't I? You're only fourteen. You have a big future ahead of you. There'll be lot's of boyfriends.

KATHY 2: I think I'm gonna marry this one.

OPERATOR 1: I think you have plenty of time before you start talking about marriage.

KATHY 2: I guess you're right. Yeah. I gotta go. I'll call you tomorrow. Bye.

OPERATOR 1: Bye.

Fade out.

SCENE THREE: Age 18

Fade in. Kathy, now 18, enters and rings the phone.

OPERATOR 1: Operator.

KATHY 3: Information, please.

OPERATOR 1: Hello, Kathy. So tonight's the big night, huh?

KATHY 3: Yeah. I'm finally graduating. I can't believe how fast high school went.

OPERATOR 1: I'm gonna miss you.

KATHY 3: I'm not leavin' until August. I'll call you every day this summer.

OPERATOR 1: You'd better.

KATHY 3: And I'll be back for all the holidays. And summer vacations.

OPERATOR 1: I'll be looking forward to those days.

KATHY 3: You were always there. Ever since that day my canary died. Over all these years, whenever I needed a friend, I could always count on "Information Please." You know, I just realized—I don't even know your name.

OPERATOR 1: Why don't you just call me "Aunt Minnie"?

KATHY 3: Ok, Aunt Minnie.

OPERATOR 1: Maybe when you come home, we'll get a chance to meet face to face.

KATHY 3: I'd really like that. I'm gonna be late for graduation. I'll call you tomorrow and tell you how it went.

OPERATOR 1: OK. Congratulations, Kathy. I'm proud of you.

KATHY 3: Thanks.Talk to you later.

OPERATOR 1: Bye.

Fade out.

SCENE 4: Six months later.

Fade in. Kathy enters and cranks the phone.

OPERATOR 2: Operator.

KATHY 4: Information, please.

288

OPERATOR 2: Yes, may I help you?

KATHY 4: *(pause)* Where's the regular operator? Minnie?

OPERATOR 2: Uh, she doesn't work here any more.

KATHY 4: What do you mean? How can I reach her? I'm only in town for a couple of days.

OPERATOR 2: Are you a relative?

KATHY 4: No. Well, sort of. I'm kind of an old friend.

OPERATOR 2: Wait. Are you Kathy?

KATHY 4: Yes.

OPERATOR 2: Kathy. I have some bad news. Minnie passed away last week.

KATHY 4: *(pause, tears)* How?

OPERATOR 2: She had a stroke. I was with her at the hospital. She told me all about you. She wanted me to give you a message if you called.

KATHY 4: Please. Tell me.

OPERATOR 2: She said to tell you not to cry for her. And to remember that there are other worlds to sing in. Do you know what she meant by that?

KATHY 4: *(smiling through tears)* Yeah. I know what she meant by that. *(Closing eyes)*
I can hear her singing.

Fade out.

CONCLUSION by PASTOR: When Steven was being stoned he saw "heaven open and the Son of Man standing at the right hand of God" (Acts 7:56, NIV). He saw the beautiful reward he was about to receive and found comfort even during a horrible death. The beauty of his new world gave him the strength to forgive the very ones stoning him.

How sad for those who die without knowing Christ. "Ye shall die in your sins:

whither I go, ye cannot come" (John 8:21). "It is appointed unto men once to die" (Heb. 9:27) and depending on our faith in Jesus, we will be standing with Him forever in heaven, or face eternal death.

God has looked down from above and has provided a way to escape the fires of hell (Rom. 5:9). God's way is the only way to have your life changed and to have a home in heaven (John 14:6). God's way of salvation is by personally receiving Jesus Christ as Savior (John 1:12).

There are five words used in the New Testament to describe death. The first word tells us that death is the sowing of a seed (1 Cor. 15:42). The second word for death is sleep (John 11:11). The third describes death as an exodus (2 Peter 1:15). The fourth word is "departure" (2 Tim. 4:6). The fifth describes death as a homegoing (John 14:1–2; Rev. 21:4). Death for the Christian is a homegoing because he will meet there in heaven his friends and his loved ones who have gone on before, and above all, the Savior who purchased his entry ticket. Around the throne of God in heaven, families separated by death shall meet to part no more. Imagine the singing in that world!

Production Notes for Other Worlds to Sing In

Cast List

KATHY 1:	8 years old. Pig tails. Cute, but sad.
KATHY 2:	14 years old. Same hair coloring as #1. Tomboyish. Bubbly.
KATHY 3:	18 years old. Pony tail. Mature for her age. Sincere.
KATHY 4:	6 months later. Same actress. A little more mature.
OPERATOR 1:	Voice-over only. Grandmotherly voice.
OPERATOR 2:	Voice-over only. Younger voice. Mid twenties.

Sets/Props

FLAT WALL	4-x-8 plywood braced behind. Painted, or wallpaper from 1930s.
CRANK PHONE	Replicas are fairly reasonably priced.
STOOL	

Costumes

KATHY 1:	School clothes, 1930.
KATHY 2:	Appropriate 1930–40 teenage.

KATHY 3:	Slacks or dress from the period; early forties.
KATHY 4:	Quickly put on a sweater from the period and take down pony tail.

Sermon Notes for "Life and Death"

Biblical References

I. Death

  A. Death

    1. Psalm 89:48 – What man cannot see death.

    2. Ecclesiastes 3:20 – All go to the same place from dust return.

    3. Psalms 103:15–16 – Like grass.

    4. Ecclesiastes 8:8 – No power over own death.

    5. Romans 5:12 – Death came to all men.

    6. Hebrews 9:27 – Man destined to die once.

    7. Numbers 16:29 – Death is natural to man.

    8. Job 30:23 – Death appointed for all the living.

    9. Ecclesiastes 7:2 – Destiny of every man.

    10. 1 Corinthians 15:21 – Death came through man.

    11. 1 Corinthians 15:26 – Death is last enemy to be destroyed.

  B. Like Sleep

    1. Job 7:21 – Lie down in dust.

    2. Mark 5:35–43 – Dead girl asleep.

    3. John 11:11 – Lazarus asleep.

    4. Acts 13:36 – David fell asleep and decayed.

    5. 1 Corinthians 15:6 – Some live and some sleep.

    6. 1 Thessalonians 4:13–18 – Asleep but will rise.

    7. Acts 7:60 – Fell asleep.

    8. 1 Corinthians 15:6 – Some living, some fallen asleep.

  C. Death of Righteous

    1. Numbers 23:10 – Die the death of righteous.

    2. Psalm 23:4 – Comfort in death.

    3. Psalm 116:15 – Precious death of Saints.

    4. Proverbs 14:32 – Even in death righteous have refuge.

5. Luke 16:22 – Angels carried.

6. Romans 14:8 – Live or die to the Lord.

7. Philippians 1:21 – Live is Christ, die is gain.

8. Revelations 14:13 – Blessed are the dead in the Lord.

9. Matthew 10:39 – Lose life for Christ will find life.

10. Philippians 1:20 – Courage to exalt Christ in life or death.

11. Hebrews 11:5 -- Enoch did not die because he pleased God.

13. Revelations 2:10 – Be faithful until death, receive crown of life.

14. 2 King 2:1 – Elijah did not die, went in a whirlwind.

15. Hebrews 13:14 – Looking for the city to come.

D. Prepare for Death

1. 2 Kings 20:1 – Put house in order.

2. Matthew 24:42–44 – Be ready.

3. Revelations 20:12 – Dead will be judged by their record.

4. Isaiah 38:1 – Put house in order.

E. Physical Life Is Short

1. Psalm 39:5 – Life is but a breath.

2. James 4:14 – Like a mist it vanishes.

3. John 6:63 – Flesh counts for nothing, spirit is life.

4. Genesis 27:2 – Don't know the day of death.

II. Life

A. Mortality

1. Proverbs 12:28 – Immortality.

2. Luke 20:36 – Can no longer die.

3. John 8:51 – Keep word, never see death.

4. John 11:26 – Live and believe—never die.

5. 2 Corinthians 5:1 – New home in heaven.

6. 2 Timothy 1:10 – Destroyed death.

7. 1 Corinthians 15:54 – Death swallowed up in victory.

8. Romans 8:36–39 – More than conquerors.

9. John 11:25–26 – Eternal life.

10. Matthew 27:52 – Bodies of holy people raised to life.

11. Luke 21:19 – By standing firm you will gain life.

12. 2 Corinthians 4:11 – Given to death to show Jesus' life.

B. Jesus Is Life

    1. John 11:25 – Jesus is life.

    2. 1 John 5:12 – With the Son has life.

    3. John 13:15 – Believe, have eternal life.

    4. John 5:24 – Crossed over from death to life.

    5. John 10:10 – Have life to the fullest.

    6. John 6:53 – Follow Christ or there's no life in you.

    7. Ezekiel 18:32 – Lord takes no pleasure in death; repent and live.

C. Long Life

    1. 1 Kings 3:14 – Do good, long life.

    2. Proverbs 10:27 – Fear of Lord, long life.

    3. 1 Peter 3:10 – Keep tongue, have long life.

    4. Isaiah 46:4 – Old age, God will sustain.

    5. Ephesians 6:3 – Enjoy long life on the earth.

    6. Genesis 35:29 – Abraham died old and full of years.

D. Heaven

    1. Acts 7:55–56 – Steven saw heaven.

    2. Matthew 7:14 – Narrow is the road to life.

    3. 2 Corinthians 5:2 – Longing to be clothed with heavenly clothes.

SECULAR REFERENCES

"I can't die; I'm booked." — George Burns.

*　　*　　*

"One way to live longer is to cut out all the things that make you want to live longer." — Anonymous.

*　　*　　*

Bumper sticker: "He who dies with the most toys is still dead."

*　　*　　*

"It hath often been said that it is not death, but dying that is terrible." — Henry Fielding, *Amelia*

* * *

"I have never seen a hearse towing a U-Haul." — Unknown

* * *

"Let us pass over the river and rest under the shade trees." — Stonewall Jackson, dying words, May 10, 1863

* * *

"Depend upon it, Sir, when a man knows he is to be hanged in a fortnight, it concentrates his mind wonderfully." — Samuel Johnson, *Boswell's Life of Johnson* (September 19, 1777)

* * *

"A man can die but once. We owe God a death." — Shakespeare, *King Lear,* V, ii

* * *

"Nothing in his life became him like the leaving it." — Shakespeare, *Macbeth,* I, iv

* * *

"That it will never come again is what makes life so sweet." — Emily Dickinson, poem

* * *

"We are always getting ready to live but never living." — Ralph Waldo Emerson, *Journals*

* * *

"The value of life lies not in the length of days, but in the use we make of them; a man may live long yet live very little." — Montaigne, *Essays*

* * *

"Old and young, we are all on our last cruise." — Robert Louis Stevenson, "Crabbed Age and Youth"

* * *

"While there is life, there's hope." — Terence, *Heauton Timorumenos*

* * *

A reporter, interviewing a woman who had reached her 99th birthday, said, "Certainly hope I can come back next year and see you reach 100."

"Can't see why not, young feller," the elderly woman replied. "You look healthy enough to me."

*   *   *

At a Las Vegas gambler's funeral, the speaker asserted, "Jake is not dead; he only sleeps." From among the gambling friends who were attending came a voice: "I got $100 that says he's dead."

*   *   *

Because I could not stop for Death,
He kindly stopped for me;
The carriage held but just ourselves
And Immortality.
— Emily Dickinson

*   *   *

Monologues.—A dramatic monologue is a literary work in which a single fictional character reveals his thoughts and feelings in a monologue usually addressed to an audience of one or more persons. In other words, a monologue is a dramatic sketch performed by one actor.

The dramatic monologue was a genre popular in early Gaelic poetry. The hermit monks of the early Irish church, living on intimate terms with their environment, established the tradition of nature poetry that is one of the distinctions of Irish and, later, Scottish Gaelic verse.

Monologues can be used to illustrate the sermon in worship the same way sketches do. Following is an example of a monologue written by Matt Tullos and published in the *National Drama Service,* volume 2, no. 5, October–November 1994.

Paul on Galatians
by Matt Tullos

Some thought I was a tad too harsh. "Foolish," I called them. "Misled! Gullible!" These words were not flowery and flattering, but they were definitely the truth. You know, friends, that there are some that respond to your teaching through soft words of direction—while there are others who listen only when you *shout!* The Galatians were such people. They, like most during that time, were babes in Christ and were having a hard time discerning the radical element of the gospel. And what was that radical element? In two words: "grace" and "faith." Difficult concepts for these spiritual infants—and then combine that with the influence of the Judaizers. . . Oh they were a strange lot. "You want to join our church? Wonderful. Have you been circumcised?" That would bring a chill down the spine of any new male believer. I must confess that they were a little more receptive to the idea of baptism. Peter was little help. I must confess that my words to him were also quite harsh. When I had heard the reports of Peter's strange behavior, I was enraged. When he was with the Gentiles he was completely Gentile. But when the Jewish Christians came to town, he was so intimidated by them that he became as Kosher as unleavened bread. But the gospel of Christ is not about rules and regulations. It is not about becoming better people. It is about being new. Being crucified with Christ. Yes, being dead! And yet newly alive! That's the newness of the gospel. My life as a Jew was filled with rules and regulations: when to walk—when to wash—how to eat—when to spit—how to work! It was as if these rules could tame the human nature. Somewhere in the history of God's nation our eyes were turned from the true and living God to our own hierarchy of rules. We idolized the law. And then came Jesus… What a jolt to the nation of Israel! What a message. You know my story. I was an enemy of this faith. I held the cloaks of the men who stoned Steven. Perhaps because I experienced such a miraculous conversion, I could not stomach the false gospel of legalism. It was precisely that false gospel from which I experienced release and freedom! I know what many of you are thinking: "Is he saying that our deeds are not important?" On the contrary, they are very important! But in truth, they are not your deeds at all! You also have been crucified in Christ. You no longer live, but Christ lives inside you. And the life you live in the body, you live by faith in the Son of God, Jesus Christ, who loves you and has given Himself for you. It is for freedom that Christ set us free. And I say to you, the church of 1994: Stand firm, and do not let yourselves be burned again by the yoke of slavery! It doesn't matter what you look like, where you come from, or what you have done in the past! All of this is rubble in the eyes of our Savior. It doesn't mean anything. What counts is that you are a new creation. Peace and mercy to all who follow this rule.

Poetry.—Poetry is a form of imaginative literary expression that achieves its effects by the sound and imagery of its language. Performance poetry, like other forms of drama, is not a new concept but is beginning to find a new popularity. Combined with music, videos, slides, dance, and other media, poetry can be an extremely effective method of worship. Poetry projects emotionally charged human experience in a metrical language. It is a form of storytelling which amplifies the imagination of the listener and causes an emotional response. We, as finite beings, use language to communicate with others; and so we also use our human language to communicate with God, even though He knows our thoughts, our souls, and our hearts. Poetry is the language of the heart. Knowing this, we have a better understanding of why King David combined the emotions of his heart with his verbal language and communicated with God through poetry.

Poetry is one of the most ancient and widespread of the arts. Originally blended with music in song, it gained independent existence in ancient times. The lyric, minus the music, maintained the same metrical qualities of the song. Meter is the central component of verse rhythm and depends basically on the relative strength and weakness of adjacent syllables and monosyllabic words. It is this rhythmic use of language that distinguishes poetry from other forms of literature and that forms the basis of the dictionary definition of poetry as "metrical writings." This definition does not, however, include cadenced poetry (as in the Bible) or modern free verse; both types of verse are rhythmic but not strictly metrical. Nor does it take into account the unwritten songs of many cultures past and present. It is, however, a useful starting point for considering what is now commonly meant by the word *poetry* .

Poetry can be constructed in many forms. The one that most often comes to mind is rhyming poetry. This, of course is constructed as the name implies, with rhyming words and the end of beats. Another popular form is free verse, which is rhymed or unrhymed poetry composed without attention to rules of meter. Modern free verse usually does not use rhyme. The emotional content or meaning of the work is expressed through its rhythm.

Lyric is a short poem that conveys intense feeling or profound thought. Ballads, often classed as narrative poems, are considered lyrics by some scholars because they are sung. By the beginning of the Renaissance the term *lyric* was applied also to verse that was not sung.

An *ode* is a dignified and elaborately structured lyric poem praising and glorifying an individual, commemorating an event, or describing nature intellectually rather than emotionally. Odes were originally songs performed to the accompaniment of a musical instrument.

The structure of the poem is not as important as the content. The end result should be the effect that it has on the audience. What set poetry apart from all other performance media are the internal truths from which poetry is written and performed. The writer and the performer must each believe deeply in the words they are presenting. "Poetry is the spontaneous overflow of powerful feelings: it takes its origin from emotion recollected in tranquillity"(William Wordsworth , *Lyrical Ballads*). "Poetry . . . is the revelation of a feeling that the poet believes to be interior and personal, which the reader recognizes as his own" (Salvatore Quasimodo , speech, 1960). "Genuine poetry can communicate before it is understood" (T.S. Eliot, *Dante*).

One dictionary definition of poetry is "writing that formulates a concentrated imaginative awareness of experience in language chosen and arranged to create a specific emotional response through meaning, sound, and rhythm."[5] In order to create that emotional response from the audience it must have been inspired by the internal truth of the poet. "Poetry is either something that lives like fire inside you—like music to the musician ….or else it is nothing, an empty, formalized bore around which pedants can endlessly drone their notes and explanations" (F. Scott Fitzgerald, letter, 1940).

In 1994, Convention Press published what we believe to be a ground-breaking book titled, *Three Voices: Poetry in Worship*. The book was a collection of works by three poets, Ragan L. Courtney, Wesley L. Forbis, and Terry W. York. The foreword of the book was written by Calvin Miller, faculty, Southwestern Baptist Theological Seminary, Ft. Worth, Texas, and we believe it best sums up the concept of poetry in worship.

> When poets perform their verses for large audiences, they too much fear their own music. They are often tentative, because they know that few of the masses will even hear subtle harps of God that accompany their verses. But when poets come together singing only to each other, the harps are audible to all.
>
> *Three Voices* is a gathering of souls come together for song. Great poets never harmonize—they never sing in unison. Yet their concert is unspeakable in

beauty. Their songs are wondrous. Their tunes walk, skip, and run to tempos each their own. In *Three Voices* you will hear such gathered music bless your doubt and cheer your certainties. Listen as Ragan Courtney "goes at last to wrestle with God." Feel the roaring of the skies as Wesley Forbis flies "the wind of the will to know." Hear Terry York call out to the God of "Honest Struggles."

Three Voices— each alone—have come to us at once in this gathering of poets. Three singers meet within us. They call to us to read their souls and listen from the inside.

— Calvin Miller

Following is an example of a "free verse" poem written by Ragan Courtney and published in *Three Voices*.

Beginning Again

Beginning again
With requiem
A somber, holy sound.
A bed of wood
In solemnity
Lowered into the ground.
Sleep in dark,
A waiting time,
A momentary affliction,
Until angels come
Rolling stones
Announcing,
"Resurrection!"

— Ragan L. Courtney [6]

Dance.—"The poetry of the foot" (Agnes De Mille, in *New York Times Magazine*). Dance in the history of human culture has been used in the forms of art, ritual, and recreation. Dance is motion that goes beyond the daily functional movements used in work or athletics. Dance is used to express emotions, moods, or ideas; tell a story; serve religious, political, economic, or social needs; or simply be a pleasing experience with aesthetic values. The well-known dancer Ray Bolger once said, "I've never been that great a dancer. It's what's inside me that comes across to an audience that has made me what I am. Dancing, according to the dictionary, is the poetry of motion. If you make this poetry come alive, you can make the audience become a part of you and dance right with you."

Throughout recorded history, including the Bible, dance has been an individual poetic means of expressing worship and praise. But since some forms of dance have been misused by secular and pagan groups, some modern religious leaders have decided to condemn dance in all forms. In other words, they've thrown out the baby with the bath water.

The many songs relating to religion support the assumption that the origins of poetry can be found in the communal expression, probably originally taking the form of dance, of the religious spirit. The dance rhythm could be marked not only by clapping, stamping, or rhythmic cries, but by chanting or otherwise intoning or singing words. Dance, then, became the forerunner of song, poetry, and instrumental music.

The physical and psychological effects of dance enable it to serve many functions. Historically it has been used as a form of worship, a means of honoring ancestors, and even a way of reaching God. "Dance is the hidden language of the soul, of the body" (Martha Graham, quoted in *The New York Times*).

Dancing is mentioned many times in the Bible, and until the Middle Ages it was often a part of worship services and religious celebrations. Although the Christian church later denounced dancing as immoral, it continued to be important in various Christian and non-Christian sects. Many Christian churches miss out on one of the most beautiful means of expressive worship because of archaic ignorance. However, many churches are now incorporating expressive dance styles such as interpretive dance into their worship services.

Dance is one of those creative arts that are impossible to teach on paper. We won't even try here. We simply want to inspire and encourage you to explore all forms of creative arts and God-given talents to be used in worship. You may want to consider developing an entire ministry department in your church that supports the creative arts

Creative Arts Ministry

The emphasis of a creative arts ministry should be placed on the word "ministry." It never should be used solely to entertain or as a way of simply allowing people to perform their talents. Though entertainment and performance will no doubt be a part, they must fit within the purpose of ministry. Otherwise, an individual should find an outlet outside of the church.

Outreach.—The ways of outreach are unlimited to a creative arts ministry. The leaders and members of the department will continue to develop new and creative ways to spread the gospel to the community and minister to the body of the church. Listed below are some of the most common methods.

1. Performances at children's hospitals, including puppets, clowns, mimes, music, skits, gifts, etc.
2. Performances at senior citizens hospitals; much of the same as the children's, but with relevant material
3. Performances at local schools and camps
4. Performances in local parks and streets
5. Tours to other churches, schools, camps, parks, etc.
6. Creative arts classes (acting, dance, painting, sculpting, music, etc.) offered at the church and open to the community at a charge substantially less than secular organizations (this has proven to be a very successful outreach tool)
7. Seasonal productions, such as Christmas, Easter, and 4th of July. (As the reputation of excellence grows, those who attend these productions remember the name of the church. Seeds are planted. When they decide they are looking for a church to attend, or have some other need, it happens that they will seek out the familiarity of that same church.)
8. Dinner theater. (This is one of the fastest growing ministries in churches today. The community is invited to an evening of performance and dinner. The performance could be a musical concert, gospel singers, a play, sketches, or any combinations of materials. The dinner could be as simple as dessert and coffee or a full-course meals. The evening would be entertaining but filled with moral and spiritual messages.

Inreach.—The creative arts ministry ministers as much to the body as it does to the world. Again, the ways are unlimited, but here are a few of the more typical.

1. Various Sunday School teachers can contact the creative arts leader (CA) with a subject that needs illustrating. The group would meet during that week and write and rehearse an illustration to be performed to that Sunday School class. Several different groups would be utilized on any given Sunday.
2. The CA group would be used to perform at special youth functions.
3. Topical issues could be demonstrated. For instance: The generation gap—a night of role playing where the parents are directed to be children and their children play the parents. Issues are discussed from the opposite point of view. This is

very effective in bringing families closer together. It can be used for a variety of issues, such as abortion, death penalty, birth control, drugs, evolution, etc.

4. The CA department would provide classes in various creative arts—dance, acting, music, art, etc.—at a fraction of the normal costs.

5. The CA group could minister to the very special needs of creatively gifted people, including those who may work professionally in the creative arts. It could help to prepare these Christians to face the rejections, failures, and frustrations unique to their arts. It could prepare those who work in the entertainment industry to stand strong in their faith and be a shining light in a dark world, eventually making changes.

Productions.—The Creative Arts Department would work with the Music Department and worship leader to plan and produce seasonal productions. Since these are productions of the entire church, all departments would work together as parts of the body.

Organization.—Ideally, the Creative Arts Department should be a separate department such as Music or Youth. It should be under the umbrella of the worship leader. The department should have its own leader, qualified in the creative arts and in the ministry.

Ideally, the Creative Arts Department should be equal to the Music Department and would work very closely with the Music Director.

Plan.—Starting a Creative Arts Department could begin slowly and build; or, with a qualified leader, it could begin in full. The leadership position could begin as a part-time salaried position: 20 hours a week plus worship services, plus special events and extra hours during productions.

Following is an initial plan for the beginning of a Creative Arts Department.

1. Choose proper leadership.
2. Publicize to anyone interested in participating.
3. Begin with a first meeting.
4. Organize officers and division heads, i.e., dance, art, voice, etc.
5. Begin with sermon illustrations.
6. Begin working on a seasonal production.
7. Begin organized instructional classes.
8. Work with Sunday School teachers.
9. Hold weekly meetings to brainstorm ideas and write new material.

This, of course, is basic. However, a Creative Arts Department by nature would grow quickly. Once momentum is begun, it will not only grow within itself but will no doubt cause overall church growth as well.

There is a healthy revival of Creative Arts beginning in the modern church. This resurgence crosses denominational and regional lines, although many churches of all denominations still refuse to accept the benefits of drama in worship. This movement will continue to grow, and the churches that incorporate creative arts into their worship will also grow. Whether we like it or not, we are competing with film, television, and theater. If we want to reach the world, we must speak to them in a language which they understand.

In the introduction to his book, *Plays That'll Preach* (Nashville: Broadman Press, 1985), Robert Don Hughes explains with eloquence the need for drama in worship:

Is the world listening to anything these days? Oh yes! Much more than ever before. Films, television—these consume more and more of our moments, not only in this country but around the world. It troubles me to think that while in the age of print the Bible was the most widely distributed message, in this modern age of media the most listened-to voices are those of currently popular secular movie producers and novelists. How do we reach the world? How do we preach to those who won't listen any longer to sermons?

Drama has been a tool for communicating spiritual truth since the world began. Simple storytelling is dramatic. The ritual activities of the Jewish priesthood were dramatic. Talk about dramatic, look at the strange antics of the prophet Ezekiel! And never in the history of this world has there been any more dramatic act than the crucifixion, burial, and resurrection of Jesus Christ.

When I was a boy, God spoke to me through drama. As a preacher's kid growing up in southern California I had learned early how to filter out my father's words. But on those occasions when Christian drama was performed in our church, my spirit came alive. One night when my parents were out visiting prospects I sat at home watching *Green Pastures* on television—and wept with a new understanding of the Father's sacrificial love.

---

[1] *Merriam-Webster's Collegiate Dictionary,* 10th ed., s.v. "worship."

[2] Ibid., s.v. "praise."

[3] Ibid., s.v. "express."

[4] Verses marked TLB are taken from *The Living Bible.* Copyright © Tyndale House Publishers, Wheaton, Illinois, 1971. Used by permission.

[5] *Merriam-Webster's,* s.v. "poetry."

[6] Ragan L. Courtney, Wesley L. Forbis, and Terry W. York, *Three Voices: Poetry in Worship* (Nashville: Convention Press, 1994), 33.

CHAPTER TWENTY

FORMS

Most viewers of a production do not realize the enormous amount of hours and work that went into producing it. A production is like a piece of machinery operating with many moving parts. If any one of those parts should fail, it would decrease the effectiveness of the entire machine. Even if the machine is able to complete its job, the failed part may cause internal damage to the machine. The same is true of a production. If it does not run smoothly, the audience may not know it, but those on the production team may be hurt.

Following you will find production forms and documents that have been designed to make the production run more efficiently. These forms were created from years of experience. Many of them may seem unnecessary, but experience has proven their worth. Many of them are for prevention of problems, and you might only be aware of their value if you did not use them. It is not necessary for you to learn those kinds of lessons, as the creators of these forms have already done that for you.

How to Use Forms

Pre-production

1. Community Emergency Telephone Numbers.—This form should be in the possession of the stage manager or production coordinator. It should be present at all rehearsals, workdays, and performances.

2. Emergency Protocol Guidelines.—Any time a large group of people is assembled, there is the possibility of an emergency situation. The risks increase during construction work. Unfortunately churches are not exempt from fires, thefts, assaults, and the like. This (double-sided) form should be given to each member of the production at the first assembly.

3. Audition Questionnaire.—In professional theater an actor will have an 8 x 10 photo with a resumé attached. Most of the auditioners for a church production will not have these. The Audition Questionnaire allows the auditioner to present a resumé in this format, thereby giving them greater insight into the casting process. It also helps the casting panel to consider placing people in other positions should they not be cast in featured roles. These should be used in conjunction with the audition top sheet. (This is a double-sided form.)

4. Audition Score Sheet.—Each member of the casting panel will have one of these score sheets. All ratings should be on a scale of 1–10, with 10 being the best performance. Totals from all score sheets will be added. Each member of the casting panel should discuss his or her reasons for scores. The final decision should remain with the director regardless of the scores.

- *Auditioner:* The name of the person auditioning.
- *Character:* The name of the character the auditioner is trying for.
- *Acting:* Rate the acting ability.
- *Singing:* Rate the singing ability, not just the voice but also the ability to "sell" the song.
- *Dance:* Rate the dance ability, keeping in mind the requirements of the character.
- *Look:* Rate the overall appearance of the auditioner as it relates to the character.
- *Comments:* Give reasons for your scores.

5. Volunteer Questionnaire.—This form is useful at the very beginning of production. It can be placed in Sunday bulletins, newsletters, flyers, and such. It can be placed in the foyer of the church or passed out in Sunday School classes. You may discover talent you never knew existed in your church.

Rehearsal/Construction

6. Creating and Developing a Character.—Each actor should be given this form to help create a character. This should be done after a discussion with the director. Then, the director should read each submission from the actors and make necessary changes and suggestions (4 pages).

7. Program Participation/Parental Release.—It is a good idea to make sure that a child's parents have actually given permission for their child's participation in your production. This is another form designed for your legal protection. The form also gives medical consent for emergency treatment.

8. Trip Permission Slip.—This is used for the same purposes as the Program Participation Parental Release form. Sometimes you may plan off-site activities such as rehearsal retreats, performances of excerpts of the program for advertising purposes, or prop-hunting excursions. For legal protection, permission from parents should be received in writing.

9. Child Photo/Parental Release.—This form is used for the same purpose as the Photo Release/Adult.

10. Photo Release/Adult.—This is a standard release form used by photographers. It is useful in protecting you and your organization from possible lawsuits. (You may want to use photos or videos for advertising or in your programs, etc.) Read the form carefully to gain a full understanding of its use.

11. Biographies/Cast and Crew.—Many times biographies of the cast and crew are printed in the program. Performers usually have other things on their minds, and it is difficult for them to write a "bio" before your printing deadline. This form allows them to fill in pertinent information, and then your publicity crew can create the biographies. These are also helpful for publicity purposes. (This is a double-sided form.)

12. General Prop List.—This is most useful during the pre-production stage. With this list you can begin the acquisition of the necessary props.

13. Record of Borrowed Property.—Most church productions rely on donations of or loans from church members for a large percentage of the needed props. To protect the church and the donor's property, it is a good idea to inspect the property and document its condition. Notice on the form a place for a snapshot or sketch.

14. Borrowed or Leased Property List.—This is a list that keeps a comprehensive account of the properties borrowed or leased. It can be modified slightly (as suggested on the description of listed form 23) to serve when your are loaning out items to others as well as when you are the one borrowing needed props or equipment for sound, lighting, costumes, and so forth.

15. Ticket Reservations.—This is the form used in the church office where tickets may be ordered. Reservations will be transferred to this form from the ticket order forms that are mailed or carried in. Telephone requests can go right onto this form. All reservations will be transferred to the box office ticket reservations form pior to each perfomance. After the transfer has been made, these ticket reservations forms should be kept safe in a file. They may be used for verifying reservations or auditing purposes at a later date.

16. Ticket Orders.—This form is used for ordering tickets by mail-in or carry-in. The forms can be mailed to a mailing list, put in the Sunday bulletin, newsletters, foyer, and so forth.

- *(Insert your titles, logos, and dates here)*: Paste over the top of this line, the name of your church, the program title, and/or any other applicable information.
- *(Insert your performance dates here)*: The days, dates, times, and cost should be pasted over this line.

Information from this form will be logged onto the Ticket Reservations form in order of the first, second, and third choices indicated as seating is available. If Ticket Order forms are not processed on a daily basis, then we suggest you have the receptionist or front office date-stamp them as they come in so that your ticket office can process them in the order received.

17. Program Advertisement Form.—This form is to be used in obtaining advertising for your program (playbill). It is to be used in duplicate and should be accompanied by a cover letter from the producer with information explaining its purpose, rallying community support, how the purchase of space is beneficial to both the buyer and production (it is a tax-deductible donation to the church), total audience capacity either for each performance or cumulatively, and any aspects your production offers which may be of special interest to the community, thereby insuring a full audience who will in fact see that ad. It is recommended that there be a sample page or pages of ads to include business cards as is, used as coupons, or personal messages to cast and/or crew, such as "Best wishes," "Congratulations," or "We love you." (This is a double-sided form.)

18. Suggested Performance Guidelines for Cast and Crew.—This should be copied and given to every member of the cast and crew. Notice the word "suggested." The form is mostly generic and has proven successful for a smooth-running production. However, feel free to change any part to suit your particular situation. (This is a double-sided form.)

19. Performance Sign-In Sheet.—This is the same as the other sign-in sheet. Post this in a place where the cast and crew enter. Make sure they understand the importance of signing in. The stage manager or production coordinator should check it often. If a key member of the production is missing there will be time to replace him or her. Stand-ins for cast or crew should be familiar with the functions they will be required to perform from having been at rehearsals, and reinforced by the scene breakdown forms (and cued scripts for crews) as determined previously.

20. Box Office Ticket Reservations.—This is to be used at the box office. It should be completely updated just before the box opens for each performance. Information is transferred to here from the Ticket Reservations form.

- *Name:* Name or names of the party.
- *No. Res.:* The total number of reservations.
- *No. W/C:* The number of "Will Call" tickets (tickets that have been pre-paid and held at the door). If tickets are reserved and not yet paid for, leave this space blank or insert a "zero" or write "none"
- *No. P/P:* The number of pre-paid tickets. Again, insert "none" if the party is expected to pay at the door. The information on the left side of this double line should already be transferred (printed or typed) onto this form before your "house is open." The information on the right side will be documented "at the door."
- *Total Tkts:* The total number of tickets sold to or presented by that party, including will call, pre-paid and new purchase.
- *CA/CH:* Write CA for cash or CH for check (number of check is optional).
- *Amt Rec'd:* The amount of money received at the box office only.
- *Comments:* Notes or special instructions concerning that party. If handicapped seating was requested when reservations were made, it should have been transferred to this column already and designated seats held to accommodate this party. (Comments that may be inserted as guests arrive would be: "Guests of..," "handicapped seating," "flowers or gifts to be sent back stage on their behalf," etc.)

Post-production

21. Strike Guidelines.—The strike is one of the most difficult times of a production. If it is not well organized, it can cause many wasted hours, wasted materials, and even injuries. This form is to be passed out to everyone participating in the strike. It will help to insure that the strike runs smoothly and without catastrophes.

22. Strike Planner.—This form is used to pre-plan the strike to help it run more efficiently and safely.

- *Order:* The suggested order that department would be in the strike. For instance, the set should not be struck first if there are any sound cables running through it. In this case sound would strike first. Some may happen simultaneously such as costume and makeup.
- *Crew:* The foreman is the person chosen to lead each department team. Other members of the crew are listed in this box. Others may join later, but these listed would have had special

instructions in advance.

- *Items to:* The designated areas where each department is placing their items. They should be easily accessible and planned in separate areas to avoid congestion.
- *Notes:* Any special requirements that might pertain to certain equipment.

23. Inventory Storage List.—When the production is over and all sets, props, costumes, makeup, effects, lights, etc. are in safe storage, this list identifies their locations. There should be a list for each department. A book should be kept containing all of the lists.

- *Item/Size:* The type of the item and, if applicable, its size.
- *Quantity:* The number of items stored in that particular box, bin, crate, etc.
- *Color/Style:* Note, if applicable, the color of the items and style. Many chorus costumes, props, and sets are separated by style and color. This is especially true of makeup.
- *Box Code:* This depends on your system of labeling. Boxes should use some kind of code to identify   contents.
- *Location:* Production properties are not always stored in the same location, especially lights and sound equipment. This section quickly locates the storage place of a particular item.

24. Inventory Sign-Out Sheet.—During the year, other persons and/or organizations may want to borrow or rent your inventory. To protect your investment, this form should be kept on file.

- *Date:* The date of the item exchange.
- *Contact #:* The name and phone number of the person responsible for the item(s).
- *Items:* The name and quantity of each item being removed.
- *Purpose:* What the items will be used for. This also helps protect your investment.
- *Auth. by:* The name of the person at your organization authorizing the release of the item.
- *Date in:* The date the item is returned.
- *Rec'd by:* The person from your organization who received and inspected the returned item.

It is suggested that you refer to the Record of Borrowed Property form (listed form "13" located in the Rehearsal/Construction section) which you should use in conjunction with this sign-out sheet when outside organizations borrow or lease items from you. Changing the "Borrowed From" line to "Borrowed By" or "Taken By" is all the modification you would need. It then allows you to document more detailed information as to the condition of the form at the time of release and the time of return. Instructions for its proper care or use can be noted under the "Condition of Item" section and then continued on the back side of the sheet.

COMMUNITY EMERGENCY TELEPHONE NUMBERS

COMMUNITY EMERGENCY NO. _____

AMBULANCE CO. _____ NO. _____

FIRE DEPARTMENT _____

POLICE DEPARTMENT _____

SHERIFF DEPARTMENT _____

POISON CONTROL CENTER _____

HOSPITAL _____ E. R. NO. _____

HOSPITAL _____ E. R. NO. _____

24-HOUR PHARMACY _____ NO. _____

GAS CO. _____ NO. _____

ELECTRIC CO. _____ NO. _____

OTHER _____ NO. _____

OTHER _____ NO. _____

OTHER _____ NO. _____

OTHER _____ NO. __ _____

SEE OTHER SIDE FOR CHURCH, STAFF, & ASSOCIATES INFORMATION

EMERGENCY PROTOCOL GUIDELINES

During any portion of the production process, the following guidelines should be considered.

MINOR INJURY OR ILLNESS

1. All injuries, regardless of how insignificant they may seem, must be made known to the Production Manager as soon as possible. This should be done by the person injured whenever possible. This includes such minor things as cuts or scrapes which can happen during workdays or even rehearsals.

    However, ANYONE, who may be aware of the occurrence whether or not he may have witnessed the incident should encourage the injured person to do so or report it himself to the Production Manager or other Staff who may also be present.

2. Standard First-Aid Procedures should be followed in each situation no matter how minor it may be.

3. If an injury is sustained which may require stitches, x-rays or other medical attention, then another adult person will assist the injured in getting the proper medical treatment. (This may be confirmed by any trained medical person who may have made themselves available to you during your volunteer recruitment.)

    If the injured person does leave the site for medical attention, ask him or her if anyone should be informed of the situation. Refer to that individual's Personal History Questionnaire for names and numbers.

    If the injured person does want someone to be notified and chooses to have someone other than himself do that, the Production Manager will do so whenever possible. If there is another close friend or family member present who might better reassure the requested party(s) of the actual situation (without undue alarm, etc) that is acceptable. NOTE: the destination of the injured person should already be determined and, if necessary, have a volunteer prepared to provide transportation to that party.

MAJOR INJURY OR ILLNESS

1. Immediately upon the discovery of an injury or illness, the pre-designated persons are to be summoned to the scene to assess the situation and give directions for:

    a) Attention to the injured party,

    b) Contacting emergency personnel: paramedic/fire/ambulance/police, etc.

    c) Retrieval of the appropriate emergency forms in the files of the Production or Stage Managers or Producer,

(1 of 2)

312

d) Insuring that the cause of the present situation has been neutralized and is no longer a threat to others.

e) Contacting immediate family or friend of injured persons with:
  * accurate and appropriate assessment of the situation,
  * destination location and approximate time of arrival to a medical facility,
  * appropriate volunteer(s) to transport the party(s) to the location where medical attention will be continued,
  * appropriate volunteer(s) to provide child care for the family as necessary.

f) Notifying appropriate Church Personnel to attend to the needs on-site, the needs of the family, etc.

2. It is a good idea to have pre-designated at least two other persons of your staff whose demeanor and experience lend themselves to leadership without hysteria at such times.

3. Follow through with appropriate accident reports to the appropriate Insurance Carrier(s).

4. **Fire**: Make the entire Production Staff, Cast, and Crew aware of alarm locations, fire extinguishers, and evacuation procedures. In the event of a small fire, make every attempt to put it out immediately. It is always a good idea to inform the Fire Department of the fire even if it has been extinguished. Regardless of the fire's size, make everyone aware without causing panic. Investigate the cause of the fire and take the necessary steps to remove the threat. When encountering more serious fires, contact the Fire Department immediately and have someone wait on the street to "flag" them down. If evacuation is necessary, keep everyone calm and have pre-designated Staff lead the way.

5. **Theft**: If a theft is discovered, the Staff should be notified immediately. Contact the proper authorities and make any reports that may be required. If a theft is caught in the act, immediately make everyone aware with as much noise as possible. Do not attempt to apprehend the thief. Surround yourself with others. Make mental notes of the thief's physical appearance and, if possible, a license number. Contact the proper authorities immediately. Investigate the security weaknesses and take steps to correct them.

6. **Assault**: Any Staff, Cast, or Crew who becomes the victim of an assault should contact the Staff immediately. Any injuries should be assessed and tended to. Immediately contact the proper authorities. Investigate the circumstances of the assault and take the necessary steps to prevent future incidents.

ANY INCIDENT INVOLVING A MINOR

ALL incidents involving a child or minor will require you to follow the guidelines listed above in MAJOR INJURY OR ILLNESS. In *every* case, the Parent(s) or Legal Guardian must be notified.

AUDITION QUESTIONNAIRE

NAME: _____

PHONE _____ (Day: Home/Work) // _____ (Evening: Home/Work)

ADDRESS _____

CITY, ZIP _____

◆◆◆

DRAMATIC EXPERIENCE:

PLAY	ROLE	YEAR PLAYED	LOCATION

COMMENTS:

----- ----- ----- ----- ----- ----- ----- ----- ----- ----- ----- ----- ----- ----- -----

MUSIC EXPERIENCE:

Soprano I _____   TRAINING: _____
Soprano II _____   _____
Alto I _____   _____
Alto II _____   _____
Tenor _____
Baritone _____
Bass _____   VOCAL RANGE: _____

COMMENTS:

----- ----- ----- ----- ----- ----- ----- ----- ----- ----- ----- ----- ----- ----- -----

DANCE EXPERIENCE: TRAINING/INSTRUCTORS

TAP: None / Beginning / Intermediate / Advanced   _____

BALLET: None / Beginning / Intermediate / Advanced   _____

JAZZ: None / Beginning / Intermediate / Advanced   _____

ACROBAT: None / Beginning / Intermediate / Advanced   _____

COMMENTS: *(OVER)*

NAME: _____

AGE RANGE:
____ 5-10	____ 20-25	____ 46-60
____ 11-15	____ 26-35	____ 61-70
____ 16-20	____ 36-45	____ 71+

Would you need assistance with transportation?_____ If yes, explain briefly: _____

SIZES:

Females: Height _____ Weight _____

Dress ____ Blouse ____ Slacks ____ Shoe ____

Glove ____ Hat ____

Measurements ____/____/____

Males: Height _____ Weight _____

Shirt ____/____ (neck/sleeve) SM MED LG XLG

Slacks ____/____ (waist/inseam) Shoe _____

Hat ____ Glove ____ Suit Jacket _____

TECHNICAL EXPERIENCE

Please **check** if yes, then give a brief statement of explanation. **Circle** any category in which you would be available to help regardless of your previous experience.

DIRECTOR:_____ *MUSIC DIRECTOR*:_____ *CONDUCTOR*:_____ *DIALECT COACH*:_____
CHOREOGRAPHER:_____ *PRODUCTION COORDINATOR*:_____ *STAGE MANAGER*:_____

SET: ___ Design / ___ Construction / ___ Painting / ___ Dressing / ___ Changes / ___ Strike / ___ Other

_____

PROPS: ___ Construction / ___ Acquisition / ___ Painting / ___ Running / ___ Other

_____

COSTUMES: ___ Design / ___ Sewing / ___ Alterations only / ___ Paper Maché / ___ Run Wardrobe / ___ Other

_____

LIGHTS: ___ Design / ___ Hang / ___ Gel & Focus / ___ Run board / ___ Run Spot, Specials / ___ Other

_____

SOUND: ___ Design / ___ Install / ___ Recording & Mixing / ___ Run board / ___ Other

_____

SPECIAL FX: describe: _____

_____
_____

MAKE-UP: ___ Design / ___ Beauty / ___ Aging / ___ Wounds / ___ Beard work / ___ Bald caps / ___ Casting

_____

PUBLICITY: describe: _____

_____

HOSPITALITY:

Food -- ___ Preparation / ___ Serving or Set-Up / ___ Clean-up / ___ Other

_____

Other -- ___ Transportation / ___ Child-care / ___ Usher / ___ Security / ___ Other

_____
_____

SEE REVERSE SIDE FOR MORE INFORMATION

AUDITION SCORE SHEET

AUDITIONER	CHARACTER	ACTING Rate 1 - 10	SINGING Rate 1 - 10	DANCE Rate 1 - 10	LOOK Rate 1 - 10	COMMENTS

PAGE _____ OF _____ .

316

VOLUNTEER QUESTIONNAIRE

The Church Play Production does not just happen. It is the result of thousands of man-hours in not only musical preparation, but in construction, painting, decorating, ushering and many other activities. The help and assistance of the church membership is most necessary. The Production **NEEDS YOU!**

Every member of the church is asked to commit themselves to some area of service. If you are not physically able to help, your commitment of prayer would be invaluable. Please complete the portion below and place it in the offering plate to let us know how you may be able to help in this strategic outreach of our church.

NAME_____

ADDRESS_____

PHONE NUMBERS: (HOME)_____
                   (WORK)_____

AGE GROUP   13-16   17-21   22-28   29-39   39-50   50+
(Circle One)

CIRCLE CATEGORY OF INTEREST

SET CONSTRUCTION	ARTIST	PAINTING	LIGHTS
SOUND	ACTING	DANCING	CHOIR
USHER	CHILDCARE	CLEANUP	FOOD
MUSICAL INSTRUMENT	DECORATING	PROPS	PUBLICITY
TRANSPORTATION	COSTUMES	MAKEUP	SPECIAL FX
SAFETY & SECURITY	TICKETS	HOUSE	CUSTODIAL

ANYWHERE YOU NEED ME

*PLACE IN THE OFFERING PLATE OR RETURN TO:*_____

CREATING AND DEVELOPING
A CHARACTER

CREATING THE PAST

The following questions will establish a basic foundation for your character. Feel free to create any additional questions that might help with character development. Try to give some type of answer to all of the questions. After you've answered all the questions, cross check to make sure there are no contradictions. You may need separate sheets of paper to do your work.

PARENT'S HISTORY

   1. What is your Mother's employment history?
   2. What is your Mother's educational bvackground?
   3. What is your Mother's maiden name?

   4. What is your Father's employment history?
   5. What is your Father's educational background

   6. Details of parents marriage if any?
   7. Circumstances of your birth. Were your parents happy about it?
   8. How did (do) your parents really feel about each other?
   9. Where are your parents now?
10. What kind of discipline did they give?
11. What were and are their sexual attitudes?
12. Any other information:

SIBLINGS

   1. How many brothers? Sisters?
   2. Where were you in the birth order?
   3. How did (do) you feel about each other?
   4. Where are they now?
   5. Any other information:

SOCIO-ECONOMICS

   1. Was your family lower, upper, or middle-class?
   2. How did you feel about your "class" position?
   3. How did your friends feel about your "class position?
   4. Did you wish for more? Less?
   5. How does your childhood socio-economic position affect you now?

(Page 1 of 4)

EDUCATION AND EMPLOYMENT

1. Describe your favorite teacher. Least favorite teacher.
2. Were you popular in school?
3. Describe closest friends.
4. Were you a good student? Grades?
5. Were you in trouble a lot?
6. Names of schools and highest degree?
7. What was your major if any?
8. Any other information:

MEDICAL HISTORY

1. Childhood diseases?
2. Did these leave any lasting effect physically and/or emotionally?
3. Surgeries?
4. Physical or psychological abnormalities, i.e. birthmarks, dyslexia?
5. Any other information:

MILITARY HISTORY

1. Were you in the military; and if so, what branch?
2. Were you in a war? Were you wounded?
3. If you were, how did it affect you physically and psychologically?
4. If you were not in the military, how did you feel about the military?

DEVELOPING THE PRESENT

THE PHYSICAL

1. What year were you born? Present age?
2. What is your physical appearance? Are you satisfied with it?
3. Are you short or tall, thin or heavy?
4. Are you strong or weak, sickly or healthy?
5. Are your movements graceful or awkward?
6. Do you have any unusual physical abnormalities?
7. Do you wear any corrective appliances?
8. Do you have full use of all your senses?
9. What is your dress style?
10. Is there a tendency to variety or monotony of voice?
11. Does any one quality of voice (nasal, guttural, etc.) give distinction to the tone?
12. Is there any artificial speech pattern adopted to affect others?
13. Any other information:

(Page 2 of 4)

THE PSYCHOLOGICAL & EMOTIONAL

1. Are you a well balanced person?
2. Are you emotionally mature?
3. Are you capable of experiencing strong emotional responses, or withdrawn?
4. Are certain emotions stronger than others, and if so, which ones?
5. Are you aware of emotional strengths and weaknesses?
6. Does this awareness have any bearing upon your emotional stability?
7. What words, phrases, events, people, etc. push your emotional buttons?
8. Are you intelligent or slow.
9. Are you fast, deliberate or slow in thought?
10. Is there any deviation from the normal state of mine? Mental lapses?
11. Do you have any secrets or desires?
12. Any other information:

RELATIONSHIPS

1. Marrital status?
2. Boy/girl friend?
3. Name and age of partner?
4. How long in the relationship?
5. How did you meet?
6. Partner's education and career?
7. How do you feel about each other?
8. Sexual attitudes?
9. Sexual relationship?
10. Your fidelity? Your Partner's fidelity?
11. Children? Names, age, sex?
12. Disciplinary problems with children?
13. Do you get along with your children?
14. Describe your casual friends.
15. Describe your best friends.
16. Any other information:

CAREER

1. What do you do for a living?
2. Salary?
3. Where are you on the ladder?
4. Are you happy with your job?
5. Are you well-liked at work, and do you like others?
6. How does your work contribute to the world?
7. Any other information:

FUTURE GOALS

1. 1 year?
2. 5 years?
3. 10 years?

TALENTS AND ABILITIES

1. Describe any natural talents and abilities you have.
2. Describe any talents and abilities you wish you had.
3. Have you developed your talents and abilities? Which ones?
4. Describe any talents and abilities you regret not developing.

CHARACTER SUMMARY

PHYSICAL SUMMARY	EMO/PSYCH SUMMARY
APPEARANCE:	INTELLIGENCE:
SPEECH:	PERSONALITY:
ABNORMALITIES:	EMOTIONS (Strong/weak):
MOVEMENT:	DEVIATIONS:
DRESS:	RELATIONSHIPS:
OTHER:	OTHER:

(Page 4 of 4)

State of_____
County of_____

Subscribed and sworn to before me this_____day of_____19_____.

PROGRAM PARTICIPATION
PARENTAL RELEASE

_____, referred to as PARENT, is the parent and/or lawful guardian of

_____,a minor, and agrees:

_____, is Producing

the Play _____for the purpose of:

_____

on_____19_____through_____19_____.

_____,

has the permission of PARENT to participate in the rehearsals, performances and all activities
thereof. _____ and the other employees and adult agents of
_____
are herewith given the following authority on the dates stated above.

To consent to any medical treatment that may be required by_____
in the place of and with the same authority as_____.

Further, in consideration of the services performed by_____and
the employees, servants and agents of_____,
are herewith released from liability for all actions taken in good faith during the Production of the
Play.

DATED_____

SIGNED_____

PRINTED NAME_____

State of _____
County of _____

Subscribed and sworn to before me this _____day of _____19____.

TRIP PERMISSION SLIP

_____, referred to as PARENT, is the parent and lawful guardian of

_____, a minor, and agrees:

_____, is organizing a trip for the purpose of:

_____

_____

on _____19____ through _____19____, from_____am/pm, through_____am/pm.

_____, has the apermission of PARENT to participate in
this trip and all activities thereof. _____, _____ and the other employees
and adult agents of _____ are herewith given the following
authority on the dates stated above:

To consent to any medical treatment that may be required by _____ in the place of and with
the same authority as _____.

Further, in consideration of the services performed by _____and the employees, servants
and agents of _____, _____, _____, and the other
employees and agents of _____,
are herewith released from liability for all actions taken in good faith during the trip.

DATED:_____

_____
SIGNED

323

CHILD PHOTO
PARENTAL RELEASE

Date

I, the undersigned parent or legal guardian of my undersigned son/daughter, do hereby give my authorization for the following waiver which is to apply to my undersigned son/daughter:

I hereby give _____, the Producer of _____, including all rights of every kind and character whatsoever in and to all work done by me and poses, acts, plays, and appearances made by me for the videotape and/or program, as well as in and to the right to use my child's name and photographs, either still or moving, for commercial and advertising purposes in connection therewith. I further give said Producers the right to reproduce in any manner whatsoever and recordations made by me hereunder of my child's voice and all instrumental, musical, or other sound effects produced by my child.

_____   _____
(Signature of Son/Daughter)   (Signature of Parent/Guardian)

_____   _____
(Printed Name)   (Printed Name)

ADDRESS/PHONE:_____
_____
_____
_____

PHOTO RELEASE
ADULT

Dated:_____

For valuable consideration received, I,_____, hereby give the absolute right and permission, with respect to the photographs that he/she has taken of me or in which I may be included with others:

    (a)   To copyright the same in his/her own name or any other name that he/she may choose.

    (b)   To use, re-use and re-publish the same in whole or in part, individually or in conjunction with other photographs, in any medium and for any purpose whatsoever, including (but not by way of limitation) illustration, promotion and advertising and trade, and

    (c)   To use my name in connection therewith if he/she chooses.

I hereby release and discharge_____from any and all claims and demands arising out of or in connection with the use of the photographs, including any and all claims for libel.

This authorization and release shall also ensure to the benefit of the legal representatives, licensees and assigns of_____as well as, the person(s) for whom he/she took the photographs.

I am over the age of eighteen. I have read the foregoing and fully understand the contents thereof:

_____
Signature

_____
Address

_____
City, State, Zip

_____
Phone

_____
Witnessed by

BIOGRAPHIES
CAST AND CREW

Please write at least two or more items in each of the sections below. Don't be afraid to list any experience or training, however insignificant you might think it is. Use a separate sheet if needed.

PERSONAL DATA

NAME: _____ CHARACTER NAME: _____

AGE: _____ DOB: _____ MARITAL STATUS: _____ CHILDREN: _____

EXPERIENCE

1. _____
   WHERE: _____ DATE: _____
   ROLE PLAYED: _____ REVIEWS: _____

2. _____
   WHERE: _____ DATE: _____
   ROLE PLAYED: _____ REVIEWS: _____

3. _____
   WHERE: _____ DATE: _____
   ROLE PLAYED: _____ REVIEWS: _____

4. _____
   WHERE: _____ DATE: _____
   ROLE PLAYED: _____ REVIEWS: _____

(OVER)

TRAINING

1. PLACE: _____
   INSTRUCTOR: _____ DATE: _____
   CERTIFICATES/AWARDS: _____

2. PLACE: _____
   INSTRUCTOR: _____ DATE: _____
   CERTIFICATES/AWARDS: _____

3. PLACE _____
   INSTRUCTOR: _____ DATE: _____
   CERTIFICATES/AWARDS: _____

4. PLACE _____
   INSTRUCTOR: _____ DATE: _____
   CERTIFICATES/AWARDS: _____

SPECIAL TALENTS/ABILITIES

_____
_____
_____
_____

GOALS

_____
_____

SPECIAL COMMENTS:

_____
_____
_____
_____

GENERAL PROP LIST

PRODUCTION: PAGE:

NO.	ITEM	HAND HELD	SET PROP	BORROW	RENT	BUY	MAKE

TOTALS

RECORD OF BORROWED PROPERTY

DESCRIPTION OF ITEM:_____

ESTIMATED VALUE:_____

BORROWED FROM:_____

       Address:_____

                    _____

       Phone_____(Day)_____(Evė)

DATE BORROWED:_____

EST. RETURN DATE:_____

_____   _____
       (Signature of Borrower)   (Signature of Lender)

ACTUAL RETURN DATE:_____

_____   _____
       (Signature of Borrower)   (Signature of Lender)

(Photo or Sketch)

CONDITION OF ITEM:_____

_____

_____

_____

_____

_____

BORROWED OR LEASED
PROPERTY LIST

PRODUCTION: DEPARTMENT: PAGE:

ITEM	QUANTITY	OWNER	DATE BORROWED	DATE RETURNED	CONDITION	PAYMENT

TICKET RESERVATIONS

PRODUCTION: _____

PRODUCTION MGR: _____

PERFORMANCE DATE ___ / ___ / ___

HOUSE CAPACITY _____

CURTAIN: _____ AM/PM

HOUSE OPENS: _____ AM/PM

NAME 1. ADDRESS 2. PHONE NO. 3.	NO. RES.	AMT. P/PD	SPECIAL REQUESTS	BOX OFFICE FORM NOTED	TICKET DISTRIBUTION			
					DATE	TICKETS	BY:	VIA:
1.								
2.								
3.								
					DATE	TICKETS	BY:	VIA:
1.								
2.								
3.								
					DATE	TICKETS	BY:	VIA:
1.								
2.								
3.								
					DATE	TICKETS	BY:	VIA:
1.								
2.								
3.								

TOTAL RESERVATIONS THIS PAGE: _____ CUMULATIVE THIS PERORMANCE: _____ PAGE NO. _____

331

TICKET ORDERS

(Insert your Titles, Logos, and Dates here)

HOW TO ORDER:

1. Select the Performance you wish to attend. Then select two alternates.

2. Print your name, address and telephone number legibly.

3. Enclose a check or money order for your donation totaling $ _____ for each ticket requested. Please do not send cash.

4. Make checks payable to: _____

5. Enclose a self-addressed, stamped envelope with your order. This will help you receive your tickets quickly. **Reservation requests will be filled in the order in which they are received. Every effort will be made to satisfy your first choice; however, due to the large number of requests, ticket distribution is final. Reservations should be made from this form only! All contributions are considered tax deductible donations and are not refundable. You may anticipate receiving your tickets after** _____.

6. **Please, enclose with this form: your check, and a self-addressed stamped envelope and mail to:**

    _____

    _____

    _____

PERFORMANCE DATES

(Insert your performance dates, times, & ticket prices here)

Please complete (type or print clearly) the form below and return with your donation as requested above. Thank you.

NAME _____   HOME PHONE _____   BUS. PHONE _____

ADDRESS _____   CITY _____   ZIP _____

Ticket Preference	Performance Date	Performance Time	Number of Reservations
1st Choice			
2nd Choice			
3rd Choice			

$ _____   **DONATION FOR TICKETS**

Cash _____ yes _____ no

Check No. _____

Money Order _____

Comments or Special Requests:

PROGRAM ADVERTISEMENT FORM

DATE:_____

I.   It is agreed that the amount enclosed, $_____, in the form of :

check no._____,   money order no. _____   or cash_____

is in exchange for advertisement space as indicated herein and that said space is guaranteed for the entire run of performances, but not to exceed _____ performances. It is understood that this agreement pertains exclusively to the production of:

_____

presented by _____

beginning on _____, 19___ which will be held at the location of _____

_____ ,

at _____ in the city of _____.

II.   I, representing _____ ,
do hereby purchase advertising space in the program referenced above as indicated below:

_____ Full Page Size at (_____ x _____) at $135.00 each

_____ Half Page Size-Horizontal at (_____ x _____) at $70.00 each

_____ Half Page Size-Vertical (_____ x _____) at $70.00 each

_____ Quarter Page Size-Horizontal at (_____ x _____) at $35.00 each

_____ Quarter Page Size-Vertical at (_____ x _____) at $35.00 each

III.   In so doing, I am providing herewith:

____ camera-ready copy to the Production Representative indicated herein.

____ camera-ready copy will be available for pick up on or before _____ / _____ /19____ .

____ camera-ready copy will be delivered (at my own expense) to Production Office on or before _____ / _____ /19_____ .

Side 1 of 2

333

III. (Continued)

_____ instructions for non-camera ready design/materials is as follows:

IV. In the event that I am submitting camera-ready copy for the sole purposes as stated herein, I understand that I may receive this copy in return only by checking this space: _____.

I prefer to receive my submitted camera-ready copy via:

_____ personal delivery service or courier (at my own expense)
_____ US MAIL
_____ Other:_____

_____   _____
Production Representative (Printed Name)   Signature of Production Representative

_____   _____
Day time Contact No. for Production   Contact Person at Production Office

_____
Purchasing Organization

_____   _(_____)_____
Contact Person of Purchasing Organization   Contact Person's Phone Number

COMMENTS:

Attach Business Card of Purchasing
Organization over this space if possible.

SUGGESTED PERFORMANCE GUIDELINES
FOR CAST AND CREW

BEFORE PERFORMANCE

1. Costumes must not be worn from home to church and vice versa. Dressing rooms are provided for you on site.

2. Do NOT park in staff or handicapped space (unless you posses a placard indicating handicapped status).

3. Upon arrival: check in if required to do so before entering dressing areas.

4. Dressing areas are as follows:

   A.

   B.

   C.

   D.

5. Call time for all cast, choir, crew members, etc., is one hour prior to show time unless specified otherwise. All performances included. NO EXCEPTIONS.

   This means that all persons required to check in must do so prior to that time. Fifteen minutes after the hour, all sheets shall be verified and replacements for that performance shall be assigned. You are more than welcome to arrive earlier.

6. Upon arrival, you must not bring any food into the sanctuary, performance areas or any dressing area. You will be notified if there is to be a designated area for food and drink.

7. Notes are to be given in a general assembly of cast and crew thirty minutes before each performance. Anyone needing to place props on or off stage must do so before this time. All "on stage" props will be placed before the "house" is open.

8. No member of the cast can be seen by an audience member while in costume. If a prop or any other item needs attention, make the Stage Manager aware of it.

9. The dressing rooms may not be locked during performances. Please leave all items of value at home. Do not ask any cast or crew member to hold something on your behalf. These persons have other responsibilities and should not take on more.

DURING PERFORMANCE

1. A call for "places" will be given 5 minutes prior to curtain.

2. Regardless of the time, no member of the cast, crew, choir, orchestra, staff, etc. will begin the performance without the final word of the Stage Manager and/or Production Coordinator.

3.   Anyone who is not on stage must remain in their proper waiting areas and out of the way of working cast and crew.

4.   Unless you are waiting for an entrance, never watch the performance from the wings.

5.   Never enter the audience in costume to watch the show from the back. NEVER!

6.   There is to be no unnecessary talking or other noise-making backstage. Any necessary talking should be a low whisper.

7.   If the Production is a period or biblical play, do not wear modern jewelry, watches, eyeglasses, etc. once in costume. It is good practice to leave these items at home.

INTERMISSION

1.   During intermission, do not socialize with any guests or other audience members. The performance is not over until the end of the show. Do not break the illusion of reality for the audience.

2.   Do not eat food while in costume and makeup. If you must drink, please be careful not to spill on costumes or makeup.

AFTER PERFORMANCE

1.   Do not bring family members, friends, etc. to any backstage or dressing room areas. These areas are restricted to Cast and Crew only.

2.   Costumes/props should be placed in prearranged places or hung neatly for the next performance. Any notes of needed repairs should be relayed to the Wardrobe/Costume Department or the Stage Manager before your departure after the performance.

3.   All personal items should be removed and taken home each night.

4.   Parents of children in childcare must get their children within twenty minutes of the close of the performance. You can ask friends and family to wait for you in the performance area or the lobby areas until you are able to meet with them.

5.   Be aware that any comments you make aloud are easily overheard by others. Therefore, comments to audience members about the performance should be kept positive in nature as this is the time people look for reasons to accept or deny all that just took place on stage.

PERFORMANCE
SIGN-IN SHEET
CAST AND CREW

PERFORMANCE: _____   DATE: _____

NAME	CHARACTER	INITIAL	CALL TIME	TIME IN	TIME OUT

BOX OFFICE TICKET RESERVATIONS

PRODUCTION TITLE: _____   PERFORMANCE DATE ___ / ___ / ___

HOUSE OPENS: _____ AM/PM   HOUSE CAPACITY _____   CURTAIN: _____ AM/PM   CHILD CARE _____

NOTES _____

NAME	NO. RES.	NO. W/C	NO. P/P	TOTAL TKTS	CA / CH	AMT REC'D	COMMENTS
TOTALS							

PAGE ____ OF ____

STRIKE GUIDELINES

The Strike is one of the most difficult times of a production. If it is not well organized, it can cause many wasted hours, wasted materials, and even injuries. To insure that the Strike runs smoothly and without catastrophes, please follow the guidelines suggested below.

1. Meet at the appointed place and time for instructions.

2. Please bring the following items: gloves, old clothes, appropriate shoes. *Optional:* hammer, hard-hat, drill (phillips bits), crescent wrench, socket set, crow bar.

3. Follow the Order of Strike as given during the instructions.

4. No horseplay.

5. No young children allowed in the strike area.

6. Carefully place screws in the designated containers.

7. Carefully remove nails and place them in the designated containers.

8. Stack all items in designated areas.

9. Do not throw items. Carry and place them.

10. Do not loiter. If you are not working or are finished, stay out of the way.

11. Keep the Cleanup Crew in mind as you strike. Try to make their job easier.

12. The Cleanup Crew should not begin until the entire Strike is completed.

13. Power tools are to be used by qualified persons only.

14. For safety and easy retrieval, all tools should be kept in a pre-designated location when not in use.

15. Should an accident happen, all work will stop immediately.

16. If someone is injured:
    A. Pre-designated persons are to be notified to give or seek medical attention.
    B. Contact the Stage Manager or Production Coordinator who will have all Emergency forms in a notebook or file.
    C. A pre-designated person will make all phone calls to emergency personnel.
    D. A pre-designated person will make calls to the injured person's family.
    E. Everyone else will get out of the way and wait for further instructions.

FOR STRIKE INSTRUCTIONS ASSEMBLE AT_____AT_____

STRIKE PLANNER

DEPT.	ORDER	CREW	ITEMS TO	NOTES
SOUND		FOREMAN:		
AUDIO VISUAL		FOREMAN:		
PROPS		FOREMAN:		
FX		FOREMAN:		
SETS		FOREMAN:		
LIGHTS		FOREMAN:		
COSTUMES		FOREMAN:		
MAKEUP		FOREMAN:		
OTHER		FOREMAN:		
OTHER		FOREMAN:		

INVENTORY STORAGE LIST

DEPARTMENT: PAGE:

LINE NO.	ITEM / SIZE	QUANT.	COLOR / STYLE	BOX CODE	LOCATION

341

INVENTORY SIGN-OUT SHEET

DATE	ISSUED TO	CONTACT #	ITEMS	PURPOSE	AUTH. BY	DATE IN	REC'D BY

GLOSSARY

AD LIB: Any lines or business improvised by an actor.

APRON: Portion of the stage that extends past the proscenium arch.

ARTICULATE: To speak clearly and distinctly so that each syllable can be understood.

BACKCLOTH: English theater expression for back drop. A scene canvas across the width of the upstage, fixed at the top and bottom.

BACK LIGHTING: Lighting that is projected from upstage onto the set and actors to enhance the three-dimensional quality.

BACKSTAGE: The whole area behind the stage, including the dressing rooms and green room, used by the actors and other members of the   production.

BARNDOOR (shutters): A four-shutter device that fits into the color-frame holder of a Fresnel spotlight to shape the beam and reduce scatter light.

BATHROBE DRAMA: A catch-all phrase describing a mediocre production. It comes from the use of department store bathrobes to pass as biblical costumes.

BATTEN: Either a long pipe or a long strip of wood used to hang scenery, lights, or draperies. Normally it is supported by lines dropped from the gridiron. Battens are also attached to the top and bottom of drops. They are used sometimes to stiffen two or more flats hinged together to form a wall.

BIT: A piece of stage action or business not described in the script.

BIT PART: A small speaking part.

BLACKOUT: To take out all the lights on stage at the same time.

BLOCKING: The physical movements of actors prescribed by the director.

BOARD: Either the sound or lighting control panel.

BOOK: The script. Sometimes refers to the prompt book.

BORDER LIGHTS: Strips of 8–12 lamps in joined compartments shining from the stage floor.

BOX OFFICE: The theater office responsible for handling ticket sales and reservations.

BRACE: An extendible wooden brace used to brace flats or door casings from behind to keep them from shaking. Also used to secure or steady platforms.

BUMP-UP: Sudden movement of lights to a higher intensity.

CALL: The time the cast and crew are expected to arrive at the theater.

CALL BACK: When an actor or soloist is "called back" for a second or third (usually not more) audition, in order to narrow the choices down.

CALL BOARDS: A bulletin board placed by the stage door on which sign-in sheets, rehearsal schedules, performance schedules, and all other information for the cast are posted.

CASTING: The process of selecting actors and actresses for the roles in a production.

C-CLAMP: A clamp used to attach a lighting instrument to a pipe batten.

CENTER STAGE: The center of the stage.

CHAIN OF COMMAND: The order of authority of the entire production team.

CLOSING: The last performance of the run of the play.

COLOR FRAME: Used on spotlights and occasionally on floodlights to hold the color gelatins. Usually of metal.

COMPS: Free tickets. "Complimentary."

CREDITS: The recognition of all those who participated in the entire production, including all suppliers who have provided material.

CROSS: To move from one place to another on the stage.

CROSS FADE: To fade or dim from one lighting set-up to another without going through a dim-out.

CUE: The word or piece of business at which point an actor is expected to begin speaking or begin some action. Also, the word or business at which point some crew member is expected to take an action.

CUE SHEET: The sheet of paper on which the stage manager or light man or sound man has written his cues.

CUE-TO-CUE: A "dry tech" rehearsal that runs the show without actors, simply moving from one technical cue to the next.

CURTAIN: The opening or closing of each show. From the use of curtains hiding the set to signify the start and finish of each performance.

CURTAIN CALL: The reappearance of the cast after the final curtain has fallen to acknowledge the audience's applause.

CUTOUT: A piece of scenery cut out of cardboard or plywood to represent trees, bushes, buildings, hills, or other objects in silhouette.

CYCLORAMA (CYC): A large, curved drop or curved plaster wall partly encircling the stage and lighted to simulate the sky.

DARK HOUSE: No performance. An off night.

DIM: To change the intensity of a light, either brighter or less bright.

DIMMER: Any device for controlling the brightness of a lighting instrument.

DOUBLE TAKE: The delayed reaction of an actor when he finally realizes the significance of something he has heard or seen.

DOWNSTAGE: The area of the stage closest to the audience.

DRAMATIC VALUES: Those values in a play that are likely to evoke an emotional response from the audience.

DRESSING (SET): Arranging furniture, props, etc. on the set for a given scene.

DRESS REHEARSAL: The final rehearsal(s) that are run exactly as a performance but without the audience.

DRY BRUSH: To paint with a brush that is almost devoid of paint. Used to get the effect of wood grain, old brick, or rocks.

ELLIPSOIDAL SPOT: An efficient spotlight with an Ellipsoidal reflector, especially useful in lighting the front areas of the stage from an overhead beam.

FILL LIGHT: Wash or soft light that fills in the light on the face from the direction opposite the key light.

FLAT: A flat piece of scenery consisting of a wooden frame covered with canvas, door skin, or plywood.

FOLLOW SPOT: A high-wattage, variable-focus spotlight usually located at the back of the auditorium or in a projection booth and used to follow the movements of a singer or dancer on the stage.

FOOTLIGHTS: A metal trough housing a number of low-wattage lamps and located on the stage floor near the front of the apron. Its purpose is to blend and tone the light from the spots and remove the shadows from under the eyebrows and noses of the actors.

FOURTH WALL: The imaginary wall that has been removed from a realistic box set to permit the audience to view the activities in the room. The imaginary wall that separates the actors from the audience.

FRESNEL: A stepped lens that efficiently throws a soft-edged beam of light up to 25 or 30 feet. Commonly applied to any spotlight having this type of lens.

F/X: Special effects.

GAG: An exaggerated line or piece of business designed primarily to elicit laughter from the audience. A running gag is the repetition of the gag at intervals, usually with added refinements to increase the laughter.

GELATIN (GEL): A paper-thin sheet of colored plastic used in a color frame attached to a spot or flood for the purpose of coloring the light emanating from that source.

GENERAL ASSEMBLY: A meeting of the cast, crew, and production staff, just prior to a performance.

GOBO: A metal cutout placed in the gate of an Ellipsoidal spot to project a pattern or an image on a wall or drop.

GREASE PAINT: A form of foundation make up that comes in sticks, tubes, or bottles.

GREEN ROOM: The room near the stage used by actors and crew members before or between acts to wait for cues or to go over lines or business.

GRID (or GRIDIRON): The steel framework at the top of the stage house to which are attached the headblocks and pulleys that support the lines used to fly the scenery or light instruments.

GROUND PLAN: The plan of the set, including the placement of furniture, that has been worked out by the director and designer.

HAND PROPS: Those properties that actors handle or use, such as glasses, food, letters, etc.

HOUSE: The entire area in front of the stage where the audience observes the performance. Also used to describe the audience.

HOUSE LIGHTS: The lights that illuminate the auditorium before and after the performance.

HOUSE MANAGER: The person in charge of the auditorium, sanctuary, or theater in which the production is taking place. Responsible for its appearance, doors, rest rooms, etc. Responsible for all activities related to the audience.

ILLUSION OF REALITY: The atmosphere created when all arts of the theater are combined to heighten the audiences appreciation of the realism of the play. The audience gets so caught up in the play that they believe that what is happening on stage is real.

INTERNAL CHARACTER: Playing the character from the inside as opposed to external gimmicks such as limping, glasses, hats, etc.

LEKO: A term commonly used to designate an Ellipsoidal spot.

LIGHT PLOT (or LAYOUT): A scale drawing including the ground plan of the set with the type and location of each lighting instrument and the area it is intended to illuminate.

LINES: The dialogue of the play.

LOIN CLOTH: A cloth worn about the hips. A period costume usually used in Passion plays.

LOVE OFFERING: Or "freewill offering." Collecting donations from the audience with no obligation concerning the show.

MASK: (verb) To conceal a set, a person, or a piece of business from the view of the audience.

MOTIVATION: The reason (either internal or external) that an actor says or does something.

MOUNT: To prepare for and undertake the production of a play.

MUSICAL: A play with musical numbers.

NOTES: Comments given at the end of a rehearsal or performance to improve the performance the following night. Notes could address mistakes that need to be corrected or positive actions that should be repeated.

OFF BOOK: To rehearse the play without the actors referring to the script (memorized dialogue).

OFF SEASON: Mounting a production at a time other than Christmas or Easter when most church plays are produced.

OFFSTAGE: All areas of the stage that are not included in the set.

OPEN UP: (Command or action.) An actor turning slightly toward the audience to be better seen.

OVERLAP: To begin speaking before another actor has finished speaking. Sometimes enhances the sense of realism.

PACE: The rate at which a scene or act is being played. The tempo.

PERIOD PLAY: A play depicting a particular point in history.

PLACES: The command given to the actors by the stage manager when he is ready to start the performance or begin an act.

PLAYBILL: The program handed to the audience containing vital information about the play: scenes, intermission, cast, crew, biographies, musical numbers, advertisements, etc.

PRE-SHOW: From the opening of the house to the opening curtain.

PRINCIPALS: The main characters in a show.

PRODUCTION VALUES: The elements of a production which singly and collectively contribute to its quality and success.

PROGRAM: See Playbill.

PROJECT: To make the voice carry to the entire audience.

PROJECTION: When an actor increases the volume of his voice to be heard by the last row of the audience.

PROMPT: To give an actor his line (or key word) when he appears to have forgotten it (usually during rehearsals).

PROPS (or PROPERTIES): Every article

on stage except the scenery. Furni-ture, rugs, drapes, etc. are known as set props. Letters, food, glasses, etc. are known as hand props. Those hand props used by only one actor such as a watch or eyeglasses are sometimes called personal props.

PROSCENIUM: The stage opening that separates the audience from the actors on the traditional type of stage.

RAMP: A sloping passageway leading from a lower to a higher level.

RUN: Usually refers to the number of performances from opening night to closing night.

RUNNING CREW: The team of individuals who actually operate the equipment during rehearsal and performance. The light board, spotlights, props, sound, etc.

SANDBAG: A canvas bag filled with sand and used to counterweight the scenery.

SET or SETTING: The arrangement of scenery to provide a background or environment in which the action of the play can develop.

SET PIECE: A single piece of scenery used alone or in conjunction with another set piece to suggest the environment in which the action of the play is sup-

posed to take place.

SIGHT LINES: Those lines of sight from the sides and rear of the auditorium that determine how much of the stage can be used so as to be visible to all parts of the audience.

SPLATTER: To apply paint to scenery in small dots by slapping the brush against one hand.

STAGE MANAGER: The person who is responsible for running the entire performance from opening curtain to final curtain call.

STATIC: When the play is lacking in movement for a long enough period of time to cause boredom in the audience.

STRAIGHT PLAY: A nonmusical production.

STRIKE: To take down and remove a set from the stage. Usually at the end of the run.

SOURCE LIGHT: Light which comes from (or appears to come from) a set piece, such as a table lamp.

UNDERSTUDY: An actor who is prepared to substitute for another actor who is unable to perform. An understudy performs a smaller featured or chorus role in the company.

UPSTAGE: Toward the rear of the stage. Also, to move upstage of another actor so that he must turn away from the audience in order to address you.

WING IT: To proceed with a performance even though the actor is unsure of his lines. Presumably he will get whatever assistance he needs from the other actors.

WINGS: Flats or drapes located at the side of the stage and set parallel to the footlights to mask the offstage area. Also, those areas offstage to the side that are masked by the wings.

WORLD PREMIER: A production that has never been performed for an audience.